Teaching Music to Students with Differences and Disabilities

Teaching Music to Students with Differences and Disabilities

A Label-Free Approach

Third Edition

Alice M. Hammel and Ryan M. Hourigan

Foreword by Dr. Tim Lautzenheiser

OXFORD
UNIVERSITY PRESS

OXFORD
UNIVERSITY PRESS

Oxford University Press is a department of the University of Oxford.
It furthers the University's objective of excellence in research, scholarship,
and education by publishing worldwide. Oxford is a registered trade mark of
Oxford University Press in the UK and in certain other countries.

Published in the United States of America by Oxford University Press
198 Madison Avenue, New York, NY 10016, United States of America.

First Edition published in 2011
Second Edition published in 2017
Third Edition published in 2025

CIP data is on file at the Library of Congress

ISBN 978-0-19-768932-5 (pbk.)
ISBN 978-0-19-768931-8 (hbk.)

DOI: 10.1093/9780197689356.001.0001

Paperback printed by Integrated Books International, United States of America
Hardback printed by Bridgeport National Bindery, Inc., United States of America

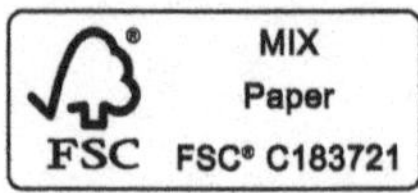

Contents

Foreword

According to Wikipedia: "A foreword is a (usually short) piece of writing, sometimes placed at the beginning of a book or other piece of literature. Typically written by someone other than the primary author of the work, it often tells of some interaction between the writer of the foreword and the book's primary author or the story the book tells."

When asked to write the Foreword for this latest edition of *Teaching Music to Students with Differences and Disabilities: A Label-Free Approach*, I was sincerely humbled by the invitation. Dr. Alice Hammel and Dr. Ryan Hourigan are not only brilliant master teachers/researchers/minds extraordinaire, but they are also deeply respected colleagues and dear friends. In addition, they are leading experts in this given field of music education. I have a mere thimble of understanding compared to the endless library of expertise they bring to the landscape. My first reaction to their outreach was: "What possible benefit can I offer to their next priceless GIFT to the profession?"

Having written many introductions, forewords, and testimonials for various texts, I started by approaching this request with a similar plan, but it changed quickly and dramatically as I embraced the knowledge and wisdom offered on each page of the manuscript. My normal reading pace quickly turned into intensive studying; I began consuming one sentence at a time, followed by a lengthy self-dialogue and a deep personal examination of my own thoughts and feelings. I found myself underlining, highlighting, and writing explanatory notes in the margins. Being a voracious reader, my normal "tempo" was replaced with a methodical embracing of each word *and* the critically important message written "between the lines," as well as the equally critically important message written "on the lines."

The authors have focused on a one-of-a-kind connection that embraces the audience/reader at a much deeper level than other similar works. The *why* is dominant, followed by the *what* and *how*. Rather than simply dictating various strategies for efficient-effective learning for the student(s), we are first availed to *why* the upcoming information is so paramount. For example (taken from Chapter 5):

Developing a Student-Centered and Inclusive Music Classroom

> Class and ensemble rules can be developed with students each year. This provides a sense of ownership in the classroom, and students are often more willing to comply with a system they created. In environments of mutual respect, students are more likely to create rules that are simple and easy to understand.

From here we are given tried-and-true success strategies (*what* and *how*) to manifest the *why* into reality. This theme is integrated throughout the book and serves as a granite building block for the understanding of the value-added for the teacher. Even following the suggested formula, the *why* is again bookended as a reassuring reinforcement (it is as though Hammel and Hourigan are walking alongside us, hand-in-hand in the journey).

Vignettes, stories, examples, scripts: the book is laced with many case studies demonstrating the *contextual* application of the *content*. Storytelling is a powerful means to guarantee learning; it connects the heart and soul of one person to another with wonderful idea-bridges. Relationships are forged and solidified, with the stories creating a blend of data points and abstract ideas, thus making it easier to grasp the meaning when it is wrapped in a compelling description of the narrative at hand. The pacing of the text is artistic, affective (as well as effective).

Throughout the book the words "students with differences and disabilities" often prefaces the to-be-explained concept. Several days into the "study," a lightning bolt hit me squarely between the eyes: the ideas, notions, hypotheses, theories, and so on, do not pertain to a select few; they are applicable to *all. Teaching Music to Students with Differences and Disabilities* is a blueprint (treasure map) to and for *everyone*. While it is designed for a specific culture-of-learners, it is adaptable to all students and to all teachers. This epiphany opened yet another landscape-of-possibilities. *Every* music educator (arguably *every educator*) should be involved (saturated, if you will) in and with this material.

Forewords are not to be misconstrued with testimonials or providers of advice. With that said, it would be irresponsible of me *not* to pass along my heartfelt enthusiasm for this thought-provoking addition (and edition) to our library of advancement supporting all learning, growing, and becoming. It is a "must read" for any teacher who cares–and who cares deeply.

I have a strong personal positive prejudice when it comes to Dr. Alice M. Hammel and Dr. Ryan M. Hourigan. Alice and Ryan are more than colleagues; they are trusted-loved partners in an aligned mission to bring the *gift of music* to every child. After all, as Tim Lautzenheiser said, "Music is a place for everyone."

Tim Lautzenheiser

Preface

The concept of *Teaching Music to Students with Differences and Disabilities: A Label-Free Approach* was developed from our travels teaching and presenting seminars, in-services, and clinics at the national, regional, and local levels, and communications with local music educators about their challenges. Music teachers often find themselves teaching either included students with disabilities or in dedicated self-contained classrooms without the support they need. As music teacher educators, we have found that a large gap exists in our methods content in the area of research-grounded best-practice approaches to teaching students with learning differences.

Teaching Music to Students with Differences and Disabilities: A Label-Free Approach is designed for faculty, in-service music administrators, in-service music teachers, and preservice music teachers. It is designed as a comprehensive manual and reference guide that introduces those in the field of music education to best practices when teaching music to students with learning differences. It includes research-based strategies for methods courses and professional development. In addition, this text will address curricular strategies for methods teachers and in-service music educators. This information is grounded in research, special education law, and best practice.

A LABEL-FREE APPROACH

A focus of this book is that a student with exceptionalities is an individual who deserves a music education that is free of labels. The philosophical premise of a label-free approach is centered in the preservation of the individual personhood of each student. Through this approach, music educators will be able to gain and advocate for support, understand their rights and responsibilities, and offer an affective and effective music education for students with and without differences and disabilities. This includes learning strategies for effective collaboration with special educators, teacher educators, and classroom teachers. We also include curriculum development ideas, lesson plan strategies, observation strategies (methods classroom), and fieldwork ideas (methods classroom).

In our experience we have found that "quick fix" strategies learned by applying a technique based on the specific disability label of a student often last for a short time until a music educator can find the next new trick to assist a student with disabilities. By applying a label-free approach, educators can create a theoretical and philosophical underpinning that will serve as an effective base of knowledge for use in each individual situation.

A further consideration when choosing this approach is that the Individuals with Disabilities Education Act (IDEA) does not specify that each teacher is to be told of the specific disability of every student. It is possible that music educators may teach students with learning differences and not have access to the label listed in the paperwork for that student. Teachers are given the list of strengths and areas of challenge for the student and are also notified of specific adaptations and accommodations that are to be used for the student. By approaching the education of students with differences and disabilities from a label-free perspective, teachers are not stymied by the possible lack of access to further information. While we recognize that educators may be able to glean valuable information through the disability categories, it is also "good teaching" to look at each student as an individual and to design instruction based on the areas of need as seen in the music classroom.

These resources are all offered within the context of learning to navigate the special education system within the framework of developing culturally responsive classrooms that are free of labels. The focus of this book is to effectively approach various learning domains when developing pedagogy for both the music classroom and the music methods classroom.

HOW TO USE THIS BOOK

Teaching Music to Students with Differences and Disabilities: A Label-Free Approach will be of most interest to in-service music teachers and music teacher educators who are seeking research and practical information regarding the inclusion of students with differences and disabilities in their classrooms. In addition, undergraduate and graduate students in music education programs will find this book useful in their future careers as music educators. Our goal was to provide a book that meets the needs of music educators at all levels of instruction.

This book is organized into four parts. Part I is focused on the current landscape of teacher preparation within the context of the special education system. Chapter 1 is intended for all music educators and music teacher educators to increase the knowledge and understanding of music educators as they plan, implement, and advocate for the appropriate instruction of students with differences and disabilities. This advocacy is a natural outcome for music educators who are aware of special education policy within the special education structure of our public schools. This chapter includes strategies used to engage and observe in special education settings to assist with a complete understanding of the ways students learn in other environments.

The label-free approach to music teaching and learning transfers focus from a student's disability to an examination of how he or she receives music information, processes this information, and expresses himself or herself musically. We introduce six teaching and learning domains in this chapter: cognition, communication, behavioral, emotional, sensory, and physical. It is hoped that as a result of this shift in concentration, music educators will center their attention on music teaching and learning, rather than on labels that are attached to students with differences and disabilities.

Part II introduces effective methods utilized in preparation to teach students with differences and disabilities in both preservice and in-service music education settings. Chapter 3 is specifically designed for engagement and fieldwork within the structure of special education. This includes observation protocols for self-contained classrooms, resource rooms, summer enrichment programs, and therapy sessions (e.g., speech or arts therapy) and how observations in these settings may enhance the understanding that music teachers have regarding the learning needs of students with differences and disabilities.

Chapter 4 uses the learning domains that are introduced in Chapter 1 and provides specific music education strategies for use in the music classroom. This chapter includes a complete introduction to Individualized Education Programs (IEPs) and 504 Plans, as well as music-specific strategies and transfers of accommodations that will enhance the ability of music educators to deliver instruction to students with differences and disabilities.

Part III provides practical applications of theory and policy from the previous chapters for use in the music classroom (e.g., behavioral strategies, curricular strategies, etc.). Chapter 5 is intended for teacher educators, preservice music teachers (methods classes), and in-service music teachers and provides many practical and effective classroom management strategies for music teachers in a variety of settings.

Chapter 6 is designed to provide specific curriculum understanding and to demonstrate how these approaches affect students with disabilities—specifically, how the fundamentals of curriculum design (e.g., materials centered, constructivism) can be used to enhance the music teaching and learning environment. Chapter 6 also provides assessment accommodations that have been seen as successful for students with differences and disabilities.

Chapter 7 offers specific ideas for conductors in instrumental and vocal music ensemble settings. Both coauthors have extensive training in these areas and not only provide rehearsal techniques but also challenge band, orchestra, and choir conductors to review and reflect on their current philosophy of teaching, considering the vast changes put in place to assist the inclusion of students with differences and disabilities in all aspects of school life. The use of technology to assist in practice techniques and classroom-tested adaptations and accommodations are presented to enhance the ensemble experience for students with differences and disabilities.

The decision to discuss students who are gifted as part of this text was intentional and purposeful. The challenges mentioned in this chapter are often not included in discussions of students with differences and disabilities. This is the topic of Chapter 8. While the premise and philosophy of the text is to encourage a label-free environment for students with differences and disabilities, the specific cognitive needs of students who are gifted necessitate a discussion that includes information about their unique differences.

This chapter includes the historical, philosophical, and practical issues involved in teaching students who are gifted. These include the history of intelligence testing, varied models for educational placement options, and common characteristics of students with this type of special need. Practical information for successful inclusion of students who are gifted in the music classroom is presented. Finally, research-derived characteristics of teachers who are successful when teaching students who are gifted are also included.

Part IV is intended to provide the most up-to-date resources and technology information for music educators at all levels. Current research articles, best-practice articles, and books and internet websites are listed for music educators to use as they seek information regarding specific disabilities. This information reinforces the overall philosophy of the text as it challenges music educators to be resourceful in their approach to teaching students with differences and disabilities. In addition, this text includes many vignettes for thoughtful and reflective discussion among in-service teachers and by pre-service music educators in methods classes. These vignettes are actual stories that have occurred in public school situations within the last few years.

For music teacher educators, this book provides strategies that are research based and provide best practice for teaching all students, regardless of the challenges they face. Chapters can be used to not only address this topic, but also embed other subjects within the context of teaching students with disabilities (e.g., assessment, classroom management, etc.). Many methods instructors are inundated with the amount of materials necessary to adequately address each topic within a given methods class. It is our firm belief that good teaching is good teaching. Therefore, this text allows you the option of covering multiple topics simultaneously.

This text was designed purposefully to chart a new direction in the preparation of music educators, music teacher educators, and in-service music educators as they design, present, and assess their practices when teaching students with differences and disabilities. The focus on creating meaningful and supportive relationships with the faculty, staff, and administration partners in the schools; the importance of a label-free environment to create truly inclusive and welcoming school experiences for students with differences and disabilities; and the extraordinary value in approaching the classroom with a "fair is not equal" philosophy are the rationales for this new direction. By preparing to create an inclusive, team-oriented environment that ensures every student receives what he or she needs, we will perhaps begin to create true equity and "fairness" for all students in our public school systems.

Acknowledgments

We would like to thank the wonderful students that we have taught over the years both in K-12 and in higher education who have given us the insight and motivation to write this book. We would also like to thank Christa Hensley, Michelle Byrn, James Byrn, Elise Hackl, Taylor Walkup, and Morgan Robinson for their vignette contributions. We would like to thank Erika J. Knapp for assisting us with gathering and updating all of the information in Chapter 9 and Alicia Faith Thomas for allowing us to use her examples of observation protocols. Thank you to Amy Hourigan, MT-BC, for her contribution to this text from the music therapy perspective and to Bruce Hammel, Virginia Commonwealth University, for his editorial support.

Thank you to Dr. Tim Lautzenheiser for reviewing the text and for writing the Foreword. We would also like to thank Norm Hirschy for his guidance and support during this process.

Finally, we would like to thank our children—Hannah, Hollie, Andrew, and Joshua—who remind us each day of the uniqueness of every child. They are the true inspiration for this book.

About the Companion Website

http://www.oup.com/us/tmtswsn

The resource materials included on this website have been developed during a decade of collection and creation by the authors. Materials include information regarding policy, teaching strategies, links, print resource lists, video case studies, and video lesson examples. Full-page Word documents of observation protocols and other materials will be available for you to download and adjust to fit your individual needs. This website will be updated regularly by the authors to remain a current reference and information source for music educators. Enjoy!

Teaching Music to Students with Differences and Disabilities: A Practical Resource, Second Edition (available separately)

Alice M. Hammel and Roberta L. Yee have created a practical resource guide to accompany the third edition of *Teaching Music to Students with Differences and Disabilities: A Label-Free Approach*. Music educators from around the United States partnered with them to contribute lesson ideas, full lesson plans, and unit plans that demonstrate the principles described in this book. Materials used to teach the lessons are also included in the resource. These practical ideas are meant to illustrate and enhance research and theory in the field in a way that is applicable to K–12 classrooms that include students with differences and disabilities.

PART I

THE CURRENT LANDSCAPE OF THE SPECIAL EDUCATION SYSTEM IN THE UNITED STATES

Chapter 1

Public School Education within a Democracy

An Equal Opportunity for All Students

CHAPTER OVERVIEW

- Unequal Opportunity
- A Brief Look at Special Education in the 21st Century
- Funding of Special Education: A Demographic Snapshot of Support
- Family Challenges and Children with Disabilities
- Teaching Music in the 21st Century: A Label-Free Approach to Teaching Music to Students with Differences and Disabilities
  - Cognition
  - Communication
  - Receptive and Expressive Language
  - Language and Culture
  - Behaviors
  - Emotions
  - Sensory Needs
  - Physical and Medical
- Conclusion
- Discussion Questions

The beginning of the school year is a time when situations similar to Mrs. Johnson's first day, described in Vignette 1.1, occur. It is when these first lessons go awry that some music teachers first begin to think of their individual students, rather than the collective group. Who is the girl who moves slower than the rest and uses a walker? Who are the students in the small group who come late each day with a teacher to assist them? Who is the boy who bounds down the hall and begins to take down one of the brand-new bulletin boards that have just been finished?

Teaching Music to Students with Differences and Disabilities. Third Edition. Alice M. Hammel and Ryan M. Hourigan, Oxford University Press. © Oxford University Press 2025. DOI: 10.1093/9780197689356.003.0001

Vignette 1.1 Mrs. Johnson

It is the first day of school. Mrs. Johnson's bulletin boards are complete, and her chairs and music stands are ready. Her class lists are prepared and the lesson plan is set. She stands at the door awaiting her first class of the day. The students begin walking down the hall and she wonders which ones will stop at her door. Her first class walks in and takes their seats. However, two of her students were escorted to her music room with paraprofessionals. The paraprofessionals then proceeded to take their scheduled break.

During class there were multiple outbursts from each of these students. Mrs. Johnson spent the entire 30-minute class pacifying these outbursts, and little was accomplished. The other students seemed frustrated and bored.

After class Mrs. Johnson realized that she needed to make drastic changes to how she teaches music in this particular class. She began to ask herself: I have no idea how to help these kids–what do I do? Whom do I talk to? This cannot happen tomorrow.

Discussion:

1. Have you heard of a similar story?
2. What should Mrs. Johnson do first?

The answer to these questions is that they are *all* our students. They all have a place in our schools and they all deserve to have an education that includes music. As music teachers, we have both the right and the responsibility to educate *all* the students in our schools. We are charged with studying each student who enters our classroom and with providing all students the music education they deserve. To do this, however, we must begin to plan for the inclusive education of all students *before* that first group heads down our hall on the first day of school.

Unfortunately, until recently this was not the educational philosophy of public schools within the United States. This chapter will introduce the process that we as a nation have experienced as we have come to the understanding of what an education for all students in the United States entails, including challenges within families, the real-world realities of inclusion in practice, and a label-free approach to teaching music in the public-school setting. This book is designed to facilitate the planning, implementation, and assessment of music education for students with differences and disabilities. It is written from a paradigm that advocates thoughtful inclusion and honors the teaching and learning relationship between music teachers and their students. It is hoped that this text will present a philosophy and a set of guiding principles for teaching students with differences and disabilities in a helpful and pragmatic manner. We believe this is possible for all music educators, and we celebrate the progress made in recent years to provide a truly appropriate music education for each student we teach.

UNEQUAL OPPORTUNITY

Unfortunately, not all students within our current public education system have an equal opportunity to learn. John Dewey regarded public education as a crucial pillar to upholding a democracy: Dewey (1916/1944, p. 84) stated:

> In order to have a large number of values in common, all members of the group must have an equitable opportunity to receive and take from others. There must be a large variety of shared undertakings and experiences. Otherwise the influences which educate some into masters, educate others into slaves.

The school experience for some students is vastly different from that of others, and in some situations, some students are given more opportunities than others. Even when one considers the recent acts of legislation and the history of litigation, our public education system is far from equal for many demographic groups. Access to quality education both inside and outside the arts, especially in music, remains a challenge for students with exceptionalities (Blair & McCord, 2016). Laws, protections, and procedures for students with learning differences have entered our public education system during the past 50-plus years, and educators are now challenged to expect achievement from all students, regardless of their background or relative strengths and areas of challenge.

Our awareness of privilege and its effect on public education has become increasingly obvious. The United States is experiencing a reckoning as we grapple with racism, classism, sexism, homophobia, discrimination based on gender identity, ableism, and religious bigotry (Diem & Welton, 2020). The intersections of portions of our individual identities and the ways we "other" those different from us have become a political rallying cry and a source of concern in public schools. To treat everyone equally is not equitable. Equity will require systemic change in our global policies, as well as in ways we treat individuals within our school systems.

The basis for some continued differences can, in part, be traced to opportunity. It is clear that an equity gap remains in the public education system. This disparity affects children in poverty, certain ethnic and racial groups, *and* students with disabilities (Hourigan, 2014). It is important to look at all aspects of public special education to understand the context that students with differences and disabilities experience as they enter the music classroom. Students have more than one identity, as everything in their lives intersects with everything else. Our ability to see each student as the composite of their life experiences and identifiers is critical. In addition, it is important to understand the current framework of the modern special education system. Hammel and Hourigan (2022) state:

> We can, while at the same time, being privileged in our citizenship and ability, also be disadvantaged by our gender, race, and class. This includes students who also might be disadvantaged by learning differences. These complexities can lead to a cognitive dissonance with those who are inherently disadvantaged because it can be complicated, messy, and uncomfortable to walk in the shoes of someone who has not shared your life experience.

This chapter offers a fundamental look at the current practice of teaching students with differences and disabilities. At the end of this chapter, we will discuss our view of a label-free approach to teaching music to students with disabilities and will begin to offer suggestions regarding implementation of this approach.

A BRIEF LOOK AT SPECIAL EDUCATION IN THE 21ST CENTURY

According to the U.S. Department of Education (2022), special education "means specially designed instruction, at no cost to the parents, to meet the unique needs of a child with a disability, including instruction conducted in the classroom, in the home, in hospitals and institutions, and in other settings; and Instruction in physical education."

The practice of special education has evolved from segregated schools and institutions in the early 19th century to an integration model in the latter half of the 20th century (Winzer, 2009). Our public schools have moved toward the full inclusion of students with disabilities in the regular classroom. Advocates for full inclusion insist that "the general education classroom is the most appropriate full-time placement for all students with disabilities" (Lewis & Doorlag, 2011, p. 4).

The specifics of these policies and their implications for music educators will be discussed in Chapter 2. However, for now, it is important to look at inclusion as a concept within the larger context of special education. It is also important to understand that the number of students needing assistance from public school programs for students with disabilities began to rise in the late 20th century and is continuing to increase (National Center for Education Statistics, 2022). This is due to many factors, including the increasing ability of service providers to identify students with differences and disabilities, improved diagnoses of childhood illnesses and injuries, and an increase in the number of babies born with low birth weight.

In practice, teachers who work in full-inclusion environments sometimes struggle with large class sizes, a perceived lack of support (either instructional or for specific skill sets), and very busy schedules (sound familiar?). In addition, pressures from a continuing standardized test-driven school culture have made full inclusion difficult to implement. Furthermore, like other federally mandated programs, special education programs are expensive (with most of the burden placed on the local school district) and are typically underfunded. These mandates require many teachers to advocate even more effectively for their special education programs as limits are increasingly placed on time, talents, and finances. Special education is a highly demanding profession. Vignette 1.2 was written by a special educator in an urban public school. This vignette shows the challenges of special education in practice.

As you can see, special educators are on the difficult front line of two reform initiatives: general special education and inclusion. These challenges often lead to a drastic turnover in the field of special education and, sometimes, to a lack of coordination or communication between special and regular (music included) education teachers (McLesky, Tyler, & Flippin, 2004). There is always a demand for special educators because of the stresses involved with special education.

Vignette 1.2 A Day in the Life of a Special Educator

I am a kindergarten through third grade, Moderate Disabilities, special education teacher. I currently have 12 students in a self-contained classroom. The teaching day runs from 8 a.m. to 3:30 p.m. The student day runs from 8:30 a.m. to 2:30 p.m. However, my students arrive at 8:05 a.m. This means that I have to have everything ready for the next day before I leave each afternoon. My students require an extremely structured environment from the moment they walk in the door until the moment they leave. There is no room for being ill prepared, or planning on the fly during the day. Part of my daily planning even requires a plan for unexpected events. And all of this planning is done without any teacher guides or textbooks from which to get my lessons/activities.

Each of my students has their own picture schedule that shows them what they will be doing each moment of the day. I develop a master schedule that has each student's activities for each moment of the day,

(continued)

Vignette 1.2 Continued

as well as the duties of each of my two instructional assistants for every moment of the day.

One of my instructional assistants must go out and get each student off the bus and make sure that each child makes it into the correct classroom safely. My other instructional assistant waits for each child at the door, greets them, and assists them with getting their personal belongings put away, taking care of morning restroom needs, brushing teeth, checking their schedule, and going to their first activity of the morning, which is designed to be an independent recreation activity. I spend this part of the morning going through backpacks, reading communications from home, and writing in each student's notebook what their individual activities are for the day. This may seem a little excessive, but most of my students are unable to communicate messages from home or events/messages from the school day. As I am sitting at the table trying to fill out student notebooks, Sam is hitting Tommy with the blocks, Karl is pulling out every puzzle in the cabinet rather than playing with the one set out for him, and Robbie has wet his pants. So, I must get up and take care of these issues before I can finish the communication notebooks. Once all of the students are in the classroom, one of my instructional assistants takes the five kids who eat breakfast at school over to the cafeteria, while the other instructional assistant continues to man the restroom/grooming activities. By 8:30 a.m. our daily goal is to have every student to the restroom, teeth brushed, hair brushed, and face/hands washed. At this point, morning announcements are given over the intercom.

The volume of the intercom bothers Mary's ears, so she begins screaming and pinching Amanda. While my instructional assistants are trying to get Mary calmed down, headphones put on, and Amanda's consequences given for pushing Mary, Will sees this as prime opportunity to bolt from the classroom. As I chase Will down the hallway, the notebooks are still sitting on the table waiting to be completed. After announcements, we start morning circle time. We work on counting, alphabet, name recognition, and spelling, colors, shapes, days of the week, months of the year, weather, seasons, sitting in chairs, raising hands, speaking clearly, and keeping our hands to ourselves. During this process, Robbie yells out every answer, someone has to sit next to Will to keep him in his chair, Mariah and Arryanna are playing hair salon rather than listening. And I have six other students that need constant verbal prompting in order to participate.

After calendar, each student checks his individual picture schedule and proceeds to the scheduled activity. Some of the five students need physical assistance to do this task. The other students are able to check their schedule independently, but then are required to wait while the teachers try to get the other students transitioned. Will never likes to do what is on his schedule because he would rather do puzzles, so we must redirect him once or twice to math group and remind him that after he does his math work, he can play with the puzzles. Luke does not like Arryanna, so he has punched her while waiting for reading group to begin. Consequences must be given for this behavior. Mariah is waiting patiently at the door for someone to take her to her general education classroom. Once everyone is settled, Mrs. D takes Mariah to her general education classroom for reading time. I am teaching four students at reading group. Mrs. F has three students for math group. Two students are listening to audiobooks, one student is at the computer, and one student is folding laundry. Everything is very calm and orderly for a few brief moments. Then, it is time to turn the tape over, so Robbie screams as if in pain and begins crying because the audiobook has stopped. This prompts Mary to throw all of the laundry she has just folded onto the floor. I have to get up to help Robbie and Mary, so Luke takes this as opportunity to pick on the other students in the group. Mrs. F gets up from her group to deal with Luke, so Will leaves math group and grabs the puzzles. After I get Robbie and Mary settled, I redirect Will back to math group and settle back in to try to teach reading. This is a very typical activity session in the room.

During the parts of the day when all of the teachers are in the classroom, there is always someone working one-on-one at a workstation with a child. For each life skills activity, such as laundry, brushing teeth, using the telephone, and so on, one of the teachers is also recording data as they are instructing the student on how to complete the activity. We also have community-based experiences in which one of the staff takes one to two students into the community to go shopping, get a haircut, go to the library, go to the YMCA, and so on. At any given point in the day, there are parents calling me, other teachers needing assistance, paperwork that needs to be completed for case conferences, progress reports, behavior plans, eligibility determination surveys, and other typical school paperwork.

At lunchtime, two teachers must be in the cafeteria with the students in order to take data on cafeteria skills, as well as monitor behavior and help the students who are unable to independently feed themselves. Two teachers must go to recess with the students in order to facilitate social interactions and appropriate play skills, and to monitor behavior as well as assist any students with mobility issues on safe use of the playground equipment. During specials classes, when most teachers have prep time, I am typically in the specials class to assist. After school, each student

(continued)

Vignette 1.2 Continued

must be escorted all the way onto the bus to ensure safety. After all of the students are gone, picture schedule cards must be collected, sorted, and put back up for the next day's activities, as well as all lesson plans and materials set out for the following day.

There are always six or seven activities happening at once in the classroom. None of the children do any activities completely independently. With only three teachers in the room, this requires us to constantly be on our toes. When people say that teachers have eyes in the back of their heads, special education teachers must have eyes all the way around their entire heads. The job of a special education teacher is extremely exhausting, stressful, unappreciated by most; but made completely gratifying and fulfilling by all of the smiles and hugs received from the students throughout the day.

FUNDING OF SPECIAL EDUCATION: A DEMOGRAPHIC SNAPSHOT OF SUPPORT

It is no surprise to learn that students with differences and disabilities in wealthy areas tend to have better services and therefore better opportunity to learn from higher-paid special educators and better-equipped (and staffed) classrooms. When we consider the ways intersections of disability and other demographics compound the problematic nature of privilege in our public school systems, we see a clear line between poverty and school funding (Hammel & Hourigan, 2022). This is especially true in urban areas. Urban school systems are typically underfunded and understaffed. In addition, there is a disproportionate representation of students from minority groups who receive special education services (Hourigan, 2014). We cannot discount the relationship between classism, race, and poverty. In addition, special educators in these areas are in a constant struggle to meet the requirements for continued federally mandated initiatives that have compounded these challenges.

Rural school systems undergo support challenges similar to those found in urban school systems. However, support for persons with disabilities in rural areas can be more often linked to access to appropriate services. Families may find themselves traveling long distances to get the healthcare and school support they need because of school consolidation and other challenges (Plucker, Spradlin, Magaro, Chien, & Zapf, 2007). Feelings of isolation and classism increase perceptions of being left on their own to teach students with complicated profiles who also have differences and disabilities (Hammel & Hourigan, 2022).

This may come at a considerable expense to the family. Rural school systems face major funding shortfalls similar to those in urban settings (Arnold, Newman, Gaddy, & Dean, 2005). Because there are fewer properties to tax in rural areas, funding must be spread among several school districts that can be hundreds of miles in diameter. If public education continues to be primarily funded by a real estate tax-based system, rural and urban schools will continue to face these challenges.

FAMILY CHALLENGES AND CHILDREN WITH DISABILITIES

Families may face enormous financial burdens in an effort to provide care to their children with disabilities. Whether it is therapy (i.e., speech therapy, occupational therapy, music therapy, physical therapy, behavioral therapy), equipment and transportation, or legal and administrative expenses, services for children with differences and disabilities can be very expensive. Because of all these challenges, an inordinate amount of stress may be placed on parents and adult family members. Because of these obstacles, family structures may disintegrate, and as a result, many children with disabilities will be raised in single-parent households or by grandparents and other family members. It is important for music educators to be aware of this as they seek to be part of the team that provides school-based family support services to the families of students with differences and disabilities (Hourigan, 2018). Families need support in many areas for a child with disabilities to have an equal opportunity to learn in public school, and we as music educators are an integral part of this support system. By carefully considering the intersective nature of each student, we can see more than differences and disabilities as we learn the entire student(s) and their families.

Music educators should take into account these considerations when teaching music to students with differences and disabilities. For example, if a child wants to start an instrument, the expense of that instrument (added to the speech therapy bill) can be insurmountable. If a student is encouraged to attend an event or participate in a trip with a music group, the challenges associated with that experience may be more than a family of a student with differences and disabilities (or any student who is part of a family experiencing financial, emotional, or health stressors) can navigate. We also must consider possible religious or cultural conflicts, as well as gender identity and any other intersection that is part of the profile of the student. All these issues are important considerations when including students with differences and disabilities in school music programs. Two parents of children who are profoundly affected by autism wrote Vignette 1.3. This vignette shows the basic challenges and stresses that families encounter while raising children with differences and disabilities.

Vignette 1.3 Parents of Children with Differences and Disabilities

My name is Ron. My wife Ann and I are raising two children with autism. Our mornings can start out rough. Our children are all about schedule. On this particular day we have had a two-hour delay because of snow. Adam, who is nonverbal, does not understand and is becoming violent. He thinks it is a Saturday because of the school delay. When he figures out that he needs to go to school, he begins a "melt down." He kicks, bites, hits, and tears anything in his path. He scratches his brother Jonathan in the eye.

This all happened after a sleepless night with Adam. Children with autism typically do not sleep well. Adam takes a "cocktail" of medications to calm him down and help him sleep. This puts enormous strain on everyone else in the household because none of us functions well on little to no sleep.

Adam's teachers and other staff members (bus drivers and paraprofessionals) have a difficult time keeping him from hurting his classmates, especially on a day like this. He does not hurt others because he is mean. He is trying to communicate his frustration.

Jonathan is off to school after witnessing this event and having his parents spend all of their time focused on his brother Adam (which happens to a lot of kids who have siblings with disabilities). He also has autism. He has a one-on-one aide and is doing rather well in school. The only issue is the lack of lasting relationships he has with his peers. His best friends are his parents. His classmates are nice to him. However, he has only been invited to a few birthday parties. Other than that, he is at home. No friends to run over and play with him after school.

After both children are home (and we find out about the damage done), we sift through the notes that come home from school for both kids. There is information about Cub Scouts, Little League, and basketball. Unfortunately none of these activities are possible for our children. Our children then go outside to play. However, one of us needs to always be alert and outside, watching their every move. Both of them got away from us when they were younger. We had an alarm system installed to let us know when doors open and close.

It is time for dinner and then bed. Once they finally sleep, we are beyond tired and know that our rest is short-lived. Inevitably one of them will be up. Potentially with a melt-down.

As parents we are exhausted. We love our children. However, it is a constant fight either at an IEP meeting or with an insurance company. We consider all of this in the midst of thinking about the future. Every day we think about what life will be like for them as adults. Will they be self-sufficient? If not, how will we pay for a lifetime of care? Many of our friends talk of college tuition. College is a temporary expense. A disability like autism lasts a lifetime.

TEACHING MUSIC IN THE 21ST CENTURY: A LABEL-FREE APPROACH TO TEACHING MUSIC TO STUDENTS WITH DIFFERENCES AND DISABILITIES

Music teachers share many of the same advocacy and funding challenges experienced by other teachers in the current educational environment. Because of equal-access provisions within the law, music teachers are under increased pressure to deliver instruction, often without preparation or support. In addition, in-service music teachers are not always prepared to work with students with disabilities (Hammel, 2001). There continues to be a considerable lack of coursework within our current undergraduate and graduate music education programs to prepare students for teaching diverse student populations, including students with disabilities (Colwell & Thompson, 2000). If programs do exist, they are often in tandem with an existing music therapy program. Current research states that only a third of all music teacher preparation programs have this requirement (29.6%), and only 38.9% have even a course available (Salvador, 2010). Often, music teacher educators themselves lack the preparation and therefore do not always include the subject of teaching students with disabilities in their undergraduate methods courses. However, research also indicates that music educators are becoming more comfortable with inclusion and adapting and modifying their curriculum (VanWeelden & Whipple, 2014). In addition, music educators have felt more support in teaching students with exceptionalities than in previous decades (VanWeelden & Whipple, 2013). When we add in the complicating profiles of students who are not privileged by race and class, we can see that music educators can feel a lack of preparation to teach the whole child in front of them and, in particular, when that child presents with differences and disabilities.

Considering the challenges presented in this chapter, how do we as music educators and music teacher educators continue to deliver quality instruction to students of all learning differences? How do we as music educators continue to deliver quality instruction and design effective curricula for students with differences and disabilities considering the challenges we face? To enhance achievement in education, students must have an equal opportunity to learn. For students with learning challenges, this opportunity coexists with various support systems within the framework of special education. John Dewey reminds us that in a democracy, all students must have access to similar experiences in education. This requires that music educators not only learn to be advocates for equity, but also construct adaptive pedagogy, curricula, and assessment that meets the needs of all students.

Research and best practice in special education is moving toward a focus on disability domains, rather than specific disabilities as listed in the Individuals with Disabilities Education Act (IDEA), in exploring the teaching and learning relationship in the classroom. This does not mean that a music teacher should not explore the nuances and obstacles associated with a single disability or diagnosis. Music teachers should use all resources available to understand the challenges and areas of strength a student brings to the classroom as a part of their disability. Moreover, music teachers should, as they do with all students, focus on the teaching and learning relationship, and what obstacles may hinder that student from learning in the classroom, through a thorough understanding of the lives of their students inside and outside the classroom. Focusing on these challenges may allow music teachers to adjust their instructional strategies and deliver higher quality instruction to students. In addition, this approach allows music teachers to focus on the whole person instead of the disability that challenges the student. In feeling less overwhelmed with labels, acronyms, and terms, the music teacher will then be able to focus on the music education of students with and without differences and disabilities.

The next section of this chapter will focus on six domains: cognition, communication, behavioral, emotional, physical, and sensory. We introduce these in the first chapter to begin the exploration of the music teaching and learning relationship and to set the foundation for discussing specific teaching strategies later in this book. It is important to remember that these categories overlap. A student may have challenges associated with multiple domains. It is hoped these strategies will make an impact on the music classroom by focusing on music teaching and learning, rather than the sometimes overwhelming litany of disability citations and descriptions. Observation protocols have been developed in this chapter to assist in obtaining an initial understanding of these areas and how they may impact your teaching and learning relationship with a student with differences and disabilities. Specific modifications (winding), and adaptations will be discussed as we progress through this text.

Cognition

"Cognition" and "cognitive function" are the generally accepted terms used to describe the ability of a student to receive, process, and commit information to memory (Davis, Gfeller, & Thaut, 1999). For cognition to occur, a person must convert sensory energy into neural information. After this occurs, our perception utilizes sensory information to make further sense of the world (including our musical world). Finally, our cognition "involves the acquisition, storage, retrieval, and use of knowledge obtained by the sensory and perception systems" (Lipscomb, 1996, p. 133).

In assessing the teaching and learning relationship, music teachers must gather and examine information regarding how students hear or receive music, remember musical concepts and understandings, and express themselves musically. In accomplishing this task, music teachers should begin by observing the student, either in music class or in other classes, to begin to understand the cognitive challenges they bring to music class. Specific adaptations and accommodations in the area of cognition will be discussed in Chapter 4. In all six of the suggested domains, an observation protocol has been provided. Box 1.1 is designed to assist music educators as they observe potential challenges in the area of cognition. This will help as you define areas of concern and establish a baseline of understanding regarding the needs of a student. In addition, within this protocol is a section designed to remind music teachers to discuss the learning needs with the student's primary teacher. This may include a classroom teacher or special educator. These discussions may also include a paraprofessional or aide who works with a student during the school day.

Box 1.1 Cognitive observation protocol (for music educators).

Student Name:_______________ Primary Teacher(s):_______________

Notes from discussion with Primary Teacher in the area of Cognitive Needs and Learning Strategies **(after reading the IEP document*)**:

Class Observed:

Strategies used in the area of input (e.g. repetition, visual icons, etc.):

- Are there any sensory challenges that may contribute to cognitive challenges (i.e. vision or hearing)
- Potential input strategies in music (including strategies to enhance sensation and perception):

Strategies used in the area of retention (multiple modes of delivery, review outside of class, etc.):

- Potential retention strategies in music (including strategies to enhance sensation and perception):

Strategies used in the area of output:

- Potential output or expression strategies in music (e.g. write instead of speak, point instead of tell, etc.):

General observations and ideas for music class:

* Please note that student or pre-clinical teachers will not have access to IEP without permission

Communication

Let's face it, if a teacher and a student cannot communicate, there probably is a learning obstacle. There are many reasons to explain why a student may struggle with communication. They may have a developmental delay; English may not be their primary language; or they may have other neurological or cognitive challenges that affect processing in the brain. In any event, it is important to understand the function of communication (both the preferred output and the current level) in a student's life and how that might affect their ability to participate and demonstrate understanding in music class. There are four areas to consider when assessing a student's ability to communicate: receptive language, expressive language, cognitive function/processing, and cultural use of language. There also may be extraneous circumstances that can hinder assessment in these areas, such as common language cues a student may or may not understand. Given that music itself is a form of communication, students who struggle to communicate (in non-music settings) may express themselves to you as their music teacher in ways they may not in any other class they attend. This is why it is important for music teachers to assess these areas in a formative manner, before the inclusion of the student in the classroom if at all possible, to understand potential challenges a teacher and student may face in the music teaching and learning relationship. A communication observation protocol (Box 1.2) has been created for use in identifying areas of strength and weakness in a student with challenges in the area of communication.

RECEPTIVE AND EXPRESSIVE LANGUAGE

Because of a multitude of challenges, students may have the inability or be limited in their ability to receive and express language. Receptive language refers to the ability of a student to receive and process information. There are a number of reasons this process may be interrupted. These reasons can include sensory obstacles, cognitive processing interruptions, or other challenges that may impede a student's ability to understand a teacher. A student may also have delays in cognitive function or processing. Expressive language is the ability to use symbols of language to express thoughts (Lewis & Doorlag, 2011). Music teachers may find that if a student has a delay in receptive and expressive language skills, they may have similar challenges in the ability to receive, understand, and express themselves musically.

Box 1.2 Communication observation protocol (for music educators).

Student Name:________________ Primary Teacher(s):________________

Notes from discussion with Primary Teacher in the area of Communication Needs and Language Learning Strategies **(after reading the IEP document*)**:

Class Observed:

Receptive Communication Strategies observed (e.g. simplified language, picture icons, etc.):

- Potential strategies in music class:

Expressive Communication Strategies observed (e.g. pointing to a picture icon, small one or two word phrases, assistive technology, signing etc):

- Potential strategies in music class:

Does the student have cultural language differences (i.e. Is English his/her first language)?

- Potential strategies in music class:

Notes:

* Please note that student or pre-clinical teachers will not have access to IEP without permission

LANGUAGE AND CULTURE

According to the National Education Association (2022), 1 in 4 children in U.S. public schools are English language learner (ELL) students. As such, there have been an increasing number of ELL students in music classrooms.

It is important to understand the cultural influences of language and the different experiences that students bring to your music classroom. Communication and language are of primary importance when allowing access to students from different cultures and language origins. This challenges teachers to be more in tune with not only language, but also cultural differences in the classroom. Through recognizing this intersectionality, we honor the culture and history that each student brings independently to the music classroom and ensemble. Therefore, the inclusion of ELL students and the way language affects our teaching and learning sequences in the music classroom are important considerations when preparing to teach students with differences and disabilities. Box 1.2 has been provided to assist music teachers in understanding strategies used in other classrooms for an ELL student. Further adaptations will be discussed later in this text.

BEHAVIORS

Because of many challenges associated with disabilities, students may struggle in the area of behavior. Research suggests that behavioral disabilities occur more often in boys than girls, and these disabilities have a tendency to become more evident in secondary education (middle or high school; Lewis & Doorlag, 2011). Most importantly, although the intelligence level of students with behavior disorders does not vary from students in the general population, students with behavior challenges tend to fall behind because of a lack of social and coping skills (Lewis & Doorlag, 2011).

Every student exhibits behavior at times that is considered inappropriate. Please consider the following when making modifications to instruction for a student: (a) Is there an antecedent to the behavior? (b) Is the behavior considered inappropriate for a student's age? (c) Is the behavior interrupting the student's learning (e.g., attention, impulsivity, hyperactivity)? (d) Is the behavior external (e.g., aggression) or internal (e.g., withdrawal)? (e) Is the behavior interrupting the learning of other students in your classroom? If the answer to these questions is yes, then it is time to consult a special education professional and create a plan that will assist in your teaching.

When a music teacher first experiences the behaviors mentioned previously, it is advisable to visit other classes to see if similar behaviors are occurring in a variety of settings and what might encourage positive and negative behaviors within the music classroom setting. In addition, it is a good idea to reach out to guardians and other teachers with similar goals to share your ideas about promoting positive behaviors in your classroom. An observation protocol has been developed to assist you in this area (see Box 1.3).

Box 1.3 Behavioral observation protocol (for music educators).

Student Name:_______________ Primary Teacher(s):_______________

Notes from discussion with Primary Teacher in the area of Behavioral Strategies (**after reading the IEP document***):

Class Observed:

Positive and appropriate behaviors observed (internal and external):

- Are there any noticeable triggers that cause negative behaviors

- Strategies to promote these behaviors in music class:

Negative or inappropriate behaviors observed (internal and external):

- Strategies to discourage these behaviors in music class:

Notes:

* Please note that student or pre-clinical teachers will not have access to IEP without permission

EMOTIONS

The emotional domain is closely connected to the previously mentioned behavioral domain. However, the IDEA defines emotional disturbance as a condition that affects students in one or more of the following ways: (a) an inability to learn that cannot be explained by intellectual, sensory, or health factors; (b) an inability to develop and maintain interpersonal relationships with peers or teachers; (c) inappropriate types of behavior or fears in normal circumstances; (d) a general pervasive mood of unhappiness or depression; and (e) a tendency to develop physical symptoms related to fears associated with personal or school problems (Turnbull, Huerta, & Stowe, 2004).

There are added challenges with students who exhibit challenges within the emotional domain. First, students may have trouble with how and when they express their emotions. For example, a student may not have the ability to self-talk their way through a difficult emotional situation. Many of us have the ability—even though we are angry, sad, or bored—to get through the moment by coping in various ways. There are many people who lack the coping mechanisms to do this. This will in turn add to challenges in the other domains mentioned in this chapter. If students also have lived experiences and trauma that exacerbate emotions during stressful situations, we are again charged with noting and ameliorating their emotions in the moment while shaping them in the longer term.

The key to helping students with these challenges is to practice coping mechanisms prior to and in between stressful episodes. We rehearse procedures with students during times of stability so that they become helpful in times of crisis. For example, model a self-talk exercise for when they are anxious (i.e., "Eric is nervous; he is safe and everything will be OK"). In addition, it is important to acknowledge and not ignore the emotion that is occurring. Both techniques allow the student an opportunity to find ways to self-regulate emotions independently. More detail regarding this domain will continue to be examined throughout this text. As with other domains in this chapter, Box 1.4 is created for music educators as we study the emotional challenges for students with disabilities.

Box 1.4 Emotional observation protocol (for music educators).

Student Name: ______________________________

Primary Teacher(s): ____________________________

Notes from discussion with Primary Teacher in the area of Emotional Strategies (**after reading the IEP document***):

Does the student have difficulty regulating emotions? Y or N

If yes, what emotion was observed as an issue (e.g. anxiety, frustration)?

What techniques did the classroom/special education teacher use to assist with emotional regulation?

How can you, as a music educator, use these techniques in the music classroom?

SENSORY NEEDS

Many students have obstacles to overcome in the area of sensory needs. While these students do have sensory challenges, there are other types of differences and disabilities that include challenges to sensory input and/or output. Students may demonstrate a hypo- (less than) or hyper- (more than) reaction to sound, sight, touch, smell, and/or taste. There are also two additional senses that involve our bodies in space (vestibular) and the way our bodies interact with others near us (proprioceptive). These seven senses are critical to every part of our daily lives. We sometimes discount them in favor of immediately looking at behaviors when an incident occurs in our classroom. By considering the seven senses (five plus two) and the ways hypo- and hyper-sensitivities affect us all, we can determine the root of some behaviors that we experience in our classrooms. Many students, with and without differences and disabilities, experience accompanying sensory challenges. An excellent first step is to observe the student in other settings and to talk with special educators and guardians. By being aware of how a student is challenged, extreme reactions to classroom activities can be predicted and sometimes alleviated. Many students who struggle with sensory challenges engage in sensory integration therapy as part of their overall services through the school system. Some will have sensory items listed in their IEP or 504 Plan and will bring them to music. An observation protocol has been developed that includes questions you may ask to understand the communication, orientation, and mobility needs of a student (see Box 1.5). This will guide you as you begin to make appropriate modifications (winding), adaptations, or accommodations in your music classroom. Specific adaptations will be discussed in Chapter 4.

PHYSICAL AND MEDICAL

A student's physical condition may or may not affect their academic performance in school. A student may have full cognitive function yet have a debilitating disorder that requires accommodation. Students with physical disabilities sometimes have difficulty achieving the skills necessary to be independent (Lewis & Doorlag, 2011). If a student has a physical disability, it is important to create a learning environment that allows not only opportunity for achievement, but also the skills necessary to achieve independence. This may require technology or low-tech strategies and tools obtained through special education or district-based funding. Increasing numbers of students with extensive health challenges are currently enrolled in public schools. This, in part, is due to advances in medicine that enable students to manage their chronic (long-term) or acute (short-term) medical conditions

Box 1.5 Sensory observation protocol (for music educators).

Student Name:_______________ Primary Teacher(s):_______________

Notes from discussion with Primary Teacher in the area of Sensory Strategies **(after reading the IEP document*)**:

Class Observed:

Sensory Challenges (Visual or hearing impairment or hypo/hyper reactions to sound, sight, touch, taste or smell):

Communication Tools Used

Mobility Needs and Strategies

Orientation Needs and Strategies

Notes:

* Please note that student or pre-clinical teachers will not have access to IEP without permission

while still attending public school (Lewis & Doorlag, 2011). When teaching students with health challenges, there are many considerations. These students may be in pain or discomfort. They also may appear fine on one day and have great difficulty the next day. Students may require medication that, depending on the time of day administered, may affect their performance in the music classroom. It is important for teachers to learn about the specific medical condition, and the way it affects a specific student, to effectively plan and offer the best possible opportunity to learn in the music classroom. Box 1.6 was designed to assist music educators in attempting to

Box 1.6 Physical or medical condition observation protocol (for music educators).

Student Name:_______________ Primary Teacher(s):_______________

Notes from discussion with Primary Teacher in the area of Physical or Medical Conditions **(after reading the IEP or 504 document*)**:

Class Observed:

Overview of physical or medical challenges:

- Specific healthcare needs:

Gross motor needs:

Fine motor needs

Notes:

* Please note that student or pre-clinical teachers will not have access to IEP without permission

identify these concerns in an attempt to provide the most appropriate learning environment possible.

It is also important to state that physical disabilities and health conditions can be temporary. If this is the case, a temporary Section 504 Plan may be designed for that student for the duration of the current challenge. Section 504 Plans can be temporary or long term and may be very useful for a student with a short-term physical or health condition. Section 504 Plans will be discussed in depth in Chapter 2. These documents can be very beneficial as you plan to include a student with a health condition or physical disability.

CONCLUSION

It is hoped this chapter will set the scene for a label-free approach to teaching music to students with differences and disabilities and the way these differences intersect with all other life experiences a student may have. We teach complex humans who come to us with a lifetime of lived moments that include the entirety of their identities. By focusing solely on differences and disabilities, we are most likely missing the whole person seeking to learn music. The remainder of this text is designed to assist music teachers and music teacher educators as they define and implement adaptations, and modifications (winding) within an inclusive philosophy. In addition, it is our goal to provide a clear understanding of policy and procedures within the public special education system. The vignettes and discussion questions included in each chapter are designed for use in methods classes or for in-depth reflection by practicing music educators to focus on the music teaching and learning relationship within music education.

DISCUSSION QUESTIONS

1. How does intersectionality factor into teaching students with differences and disabilities?
2. Discuss inequities within our current public school education system.
3. Describe how public school programs are funded. How does this funding affect students in urban and rural settings?
4. Describe in detail the six categories of disabilities and the label-free approach.
5. What hyper- and/or hypo-sensitivities do you experience within the five plus two sensory challenges?

Chapter 2

The Current Structure of Special Education in Our Schools

A Brief History of Legislation and Litigation in the United States

CHAPTER OVERVIEW

- Keystone Legislation and Educating Students with Exceptionalities
  - Parallel Movement in Congress on Behalf of Children Who Are Intellectually Gifted
  - Public Law 94-142
  - The Movement to Full Inclusion
  - Further Legislation Regarding Gifted and Talented Students
- The Effect and Future Influence of the No Child Left Behind Act on Special Education
  - A Closer Examination of the Individuals with Disabilities Education Act
  - Zero Reject
  - Nondiscriminatory Evaluation
  - Free and Appropriate Education (FAPE)
  - Least Restrictive Environment
  - Procedural Due Process and Parental Involvement
- The Influence of Race to the Top (RTTT) on Current Policy
- Common Core State Standards (2010)
- The Every Student Succeeds Act (2015)
  - *Endrew F. versus Douglas County* (2017)
  - New Focus on Early Intervention
  - A Different View of Due Process: House Bill 1107 (Indiana)
  - Important Non-Educational Legislation to Consider (The Americans with Disabilities Act)

Teaching Music to Students with Differences and Disabilities. Third Edition. Alice M. Hammel, and Ryan M. Hourigan, Oxford University Press. © Oxford University Press 2025. DOI: 10.1093/9780197689356.003.0002

- The Intersectionality Between Poverty, Race, and Special Education Policy
- Applications and Considerations for Music Educators
- Discussion Questions

KEYSTONE LEGISLATION AND EDUCATING STUDENTS WITH EXCEPTIONALITIES

Before we continue with the expansive history of special education in the United States, it is important to remember that even if a piece of legislation is dated, it still influences the next steps. In this chapter you will see how each law expands on the previous sets of legislation. Some would say in a positive way. Some would say in a negative way. We say it is both. Education policy has become more politically charged, and will continue to be so as we move into the middle of the 21st century.

Legal wrangling, court decisions, and the timeline of a bill as it becomes law are not always met with public scrutiny or interest. However, there are many seminal moments that have shaped policies, legislation, and litigation in the areas of civil rights and the education of students with differences and disabilities. The keystone legislation examined in this chapter has continued to define us as a country and to shape our public policy. Influenced by the civil rights movement, parents and advocates of students with differences and disabilities learned that true progress for their causes is steeped in the courthouses and lawmaking bodies of our states, districts, and in Washington, DC. It is through legislation and litigation that change becomes reality. And it was through this paradigm shift that the lives of students with differences and disabilities, and their families, improved. In addition, advocates learned it is also possible to improve the quality of life for all students. Through inclusion and an increasingly widened lens when viewing differences and diversity, *all* students (those with and without differences and disabilities) in our schools have the opportunity to learn and grow with those who are different. The path for all, then, is expanded and enriched for the experiences shared through an inclusive and diverse environment.

While Linda Brown (Vignette 2.1) and all other students who are African American are now eligible to attend their neighborhood schools, students with differences and disabilities are often bused far from their neighborhoods to be educated with other students because the school system has decided to segregate them according to ability and disability. If Linda had autism today, she might have to ride a bus for an hour and a half (each way) to school every day when her local elementary school is no farther from her

Vignette 2.1 Linda

Linda was six years old and was very excited at the thought that she may be allowed to attend school down the street from her house. She had played with her friends in the neighborhood and almost all of them went to the Sumner School, their local elementary school. One day, Linda and her Dad walked the few blocks to the Sumner School together. Linda remembers how big the school looked. School buildings and steps can look very large when you are a very small child. She walked up the steps with her Dad and entered the school office. Her Dad then went into the Principal's office while Linda stayed in the waiting area. Before long, Linda began to hear raised voices and she could tell her Dad was not happy with whatever the school principal was telling him. Then, her Dad walked out of the office, took her small hand in his, and the two of them walked home. Linda would not be attending Sumner School with her friends. Instead, Linda must attend another school built for students like her that was farther away from her neighborhood and farther away from the friends she played with each day. What possible reason could exist for Linda to be considered unacceptable to a local elementary school? What disability must she have had to not be admitted? In reality, Linda did not have a disability. The answer is that Linda and her family were African American and the year was 1951. Linda's last name was Brown, and her family became part of the class action lawsuit that eventually included over 200 students in several states by the time the case was heard by the United States Supreme Court in 1954.

home than the Sumner School was in 1951. We clearly still have a long way to go in delineating the rights of all citizens to equal access under the law.

The *Brown v. Board of Education* (1954) case was very important to the cause of those seeking to have students with differences and disabilities included in the public schools. The Supreme Court ruled, in *Brown v. Board of Education*, that it is unlawful to discriminate against a student for reasons that are not justified (Cartwright, 1995). The *Brown v. Board* case challenged an earlier Supreme Court case that held that "separate but equal" facilities for transportation were acceptable. This earlier case was heard in 1896 and was titled *Plessy v. Ferguson*. While we know Linda as the face of the *Brown* case, this case was actually a class action lawsuit that combined several lawsuits from five states that were all sent to the Supreme Court at the same time, and all were challenging the idea of "separate but equal" and discrimination without cause.

Much legislation and litigation in the area of education over the past 55 years has a foundation in this very important court ruling. Moreover, this decision is a symbol of the beginning of the advocacy movement, as well as an ongoing discussion in the United States, regarding students with differences and disabilities and their place in American society (Paul & Warnock, 1980). The *Brown* case challenged the educational placement of students who were African American, yet the decision resonated throughout the differences and disabilities community as well.

Parents and supporters of children with differences and disabilities continued to organize within schools and communities throughout the 1960s as advocacy groups worked on their behalf and utilized techniques from the civil rights movement to further their cause. Because much of the overall discussion in education during that time had a focus on the improvement of educational opportunities for all students, those working on behalf of students with differences and disabilities were timely and justified in adding their voices and opinions (Melcher, 1976).

An important piece of legislation during this time was the Elementary and Secondary Education Act of 1965. This act focused on education for the "disadvantaged." The specific goal was to "strengthen and improve educational quality and educational opportunities in the Nation's elementary and secondary schools" (Senate Committee on Labor and Public Welfare, 1965, p. 1340). The Elementary and Secondary Education Act was amended to include specific financial support for school systems that included students who lived in poverty (Senate Committee on Labor and Public Welfare, 1965, p. 1).

The Elementary and Secondary Education Act was part of a general legislative focus on the protection of students who were economically disadvantaged. This created a stir within the movement for those with disabilities. These advocates began asserting that if education were to be provided to create equity for students who were economically disadvantaged, then students with disabilities were also to be provided with equity as they were disadvantaged as a result of their particular need as well. As a result of this advocacy, funds were allocated for services to students who were considered at risk because of educational and economic needs (Senate Committee on Labor and Public Welfare, 1965). Soon, federal courts rendered decisions in Pennsylvania (1971) and the District of Columbia (1972) to establish "a free and suitable publicly supported education despite the degree of a child's mental, physical, or emotional disability or impairment" (Atterbury, 1990, p. 6).

In 1973, the Health and Rehabilitation Act was passed by Congress (Public Law 93-112). This piece of legislation helped increase equal access to facilities, services, and treatment for students with disabilities. Sections 503 and

504 of the act included antidiscrimination language reminiscent of the civil rights movement that had been adapted to prohibit discrimination against persons with disabilities (Congressional Information Service [CIS], 1972). We will discuss Section 504 later in the chapter as it applies specifically to students with differences and disabilities.

PARALLEL MOVEMENT IN CONGRESS ON BEHALF OF CHILDREN WHO ARE INTELLECTUALLY GIFTED

As legislation and litigation began to shape the education of students with differences and disabilities, the needs of students who are intellectually gifted were also an important consideration. In 1972, the U.S. commissioner of education was tasked with determining the quality and quantity of programs in public schools for students who are considered gifted and talented. The report was termed the Marland Report.

The Marland Report noted the lack of services and programs for students who are gifted. At that time, 96% of students identified as gifted were not being served through their school systems. As a result of the Marland Report, $2.56 million was allocated for gifted education in 1974 (approximately $1.00 for each student who was gifted in the United States; Marland, 1972).

Further studies, reports, and legislation have been proposed subsequent to the initial acts; however, gifted education is still sparsely funded (approximately 2 cents for every $100 spent on education; Kettler, Russell, & Puryear, 2015).

As part of the report, the U.S. Office of Education stated in 1972:

> Gifted and talented students are those identified by professionally qualified persons who by virtue of outstanding abilities are capable of high performance. These are students who require differentiated educational programs and/or services beyond those normally provided by the regular school program in order to realize areas of their contribution to self and society. (Walker, 1991, p. 16)

Areas included in their definition of giftedness were general intellectual ability, specific academic aptitude, creative and productive thinking, leadership ability, visual and performing arts, and psychomotor ability.

Public Law 94-142

Public Law (P.L.) 94-142 (1975) was the first legislation that specifically mandated a free and appropriate public education for all students with differences and disabilities. This law, the most comprehensive ever passed by Congress regarding education, has a direct effect on music teachers in schools today (Heller, 1994). P.L. 94-142 requires that:

> All children ages 5-21, regardless of the nature or severity of their handicaps, are provided a free and appropriate public education. In addition, all handicapped children will be educated to the maximum extent possible with non-handicapped peers. Special classes, separate schooling, or removal of a handicapped child will occur only if the severity of the handicap impedes the education of a child within the general education classroom with the use of supplementary aids and services. Each child identified as having a handicap will have an Individualized Education Program (IEP) to match their educational needs, and all children and their families will be offered the right to due process under the Constitution of the United States. (20 USC 1412 Section 612 89 Stat. 780).

We will outline this law in more detail later in this chapter. P.L. 94-142 was, and still is, a very controversial piece of legislation. It was signed into law in December 1975 (CIS, 1975, p. 1021). Music is specifically mentioned in the language of P.L. 94-142 as being an integral part of the education of students:

> The use of the arts as a teaching tool for the handicapped has long been recognized as a viable, effective way not only of teaching special skills, but also of reaching youngsters who had otherwise been unteachable. The committee envisions that programs under this bill could well include an arts component and, indeed, urges that local educational agencies include arts in programs for the handicapped funded under this act. Such a program could cover both appreciation of the arts by the handicapped youngsters and the utilization of the arts as a teaching tool per se. (Senate Committee on Labor and Public Welfare, 1977, p. 324)

THE MOVEMENT TO FULL INCLUSION

Through subsequent decades, litigation has continued to refine legislation, and the path to full inclusion has been delineated with more clarity. The Supreme Court decided a groundbreaking case, *Hudson v. Rowley* (1982), stating that while a student has a guarantee to an appropriate education, he or she is not automatically guaranteed "maximum possible achievement" in an educational setting. By deciding the case this way, the question of whether a school system is required to ensure maximum possible achievement was answered. Maximum possible inclusion in the least restrictive environment is a right of all children (Cartwright, 1995); however, maximum achievement is not the responsibility of the school system.

In 1986, P.L. 94-142 was clarified with the passage of P.L. 99-457. The scope of this law includes early intervention and early childhood education. This law expanded the range of age for students with disabilities to receive services to include every child aged 3 to 21. Students are guaranteed these services without regard to the type or severity of their disabilities. States were also offered funding through the federal Department of Education to provide early intervention programs to young children with disabilities (CIS, 1986).

P.L. 94-142 was amended and renamed the Individuals with Disabilities Education Act in 1990. The law quickly became known as IDEA (CIS, 1990). IDEA significantly altered P.L. 94-142 in four ways: (a) children were re-termed *individuals*; (b) the term *handicapped* was changed to *persons with disabilities*; (c) transition plans were put in place for students preparing to enter the workforce or education beyond secondary school; and (d) autism and traumatic brain injury were added to the list of identified disabilities (Cartwright, 1995; Hallahan, 1997). The addition of transition services opportunities increased the options that students with disabilities had when transitioning from school to work or higher education. The term *handicapped* was eliminated from the special education language and "person-first" language was introduced as an alternative. Additionally, related services were redefined "to include therapeutic recreation, social work services, and rehabilitation counseling" (CIS, 1989, p. 5). Through this legislation, the secretary of health, education, and welfare is required to "give priority to programs that increase the likelihood that severely handicapped children and youth will be educated with their non-disabled peers" (CIS, 1989, p. 7). Box 2.1 represents a list of disabilities identified in this important piece of legislation.

Box 2.1 Disabilities included in the Individuals with Disabilities Education Act

Autism

Deaf Blindness

Deafness

Developmental Delay

Emotional Disturbance Hearing Impairment

Intellectual Disability

Multiple Disabilities Orthopedic Impairment Other Health Impairment

Specific Learning Disability Speech or Language Impairment Traumatic Brain Injury

Visual Impairment, including Blindness

An important IDEA amendment became law in 1997. This legislation (P.L. 105-17) reorganized IDEA into four parts: (a) general provisions for students with disabilities; (b) assistance for education of all children with disabilities; (c) the inclusion of infants and toddlers with disabilities; and (d) national activities to improve education of children with disabilities. In addition to these modifications, the Individualized Education Program (IEP) team was expanded to include a general classroom teacher (which may be the music teacher), and further clarification and guidelines for increased funding and early education programs, as well as transition programs, were put in place (20 USC 14 et seq.).

A controversial point of this legislation is the alteration of the policy regarding disciplinary actions taken against students with differences and disabilities. The act "allows application to children with disabilities of the same relevant disciplinary procedures applicable to children without disabilities, if the behavior is determined to be not a manifestation of the disability" (CIS, 1997, p. 4). According to IDEA 1997, students with differences and disabilities cannot be denied educational services, regardless of the behavior of the student (Council for Exceptional Children, 1998). This means that if a student with a disability commits an infraction of a school rule, and that behavior takes place as a manifestation of the disability, the student may be disciplined differently than if the behavior was not related to the disability. The law protects students with disabilities from being repeatedly suspended, or expelled, thus denying them equal access to education.

Further reauthorizations to IDEA took place in 2002 and 2004. During this process, new procedural safeguards, highly qualified teacher provisions, and a focus on reduction of overrepresentation of some ethnicities, genders, and socioeconomic levels were added. Other new considerations included a reduction in IEP paperwork, closer monitoring and enforcement of compliance, No Child Left Behind, assessment issues, discipline, and the identification of students who have specific learning disabilities. Of these changes, No Child Left Behind (NCLB), the IEP team composition, and the identification and provision of services to students with specific learning disabilities became the most important new considerations for music educators who taught students with disabilities in their classrooms at that time.

No Child Left Behind affected music educators in a profound way. Because of the demands placed on schools to achieve adequate yearly progress, music educators were routinely asked to assist in classroom reading and mathematics goals, and students were sometimes denied access to music because they were instead receiving remediation to prepare them for this testing. Because the music educator is considered a member of the team, it is empowering and practical for them to know and act upon his or her full membership in the process. Finally, the new process for identification of students with learning disabilities involved a school-wide initiative as students were assessed and received remediation in a more holistic setting. This setting often included the music classroom.

More changes to IDEA came later in December 2008 when an amendment to a 2006 directive concluded/decided/clarified that a school system must cease provision of services to a student with differences and disabilities upon written notification from the parents requesting an end to all special education measures (34 C.F.R. § 300.300(b) (4)). Action upon this request is to be immediate and no services are to be provided unless the parents ask that the special education process begin again (Zirkel, 2008b). As a music educator, and therefore a member of the special education team for a student with differences and disabilities, you should be made aware if this situation occurs in your school.

FURTHER LEGISLATION REGARDING GIFTED AND TALENTED STUDENTS

The Jacob K. Javits Gifted and Talented Students Education Act was passed by Congress in 1988 (Winner, 1996). As part of this act, funding was made available for programs that serve students who are gifted (Walker, 1991). One primary purpose of the Javits Act was to increase the accurate identification of and provision of services to students from diverse backgrounds (VanTassel-Baska, 1998). In the 30 years since the passage of the Javits Act, little has been accomplished in this area that can be directly attributed to it, as the act has been historically and critically underfunded. Testing and other methods of identification for students who are gifted have increasingly been refined to increase the identification of students from diverse backgrounds, and cultural sensitivity has also been raised to address this issue as well.

THE EFFECT AND FUTURE INFLUENCE OF THE NO CHILD LEFT BEHIND ACT ON SPECIAL EDUCATION

In 2001, Congress passed the No Child Left Behind (NCLB) Act. This legislation significantly altered the way in which schools and students were assessed (Simpson, LaCava, Sampson, & Graner, 2004). A controversial portion of NCLB is that each school was required to make adequate yearly progress (AYP) toward closing the achievement gap in reading and mathematics. The deadline for AYP to have been met was the 2013–2014 school year. This mandate included every student in every school district (including students with differences and disabilities; http://www2.ed.gov/nclb/landing.jhtml). Schools were under tremendous pressure to meet AYP, and standardized test scores, graduation rates, and attendance records were evaluated yearly. In addition, students were grouped for sub-evaluation. These groups included race, socioeconomic status, and disability. Students with disabilities failed to meet AYP at a greater rate than other students, and they contributed to failing school scores more than other subgroupings (Simpson et al., 2004). This failure created an even more palpable sense of stress in schools as they struggled to meet AYP while attempting to meet the needs of all students in their school. Moreover, federal funding was tied to successful AYP under NCLB (NCLB, 2001). Many schools were forced to restructure and move special education programs around from school to school. Vignette 2.2 is a story about a child who suffered from the results of NCLB and AYP and is still affected today.

Vignette 2.2 Ms. McCallister

As a parent of a student with Down syndrome, the best way to show how IDEA works is to talk through the Individualized Education Program (IEP) process for my son Sean. Sean is an eighth-grade student at a Midwestern middle school. There are six basic principles of IDEA. Each of our IEP meetings with Sean's team touches on all of these principles. First, Sean has been interested in programs at his school that are not traditionally part of the special education curriculum. However, according to federal law (Zero Reject), he is eligible. Last year he was interested in the theater club. Therefore, the school district was responsible for making this program accessible.

The second of the six of IDEA principles was evident when we moved into our new home three years ago. Every student who seeks special education, whether they eventually receive an IEP or a 504 Plan, must be evaluated by a medical health professional who is qualified to do so. This falls under the Nondiscriminatory Evaluation principle of IDEA. When we moved here, we were required to provide documentation of Sean's diagnosis. After this point, he became eligible under the Free and Appropriate Education (FAPE) principle of IDEA. An IEP was created in collaboration with the special education team and other educators, and we met to discuss the best possible education environment for Sean. In this meeting we discussed the best scenario for Sean to be educated with his peers, with proper support. The least restrictive environment (LRE) was determined to be including him in all regular education classes with a paraprofessional. The IEP was completed, and my husband and I signed it.

Later in the year, we noticed that Sean's paraprofessional had not been effective. She did not keep Sean on task. We exercised our right to due process, another principle of IDEA, and scheduled another IEP meeting to address the problem. A new paraprofessional was assigned to Sean. Overall, with our move, the special education process has worked, as it should. That is not to say that we have not seen some adjustments that need to be made. Sean is doing well and is about to begin high school.

A CLOSER EXAMINATION OF THE INDIVIDUALS WITH DISABILITIES EDUCATION ACT

Six overarching principles that have been a part of IDEA since its inception in 1975. These principles are (a) zero reject, (b) nondiscriminatory evaluations, (c) free appropriate public education, (d) least restrictive environment, (e) procedural due process, and (f) parental involvement (Lewis & Doorlag, 2006). These principles also create an important framework for music educators as we continue to improve our abilities to include and educate students with differences and disabilities in our classrooms. Turnbull, Huerta, & Stowe (2006) state: "So many people fail to understand IDEA wholly and conceptually because they lack a framework" (p. 17). Our goal in the next section is to frame the basic underlying elements of IDEA in a way that is useful for music educators.

Zero Reject

Perhaps the most important principle is that of "zero reject." This means a student cannot be excluded from a classroom or educational setting merely because they have a disability. Even if a student has committed disciplinary actions that cause the system to change the specific setting for that student, they still have the right to an education. This includes students who may have been expelled from a traditional school situation (Turnbull et al., 2006). The most important aspect of this principle is that *all* means *all*. The equal access discussed earlier applies to both music educators and general classroom teachers (Turnbull et al., 2006). As a result of the application of zero reject for a considerable period of time, the attitudes of children toward their peers with disabilities have changed. As we know, education is not purely "book knowledge." We have also learned a great deal about society and the place we hold, as well as the places our peers hold, as we work together in inclusive classrooms (Colwell, 1998; Darrow, 1999; Johnson & Darrow, 1997; Wilson & McCrary, 1996).

Nondiscriminatory Evaluation

Once a school system has admitted a student with differences and disabilities, under the provision of zero reject, the next principle is that of a nondiscriminatory evaluation. This process, sometimes referred to as a "child study," includes several professionals within the school system. A student is evaluated and observed by professionals assigned to the team. This team then meets to discuss the most appropriate educational setting, provisions, accommodations, and related services (speech therapy, occupational therapy, music therapy, physical therapy) that may be utilized to provide the student with equal access and support within the educational environment

(Adamek & Darrow, 2018). The team will also include administrators, classroom teachers (sometimes the music teacher), and professionals who assisted in the evaluation and observation procedures. In addition, parents are also an integral part of this team (Turnbull et al., 2006).

If you think a student in your classroom may have a disability, the first and most appropriate step is to discuss your concerns and observations with the classroom teacher or a colleague who works within the special education structure of your school (Turnbull et al., 2006). As music educators, we are not specifically qualified to presuppose disability categories or cite specific labels we think are appropriate for students. It is our responsibility to seek assistance, as a part of the total school team, from those professionals who are qualified and charged with the responsibility of conducting assessments of students who may have differences and disabilities (Adamek & Darrow, 2018).

Free and Appropriate Education (FAPE)

Once a student has been identified as having a special educational need, the next principle of IDEA, the provision of a Free and Appropriate Education (FAPE), becomes important. This is the part of the process where the specific educational placement of a student with differences and disabilities is determined. As part of the application of a FAPE, an IEP (Individualized Education Program) is created. The first step when creating an IEP is to determine the most appropriate placement. This step includes a statement of the present level of functioning of the student, noting his or her areas of strength and challenge (Lewis & Doorlag, 2006). It also states how the student is particularly affected by the specific school setting.

Under the FAPE provision, the second set of statements in an IEP is a list of the specific level of academic functioning of the student. These statements describe specific goals for the forthcoming academic period and any particular benchmark periods used to evaluate progress throughout the school year. These benchmark goals are important for music educators as we include students with differences and disabilities in our classrooms. It is highly recommended that we consider the goals included in a student's IEP as we plan modifications and adaptations to our lesson plans and classroom environments. In fact, it is our legal responsibility to be aware of, and to provide, accommodations for all students who have been identified as having special educational needs (Hammel, 2004).

One of the first "items of business" as a music educator begins a school year, or begins to teach at a new school, is to identify and study all students with differences and disabilities who will be a part of music classes and ensembles. While this may seem a daunting task, it is enormously helpful when creating a curriculum, creating a scope and sequence for teaching, and writing individual lesson plans for classes. Remember, it is also our responsibility according to the law (IDEA). Once we have begun to study and apply adaptations and modifications, the process becomes more streamlined, and we are much better informed through having participated in these preparation guidelines (Hammel, 2001; Hammel & Gerrity, 2012). An excellent example of a real-life story about this process is "Amy and Drew: Two Children Who Helped Determine What Free and Appropriate Public Education Means" (Hammel, 2017). This article traces the challenges of these determinations on the subsequent supreme court decision that followed.

Least Restrictive Environment

Education in the least restrictive environment (LRE) is a principle that has been somewhat confusing for music educators in the past (Hammel, 2004). This part of IDEA states: "to the maximum extent appropriate, students with disabilities will be educated with students who are not disabled" (Turnbull et al., 2006, p. 67). The IDEA also states that the LRE is the environment where a student learns best. This includes the application of appropriate and supplementary aides and services (Burkett & Hammel, 2007). Many students learn best in a general classroom environment with heterogeneous grouping. Some students, however, learn best in an environment that is homogenous, has a smaller student-to-teacher ratio, or at a different time of day (e.g., morning instead of afternoon). Although we would never deny a child access to a music education, there are times when changes to the classroom setting may greatly increase (Zigmond, 1997). The fundamental assumption of an inclusive philosophy is to start with a student in a general classroom setting. As a team studies the level of functioning, adaptations necessary, and addition of personnel and services, they may determine that a student with differences and disabilities may need to participate in a classroom other than the traditional setting (Turnbull et al., 2006). This can also be an issue when the behavior of a student is such that it is inappropriate for the student with differences and disabilities, as well as the other students in the class, to participate in an inclusion setting. Webber (1997) states: "The practice is especially controversial when applied to students with emotional and behavioral disorders who have the potential to become aggressive and/or noncompliant" (p. 27). The educational setting agreed upon by the team after all options have been discussed is then considered to be the LRE for that student (Lewis & Doorlag, 2006).

Procedural Due Process and Parental Involvement

The final principles of IDEA are procedural due process and parental involvement. If the parents of a student with differences and disabilities consider the placement of their child to be inappropriate, they may request a review of placement, services, and personnel. If the process continues to a formal review, it is known as "procedural due process" (Turnbull et al., 2006). Each state has separate procedural laws that govern due process. Parents are encouraged to participate throughout the process to advocate for their child. These reviews conducted by the team, as well as the continued encouragement of parents to participate, are important elements of the system of checks and balances within the special education framework (Turnbull et al., 2006).

Vignette 2.3 is an example of how federal policy can directly impact an individual child. Especially students with learning differences. Students within a school who struggled to meet the standards of NCLB were often

Vignette 2.3 Toby

My name is Mike. I am the father of a 12-year-old boy on the autism spectrum named Toby. In 2006 we moved to a small Southern community that, at the time, we felt had outstanding services for our son (who was three at the time). For about a year he was attending an early intervention program in our public schools. The teachers were fantastic and he made incredible progress. Upon getting ready for kindergarten in the same school, we learned that George Washington Elementary did not make Adequate Yearly Progress (AYP) for the fourth year in a row. After doing some investigating, we learned that this was part of a federal program called No Child Left Behind where schools were evaluated by the improvement of their test scores.

George Washington Elementary was closed and we were forced to change schools. This has been particularly difficult for Toby. Change is very challenging, and it took several weeks for him to adjust to his new school. After one year at his new school, an additional elementary school closed, forcing a restructure once again. Toby was then moved to a third school in three years. Toby is now 12 and has attended five different schools in the district. It is my opinion that federal policymakers are often one-sided when considering what is best for American students, especially those with differences and disabilities. Toby has finally had multiple years in the same school and seems to be doing great. However, as each school year begins, he becomes anxious about his first few weeks. It is hoped that consistency will be a part of future discussions in the years to come when evaluating the best learning environment for all children.

Discussion Questions:

1. What can be done to make Toby feel more comfortable in his learning environment?
2. How could music play a role?

temporarily also denied access to music if they were required to attend remediation and tutoring sessions prior to testing days (Simpson et al., 2004). It is important to note that the test scores of students with disabilities from this era still have a profound influence on and in our educational system, especially when used to evaluate a school district or even an individual teacher. Further, we often forget the effect on the student who is forced to take exams that could impact self-esteem and self-worth. This will continue to be a challenge for the time being.

THE INFLUENCE OF RACE TO THE TOP (RTTT) ON CURRENT POLICY

In 2009, the Obama administration promised to remove the emphasis on testing for children enrolled in special education. In his speech on November 4, 2009, he stated:

> This Bush administration policy placed heavy emphasis on the development of standardized tests, which created a rigid set of guidelines for education performance and provided little room for creativity in curriculum. States had every incentive to set the bar low in order to avoid having large numbers of their schools labeled as "failing" under NCLB. Thus not only were special education and English as a second language (ESL) students being left behind by schools that did not wish to lower their performance grade, the system also failed in its most important objective: encouraging higher educational standards across the board.

Race to the Top (RTTT) was structured as a grant competition instead of a federal mandate. Pathways were created for local school districts or states to apply for these grants based on categories (e.g., teacher quality, student performance, etc.) (Hourigan, 2011). There were a few controversial components of RTTT. First, all professional development was required to be "data-informed" and to address the "high needs" of the students (Whitcomb, Borko, & Liston, 2009). This caused professional development to, once again, be tied to test scores. Second, one of the grant funds, "The Teacher Incentive Fund (TIF)," called for the idea of "performance pay." Grants were awarded to districts that showed connections between test scores and teacher pay raises (U.S. Department of Education, 2009). Essentially, if you really look at NCLB and RTTT, there was not much difference. One program punished schools for not meeting expected test scores by not funding them. The other just did not award grant funds based on some of the same principles (Hourigan, 2011).

It is important to look at the influence of charter schools and school choice that started under the Obama administration, and its future influence on the Trump administration. Under the Trump administration, Betsy

DeVos (secretary of education) attempted to change IDEA to allow states to decide the funding model for special education. This would set up a "have" and "have not" system where states who see equal rights for students with disabilities would have one funding model and others would have another (Jimenez and Flores, 2019). School choice also challenges students with disabilities in two significant ways. First, it removes funding by taking students away from schools. Second, charter schools do not and are not required to follow federal law. School choice is still a current issue and will continue to be a challenge for special education advocates.

COMMON CORE STATE STANDARDS (2010)

In 2010, a large contingent of private foundations (primarily the Bill and Linda Gates Foundation), academic leaders, and federal agencies, as well as the U.S. Department of Education, published the Common Core State Standards (CCSS) initiative for school reform (Wexler, 2014). The idea was to unify content for students and prepare students for "college and career." By 2013, the CCSS was adopted by all but a few states (Haager & Vaughn, 2013).

The creators of the CCSS argue that a rigorous set of common standards is good for students in special education. In fact, the CCSS call for a standards-based IEP; they suggest compliance with IDEA as well as "high-quality, evidence-based, individualized instruction and support services." In addition, the CCSS suggests the use of Universal Design for Learning as a tool for students with learning differences (McNulty & Gloeckler, 2011).

The jury is still out on how the CCSS will affect all students, including those with disabilities. College and career look very different for this population of students. Some students with disabilities need different goals for their future college and career transition, and there is a movement underway titled "Reclaiming the Conversation on Education" that is spearheading a possible descent of Common Core (Wexler, 2014). As of 2022, these standards are still adopted in 43 of 50 states.

THE EVERY STUDENT SUCCEEDS ACT (2015)

The Every Student Succeeds Act (ESSA) of 2015 reauthorized the previous K-12 education law, the Elementary and Secondary Education Act (ESEA) of 1965. Prior to the passage of the ESSA, the ESEA was known as No Child Left Behind. The ESSA encompasses most of the education programs for American public schools today, including Title I (school improvement for low-income students); Title II (preparing, training, and recruiting high-quality teachers); Title III (English language learners); Title IV (twenty-first-century schools); Title V (state innovation and local flexibility); Title VI (protections from discrimination/programs for Native American students); Title VII (impact aid); Title VIII (general provisions); and Title IX (education for the homeless) (www2.ed.gov).

There are a couple of new provisions since 2015 that impact our examination in this text. First, in regard to gifted and talented students, ESSA retained the previously mentioned Javits Gifted and Talented Education Program, and report cards must include data related to performance at an advanced level. In addition, under Title I and II funding, schools must include information regarding how teachers will identify gifted and talented students (Every Student Succeeds Act, 2017). The most important repeal as part of the ESSA is the Adequate Yearly Progress clause from NCLB. Through ESSA, states can choose a statewide accountability system and action to assist the 5% of low-performing schools. This will be handled locally, not federally (Every Student Succeeds Act, 2017). In addition, the following provisions are part of the ESSA: (a) access to the general education curriculum; (b) access to accommodations on assessments; (c) concepts of Universal Design for Learning are mandated; (d) includes provisions that require local education agencies to provide evidence-based practice and procedures; (e) interventions in schools with consistently underperforming subgroups; (f) requires states in Title I plans to address how they will improve conditions for learning, including reducing incidents of bullying and harassment in schools, overuse of discipline practices, and reducing the use of aversive behavioral interventions (such as restraints and seclusion; Every Student Succeeds Act, 2017).

ENDREW F. VERSUS DOUGLAS COUNTY (2017)

Probably the most significant court case in recent decades happened in Douglas County, Colorado. In this case, a student (Drew) was diagnosed with autism spectrum disorder. In the second grade Drew exhibited behaviors that were challenging and affected the teaching and learning atmosphere of the classroom (*Endrew F. v. Douglas County School District RE*, 2017). The school district did very little to address these behaviors and Drew regressed. Just before fifth grade, Drew's parents withdrew him from public school and enrolled him in a private school that could address his needs.

The family had saved enough money to send Drew to the private school for one semester. During that semester, Drew began to meet and exceed his IEP goals. The family then returned to public school and requested services similar to those at the specialized private school. Their requests were denied. Drew's family then sought reimbursement for his tuition. The case went all the way to the Supreme Court of the United States (https://secureservercdn.net/198.71.233.69/d25.2ac.myftpupload.com/wp-content/uploads/2017/04/Endrew-F-opinion.pdf). The Supreme Court stated the following: "Specifically, the IEP proposed by the District was not reasonably calculated for Petitioner to achieve academic success, attain self-sufficiency, and contribute to society that are substantially equal to the opportunities afforded children without disabilities." The overarching takeaway from this litigation is the statement made by the Supreme Court that every student deserves to have meaningful and achievable goals each day they attend school. We mention this case specifically because this case, along with the case in Indiana (see below), shows that school districts are under pressure to provide appropriate educational settings for students within a least restrictive environment (LRE). Furthermore, caregivers are becoming more assertive in seeking their child's rights within the public school system.

New Focus on Early Intervention

As of 2022, IDEA is now separated into "Part A" (general outline of the law), "Part B" (school-aged children), and "Part C" (Focus on Early Intervention). Part B serves children aged 3–21, and Part C, which is new, serves children with developmental delays from birth through age 2. This federally funded addition allows access to early intervention through a $436 million grant from the U.S. Department of Education (idea.ed.gov, 2022). Previous to this historic change, not all families had guaranteed access to early intervention.

In October 2022, the U.S. Department of Education released guidelines to follow policies mentioned in the previous paragraph for Part B. They include guidelines for early childhood programs, including Head Start programs.

A Different View of Due Process: House Bill 1107 (Indiana)

Recently certain states have proposed changes to due process as part of P.L. 94-142. In January 2022, the State of Indiana House of Representatives passed House Bill 1107. This bill passed in 2022 and will shift the burden to prove that students are receiving adequate special education services to the school, rather than the parents. Advocates for this change argue that parents are not trained in special education law, nor do they have the financial resources to carry the burden of proving their students are learning in an LRE. Whether this bill has traction nationally is yet to be determined.

Important Non-Educational Legislation to Consider (The Americans with Disabilities Act)

The Americans with Disabilities Act (ADA; P.L. 101-336) was passed in 1990. A highlight of this legislation is the guarantee of nondiscrimination to all persons with disabilities in employment, transportation, public accommodations, state and local government, and telecommunications situations. Students with differences and disabilities are not specifically addressed in the ADA; however, the practices utilized by employers and those in higher education when interacting with students with differences and disabilities are an important component of this legislation. Nondiscriminatory practices and accessibility to all public buildings are the largest legacies of this act (CIS, 1990). A significant amount of litigation has refined this legislation, and the ADA has been a prominent feature in lawsuits involving discriminatory practice and lack of access to public buildings and spaces.

The ADA was amended in late 2008 as the Americans with Disabilities Act Amendments (ADAA). These new regulations took effect in January 2009. The most important portion of this amendment connects the ADAA with Section 504 Plans by expanding the options for eligibility and monitoring the enforcement of provision of services for students who have both IEP and 504 Plans (Zirkel, 2008a). The expansion of the "major life activity" category includes the addition of reading, thinking, concentrating, sleeping, bowel functions, bladder functions, digestive functions, and eating (see Box 2.2). As music educators, it will become increasingly important to be aware of the students in our classrooms who have differences and disabilities. With the implementation of new ADAA measures, it is likely that more students will be eligible for Section 504 Plans.

Box 2.2 (below) is an example of an eligibility form for a student seeking a 504 plan. With the expanding eligibility criteria for Section 504 Plans, and the increasing common characteristics of 504 Plans and IEPs, it is necessary for music educators to be vigilant regarding the needs of all students with identified differences and disabilities. As seen in the Student Eligibility Form created by Zirkel (2009), students with physical challenges that substantially affect their ability to learn in the music classroom will have specific needs that we must acknowledge and meet. When traveling with music students, these relatively new student needs, as stated in their 504 Plans, may be very important and may change a well-planned itinerary or number of stops a group must make en route. In general, as a music educator, the awareness of the physical, emotional, academic, and social needs of our students is both our right and responsibility.

Box 2.2 Section 504/ADA Student Eligibility Form

(Shaded Areas Denote Changes Due to ADAA, Effective 1/1/09)

Child's Name: ________________ Date of Birth: __________

Eligibility Team Members: Fill in names, and check areas of knowledge for each team member:

Names:	about the child	about the meaning of evaluation data	about accommodations/ placement options
Note: Make sure there is at least one check in each column.			

Sources of evaluation information (check each one used):

____ aptitude and/or achievement tests ____ teacher recommendations
____ adaptive behavior ____ others(specify):__________

1. Specify the mental or physical *impairment* ________________ (as recognized in *DSM-IV* or other respected source if not excluded under 504/ADA, e.g., illegal drug use)
2. Check the *major life activity*:

____ seeing	____ hearing	____ walking	____ learning
____ performing manual tasks		____breathing	
____ reading	____ thinking	____concentrating	____ sleeping
____ bowel functions	____ bladder functions	____ digestive functions	____ eating

Or specify alternative of equivalent scope and importance: ________________

3. Place an "X" on the following scale to indicate the specific degree that the impairment (in #1) limits the major life activity (in #2).
   - Make an educated estimate **without** the effects of mitigating measures, such as medication; low-vision devices (except eyeglasses or contact lenses); hearing aids and cochlear implants; mobility devices, prosthetics, assistive technology; learned behavioral or adaptive neurological modifications; and reasonable accommodations or auxiliary aids/services.

- Similarly, for impairments that are episodic or in remission, make the determination for the time they are active.
- Use the average student in the general (i.e., national) population as the frame of reference.
    - Interpret close calls in favor of broad coverage (i.e., construing items 1-3 to the maximum extent that they permit). Thus, for an "X" at 4.0 or below, fill in specific information evaluated by the team that justifies the rating.

4. If the team's determination for Item #3 was less than "4," provide notice to the parents of their procedural rights, including for an impartial hearing. If the team's determination was a "4" or above, the team also should determine and document the reasonable accommodations necessary for the child to have an "appropriate education" in accordance with Section 504 and the ADA.

THE INTERSECTIONALITY BETWEEN POVERTY, RACE, AND SPECIAL EDUCATION POLICY

This chapter would not be complete without examining how the policies above, along with current educational practice, intersect race, poverty, and disability. If you follow funding and support, these three groups of students (those who live in poverty, BIPOC students, and students with exceptionalities) often share the same struggles. Currently about one in five students live in poverty. Fifteen percent of students in our public schools receive special education services (increase of 13% over 10 years), and roughly 40% of U.S. public school students are BIPOC students (Black, Indigenous, or People of Color) (National Center for Education Statistics, 2022).

Because our educational system relies primarily on local property tax support, the inequities in education are exacerbated in some areas of the country. We all see what we are about to examine in all parts of the United States. Wealthy schools have robust arts, special education, curricular, and extracurricular opportunities. This has been part of the educational debate or schism for decades. We reference the work of Jonathan Kozol, all the way back to 1967, who pointed out these same inequities in his text *Death at an*

Early Age: The Destruction of the Hearts and Minds of Negro Children in the Boston Public Schools. In this book he includes an account of his dismissal for teaching the poem "The Ballad of the Landlord" (Langston Hughes), which details the exploitation of Black tenants by white landlords.

The school reform efforts listed above have a compounded effect on the aforementioned three groups. The reform efforts also influence each other, and that is compounded by our current climate. No Child Left Behind, as mentioned above, allowed school districts to move students where they could influence (or not influence) high-impact test scores. These tests are not accessible by any stretch of the imagination to a large portion of the student population, and are still part of the education system today (Darling Hammond, 2007). Race to the Top, as well as the influence of school choice, is a critical and controversial issue as well for all three groups. School choice assumes that all students can travel and that the same educational services will be provided (and federal law followed) at the school of choice. In most instances this is *not* the case.

As an example, the New Orleans public schools became largely charter school based following Hurricane Katrina. Students with disabilities were systematically denied admission to most schools (Hammel & Fischer, 2014). Families of some students with differences and disabilities were left to travel from school to school, hoping to be admitted somewhere. The result was complicated and, in some cases, catastrophic to the education of these students.

The larger question is: What happens when students leave and their federal, state, and local monies go with them? What is left for the remainder of the students at the home school? The answer is they get less educational resources. Most of these students will be poor, students with disabilities, and people of color (Hammel & Hourigan, 2022). Essentially, we are moving backward in time to a segregated educational system for the "haves" and the "have nots."

APPLICATIONS AND CONSIDERATIONS FOR MUSIC EDUCATORS

As legislation, litigation, and public policy continue to refine our educational approaches, the result will be that the procedures we follow to include students with differences and disabilities in our classrooms will change. An awareness of these regulations and policies is part of our responsibility as music educators. Moreover, the careful application of guidelines as presented through contact with our school administrators and special education teams, and through professional development opportunities, will lead to an improvement of our ability to provide the most appropriate education for our students with differences and disabilities.

While the specifics of legal details may sometimes be confusing, and the field of special education continues to define itself, the most important caveat to remember is that each student with differences and disabilities is an individual child. When we consider the seemingly cavernous world of acronyms and definitions, we sometimes forget that we are considering the present and future possibilities for a child. Taking a moment to remember the individual child and the lifetime ramifications of decisions we make often brings into focus the true importance of the education of students with differences and disabilities.

DISCUSSION QUESTIONS

1. Discuss how the advocacy efforts employed during the civil rights movement were mirrored by those advocating for persons with differences and disabilities
2. How did P.L. 94-142, and later IDEA, expand during its 50-year history?
3. What are the six principles of IDEA, and how does each apply in the music classroom?
4. Describe "least restrictive environment" and state how this may be achieved in the music classroom (at least three examples).
5. How would you respond if a school choice referendum was put on a ballot for an election in your community? Would you support such legislation?

PART II

PREPARING TO TEACH MUSIC TO STUDENTS WITH DIFFERENCES AND DISABILITIES

Chapter 3

Preparing to Teach

Practicum and Engagement Opportunities in Special Education for Preservice and In-Service Music Educators

CHAPTER OVERVIEW

- Becoming Acquainted through Observing, Assisting, Discussing, and Planning
- Types of Practicum Opportunities in Special Education for Preservice and In-Service Music Educators
  - Practicum Opportunities in Self-Contained Classrooms
  - Practicum Opportunities in Resource Rooms
  - Practicum Opportunities in Inclusive Classrooms
  - Practicum Opportunities in Summer Enrichment Programs
  - Practicum Opportunities in Specific Therapy Environments
- Music Therapy and Music Education
- Creating Practicum Experiences with Students with Differences and Disabilities for Preservice Music Educators
- Conclusion
- Discussion Questions

There are varying degrees of undergraduate and graduate preparation for teaching students with differences and disabilities. Music educators may have had a general special education class or the opportunity to study topics regarding students with differences and disabilities embedded within a music methods course. The topic of students with differences and disabilities may have been included in an educational psychology course or a course about teaching music to students with differences and disabilities that was part of the curriculum (Heller, 1994; York & Reynolds, 1996). More often, music educators have little or no background or instruction in this area (Gerrity, Hourigan, & Horton, 2013). Therefore, music educators must be resourceful in gaining insight into the skills, strategies, and

Teaching Music to Students with Differences and Disabilities. Third Edition. Alice M. Hammel, and Ryan M. Hourigan, Oxford University Press. © Oxford University Press 2025. DOI: 10.1093/9780197689356.003.0003

understandings that accompany the experience of teaching students with differences and disabilities.

Further, music teacher educators often have little or no preparation in how to educate future music educators regarding the inclusion of music students with disabilities, or how to plan, implement, and assess lessons in self-contained and inclusive music classrooms. Often, this lack of understanding results in either glossing over the topic or ignoring it altogether. Licensure requirements can leave little room for "special" topics in the methods classroom.

Engagement with special education faculty and staff in a variety of environments can assist music educators in finding ways to reach students with differences and disabilities. This chapter may appear to be designed for the music teacher educator. However, practicing music educators are encouraged to utilize the observation protocols and other strategies to obtain on-the-job and authentic experience through self-imposed observation, and discussion within the special education framework. This may be beneficial to music educators in understanding the subculture of students, parents, educators, and administrators that surrounds students with differences and disabilities. This type of engagement may need to be conducted during preparation/planning time or through permission from an administrator.

For music teacher educators, this chapter is designed as a guide to develop practicum opportunities for preservice music educators. Included in this chapter will be strategies for engagement in self-contained classrooms, resource rooms, inclusive settings, and summer enrichment programs. This chapter is also designed to offer insights into this process and to provide strategies for optimizing the practicum experience for music teacher educators, preservice music teachers, and cooperating teachers.

As mentioned in earlier chapters, the goal of the current special education system is to offer an appropriate education for students within the least restrictive environment. Students who need special education attend classes in public school in a variety of settings to meet their specific needs. Parents of music students with differences and disabilities are becoming more active in advocating for equal access to curricula. Therefore, music educators often find themselves teaching at least part of their day within one or more different types of special education classes (described in this chapter). Music teacher educators can establish outstanding engagement experiences for students in music methods courses. Before these experiences are described in detail, the following section will review types of special education settings and will provide an initial observation protocol to give music educators and music teacher educators ideas regarding the instructional goals in these learning environments.

BECOMING ACQUAINTED THROUGH OBSERVATION, ASSISTING, DISCUSSING, AND PLANNING

Many school sites mentioned in this chapter may be different from other teaching and learning settings. Depending on the setting, it may be difficult initially to ascertain the curricular goals and objectives of these classrooms. Through research (Gerrity, Hourigan, & Horton, 2013; Hammel, 1999) and personal experience in teaching practicing music educators, we have found that music educators learn to teach students with differences and disabilities in a sometimes unique way. Several components (observation; serving as a one-on-one assistant; discussion and coaching; reflection; and planning) are crucial for successful practicum experiences in which preservice and in-service music teachers gain as much as possible through observation and participation.

Observation has been mentioned (and protocols added) in previous chapters. Observation should happen at two levels. First, as discussed in Chapter 1, music educators should observe with the intent to understand the student's needs regarding the teaching and learning relationships that must develop between teacher and student. In the next section of this chapter, we focus on the second level of observation, centered within the student's primary placement. These placements may have an impact on how music educators design, deliver, and assess instruction within the music classroom.

Serving as a one-on-one assistant allows music educators a small window into what a classroom and learning environment is like for a student with differences and disabilities. It will become clear how a student communicates, processes information, and uses successful adaptations, as well as how their unique personality traits affect them in the learning environment. Often our in-service and preservice students form bonds with students with differences and disabilities that are powerful and add to a rich learning environment for both student and teacher. This opportunity may also allow music educators to learn techniques from the current paraprofessional working with the student with differences and disabilities that may be useful in the music classroom.

Whether you are an experienced music educator or an aspiring in-service music educator, it is important to receive some coaching from experienced special educators or therapists when teaching students with differences and disabilities. There are nuances that music educators may not be accustomed to including as part of a typical music lesson (e.g., self-care, hand-over-hand assistance), and music educators will need strategies regarding how to include these adaptations appropriately. In addition, an experienced special educator may not know music content; however, they do know the challenges that students face in the areas of language (e.g., speaking too fast or using too many words), physical needs, and cognitive and sensory limitations. It is important to implement these ideas and to encourage a dialogue among all members of the team.

Reflection can occur in several ways. There are, however, important considerations when reflecting upon the improvement of music teaching with students who have learning differences. First, write strategies and thoughts down as soon as you finish teaching. Find time to sit and reflect on what just happened and how it may impact future lessons with students or the overall environment in the music classroom. Second, when finishing a long-term field placement (i.e., preservice or graduate-level practicum), take the time to reflect on the overall experience and how this influences your philosophy of music teaching. Students with differences and disabilities overcome obstacles that we often would never attempt, and their experiences in music will impact them for a lifetime. Our ability to reflect on their goals and achievements will result in stronger teaching practices.

After reading the Individualized Education Program (IEP) or 504 Plan, attending an IEP or 504 Plan meeting, observing, and assisting students in their primary classroom setting, and reflecting on these experiences, music educators will be able to provide the foundation for planning future lessons with students with differences and disabilities. As part of this planning process, it is also important to be resourceful. Chapter 9 is devoted to providing current research and practitioner-oriented materials in music education, websites, and online tools.

In the area of music teacher education (i.e., practicum settings), we have found that peer-planned lessons (undergraduate students planning lessons together) in small groups work well for initial experiences in teaching music to students with differences and disabilities (Hourigan, 2007). This has also worked well with other studies involving practica (VanWeelden & Whipple, 2005). This allows for a step between observations and "solo" delivered lessons that can increase the confidence of new teachers who are attempting to teach for the first time. More on how this is implemented will be discussed later in this text.

Understanding a Continuum of Services for Students with Learning Differences

Section 300.115 of the Individuals with Disabilities Education Act requires that "[e]ach public agency must ensure that a continuum of alternative placements is available to meet the needs of children with disabilities for special education and related services" (U.S. Department of Education, n.d). In addition, this continuum must include "instruction in regular classes,

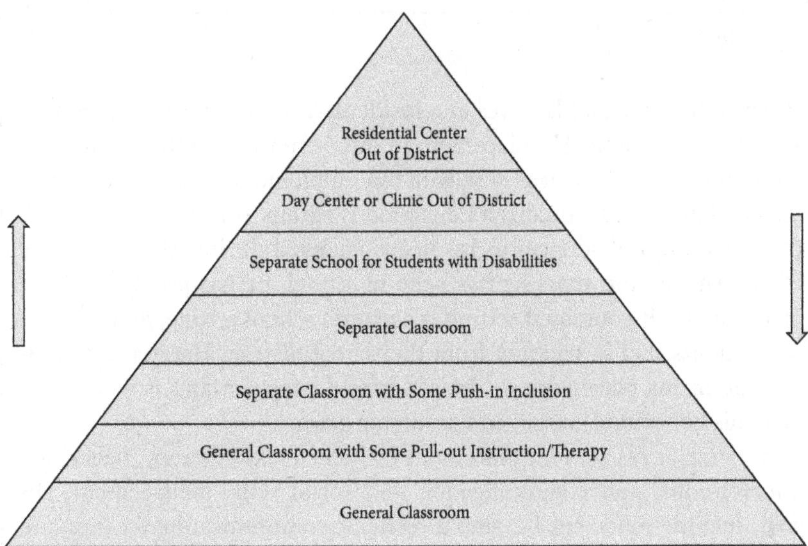

Figure 3.1. Continuum of services.

special classes, special schools, home instruction, and instruction in hospitals and institutions" and "make provision for supplementary services (such as resource room or itinerant instruction) to be provided in conjunction with regular class placement" (U.S. Department of Education, n.d). Figure 3.1 is an example of what a school district provides as a model for evaluating placement for a student.

Cautionary Considerations

Do not assume that the inclusion classroom is always the least restrictive environment (LRE). Some students with learning differences function best in a self-contained classroom free of the distractions of an included classroom. Often, these can be opportunities for reverse inclusion, where a general education class can join a self-contained classroom for music. The options along the continuum of placement and services for students with disabilities are varied, and music educators are not always familiar with the way music may be part of these placements. Below are three vignettes about three students who experience school at different points along this continuum. Each placement described is the LRE for that student. LRE can change during the time a student is in school, and is assessed each year when the IEP is being updated. Vignettes 3.1–3.3 help explain this process from three different vantage points.

Vignette 3.1 Harry

Harry is 16 years old. He lives at a residential center more than an hour away from his home. His placement in this center is his LRE because it is the setting where he learns best, with the supplemental aides and services included in his Individualized Education Program. Harry moved through the continuum of services as his needs changed during his educational career. During the years he has been in school, he has previously been placed in a self-contained setting, a separate school setting, and a center for students that is separate from the school district. Harry is now succeeding in his placement at the residential program and is working to meet his behavioral, social, and academic goals.

Services at his current placement include weekly therapy, behavioral interventions, and communication and social skills management. His goals include following 1–2 step directions, communicating feelings and needs in two ways, and indicating when he becomes tired or frustrated. Some self-care skills included in Harry's program are to independently make his bed and take a shower. Harry also has opportunities to go into the community to eat and shop with students and staff from his program.

The overall goal for Harry is to have him return to his local school system and live at home. Once he has accomplished the behavioral, academic, and social goals set for him, and when it is determined that the residential center is no longer his LRE, he will move to the next step placement in the continuum (the center in his town not associated with the school system), which will allow him to live at home and continue his goals.

In this particular residential center, there is no regular music instruction or therapy. When Harry is able to return to his community, there will be opportunities for music and theater (another favorite of his) instruction and therapy again. The current placement is focused on the specific skills and behaviors Harry needs to be successful in his home community as he transitions to adulthood.

TYPES OF PRACTICUM OPPORTUNITIES IN SPECIAL EDUCATION FOR PRESERVICE AND IN-SERVICE MUSIC EDUCATORS

Practicum Opportunities in Self-Contained Classrooms

Self-contained classrooms exist in public schools for a variety of educational reasons. The most common use of the self-contained setting is for students who would not be successful in an inclusive or integrated classroom.

Vignette 3.2 Ann

Ann is 12 years old. She attends a local middle school and is in a self-contained class with six other students. Ann rides the bus to school and a staff member is with her all day. This small classroom with a one-to-one aide is her LRE. This is the environment where Ann learns best, with the supplementary aides and services provided to her through her Individualized Education Program. Ann has always been in a small self-contained classroom and has just this year been able to ride the bus to and from school without a staff member accompanying her. Ann is succeeding in this placement and is progressing toward her academic, social, and communication goals.

Services provided to Ann include occupational therapy, physical therapy, and targeted communication and social skills experiences. Her goals include sorting items, identifying coins, tracing letters, and verbally communicating her wants and needs. Ann struggles to appropriately signal her frustrations before she begins self-harming or throwing items. She is in a social skills group twice a week and is proud of her progress in regulating her frustrations.

The long-term goal for Ann is to have her remain in the school system until she ages out at 22. Her transition plan may include teaching her to work in a supervised setting with others who have disabilities after she finishes high school. There are several group homes in the area and her family is hopeful that Ann will be able to live in a structured space with other adults and staff members when she is an adult.

Ann receives music instruction twice a week. A music teacher comes to her classroom to provide chronologically and developmentally appropriate instruction. The school system designed a special curriculum for students in grades 6–12 who are in self-contained classrooms. The music teacher has sequenced lessons to fit the needs of the students in each classroom. Ann and her classmates look forward to music and happily put away their work when they see the music teacher come in the door. Her family is hopeful that Ann will be able to participate in musical activities as an adult as she really enjoys music at school.

However, many self-contained classrooms are used to group students together who have similar needs (i.e., students who are intellectually gifted). More often, a self-contained classroom contains students who have a variety of learning needs. Typically, a self-contained classroom has one lead teacher who is a certified special educator and multiple paraprofessionals to assist

Vignette 3.3 Mary

Mary is 8 years old and participates in school in an inclusion classroom. She has a special education teacher in the classroom who also works with two other students in the class. Mary began preschool at age 2 with special education services and is doing well in the inclusion classroom with the supplementary aides and services available through her Individualized Education Program. The inclusion classroom, with services, is the LRE for Mary. She is progressing toward her academic, behavioral, and social goals in this setting.

Mary has a variety of services through her elementary school. She has occupational therapy three times a week and speech therapy four times a week. These are provided through therapists who come to the classroom and take Mary with them for a period of time. Mary is also part of a social skills group twice a week. She has a Behavioral Intervention Plan that is monitored by her classroom teacher and her special education teacher. Mary is working to decrease the number of meltdowns she has during the school day by requesting a break or a sensory item to help when the sights, sounds, and expectations of her inclusion classroom become more than she can absorb at the time.

The overall goal for Mary is to support her as she continues her education in the inclusion classroom. Currently, it is projected that Mary will be able to receive an academic diploma and graduate with her class from high school. The services she currently receives will continue as long as she needs them and will be reviewed annually. Her teachers and therapists are hopeful that Mary will be able to live and work independently in the community when she is an adult.

Mary attends music with her inclusion class once a week. Her special education teacher stops by frequently to see how the three students in the class are doing; however, they have all been participating well without any behavioral, academic, or social difficulties. Mary really enjoys music and is allowed to wear headphones when the class becomes especially active or her sensory system is overloaded. Mary appreciates that her music teacher keeps a basket of chewy sensory items for Mary to use when necessary. Recently, Mary played a large welcoming drum in a class program because she was able to keep a steady beat while others were singing. Mary really loved the vibrations from the drum and was able to participate without assistance in the program.

Box 3.1 Types of Instruction for Self-Contained Classrooms

Skill-specific group: Students are grouped together based on shared skills or abilities.

Heterogeneous Grouping: Students with mixed levels of understandings or skills are grouped together to learn from their peers.

Flexible Grouping: Using several types of groups at the same time.

Learning Centers: Organized self-instruction areas of a classroom used to promote independent learning.

that lead teacher. Within these classes it is important to observe the variety of instruction taking place. There are often several different methods of instruction occurring together or in tandem (Box 3.1).

There are many advantages to establishing a practicum setting in a self-contained classroom. First, there will obviously be a number of different students with differences and disabilities in this classroom with a wide range of learning styles. Second, many self-contained classrooms are grouped by disability. Therefore, in-service and preservice music educators can gain strategies and understandings about how to teach students within a specific learning category. We have provided a practicum observation protocol (Box 3.2) for use in gaining insight into the goals of a self-contained classroom. The form provided is a framework regarding the types of questions used for effective reflection. However, you should still ask questions of the music teacher (who teaches in this setting) and the special educator when given the opportunity.

Practicum Opportunities in Resource Rooms

A resource room is a type of self-contained classroom. It is designed for students who are partly or completely included in regular education classrooms. Students can attend these classrooms for a variety of reasons. Typically, students attend resource rooms for assistance in specific subject areas or more detailed accommodations including intensified one-on-one instruction.

In-service and preservice music educators may use an observation in a resource room to gain understanding of the instruction most beneficial when working with a specific student or small group of students. These strategies may also be used to teach music. For example, if a child attends a resource room for help in language or reading, similar learning goals could be applied to music class (e.g., visual vs. aural learning tools).

Box 3.2 Fieldwork Observation Protocols for Self-Contained or Resource Classrooms

Name: ________________________

Type of classroom setting (e.g. self-contained moderate disabilities):_______

Grade range:_______

Special Educator(s): _______________ Music Educator: _______________

Physical arrangement of classroom (e.g. centers; desks in rows):

Instructional goals articulated by the music educator (if visited by a music education student):

- How might these techniques be used in the music classroom:

Instructional adaptations articulated by the special educator:

Types of learning groups observed (e.g. skill-specific or heterogeneous):

Specific music teaching and learning ideas for future use in self-contained music classrooms:

Assessment strategies used by the music educator/special educator:

Practicum Opportunities in Inclusive Classrooms

An inclusive classroom, as a philosophy of teaching, has been discussed at length in previous chapters. There are, however, important factors to consider when observing and assisting a student within an inclusive setting to gain the appropriate understanding of how and why a student is included within that specific setting. A student may be included for a variety of reasons. These aims may include academic, social, and experiential goals.

Inclusion or Mainstreaming

The first consideration is whether a student is truly being included or is merely being mainstreamed into a classroom. Inclusion is a concept based on the idea that when initial placement decisions are made for a student (for

LRE purposes), the regular education classroom must be considered first before other settings and services are considered as additional assistance is needed. Some school districts claim to be "including" students in regular education classrooms but are essentially still mainstreaming them based on the old paradigm. Mainstreaming is an older concept based on the idea that a student may be mainstreamed into a subject (e.g., math, English, or a general education classroom) from a special education setting. Often mainstreaming was based on the premise that the student would be mainstreamed into the general classroom if their behavior and/or academic needs did not "interrupt the learning of others in the classroom." We have found that the inclusion philosophy is far more beneficial for students with and without differences and disabilities, and that mainstreaming, while seemingly well intended at the time, does not reflect a true inclusive philosophy, or provide the most appropriate and LRE for all students. However, not all students function well in either an inclusive or a mainstreamed schedule. There are instances where students need to start in an exclusively self-contained classroom. For these students, the self-contained classroom is the least restrictive environment and will remain so until they are able to function best in a more inclusive environment. These particular students may well benefit from being mainstreamed into a class such as music.

In inclusive settings, the special education team is concerned with the whole school experience and the peer relationships that may develop as a result. The idea is that if students are isolated from their peers, they will make assumptions about each other. In inclusive schools, all students are encouraged to attend and participate as a community of learners. The overall goal of inclusive schooling is to assist all students as they develop an increasing social awareness, understanding, and appreciation for differences within their community.

It is important that students who are included within regular education classrooms are placed correctly and are well supported. In addition, it is critical that teachers who have a lack of experience in teaching students with differences and disabilities are also well supported in their efforts to provide the best education for all of their students. If a student participates in music class and is part of an inclusive environment, it is important to visit them in a class other than yours. A practicum protocol has been developed for use when visiting a student in an inclusive environment (Box 3.3).

Practicum Opportunities in Summer Enrichment Programs

Many students with differences and disabilities or who are at risk continue with some sort of school program (if available) during the summer. Proponents of such programs advocate that students with differences and disabilities need

Box 3.3 Fieldwork and Observation Protocols for Inclusive Classroom Settings

Student's name: ______________________

Grade range:_______

Special Educator(s) (including paraprofessionals and contact information):

Music Educator: ______________________ (If visited by a music education student)

Does the child have a full-time paraprofessional with them at all times?

- How does the paraprofessional assist with instruction?
- How might these strategies work in music?

Do the other students in the classroom appear to assist the teacher with this student?

Does the student appear to have a social group or a friend?

Instructional adaptations, accommodations, or modifications used either in music or other classes and settings:

How might these adaptations, or modifications be used or changed in the future?

Notes:

continuing education in the summer to maintain skills. Often schools that offer summer programs spend less time reviewing during the fall semester.

We often send in-service music educators to these types of settings when teaching our summer graduate courses on teaching music to students with differences and disabilities. Summer enrichment programs are often easily accessible for teachers and provide a wealth of information, including getting to know special educators, teaching and classroom management techniques, and a knowledge of the individual students they may be teaching in the fall semester. Often these programs group students into self-contained classrooms based on ability (use the practicum protocol provided earlier; see Box 3.2).

Practicum Opportunities in Specific Therapy Environments

Many students in special education receive related services provided by the school district. These services often include speech, occupational, and physical therapy. Other adjunct therapies are utilized when deemed necessary by the IEP team. In addition, some school districts have music therapy or other arts-related therapy programs. In certain instances, it is important to visit students or observe them in these specific therapy settings. Music educators will gain insight into specific learning challenges and language or physical obstacles that may be obstructing the ability of students to learn in the music classroom or ensemble. For example, if a child has speech challenges, it may be beneficial to observe the student in speech therapy. Consulting with the speech therapist after the session may provide insight into improved communication within the music classroom. Understanding how to make specific accommodations in these areas can be critical to a successful music experience. A practicum protocol has been developed to give music educators (both preservice and in-service) suggestions regarding what to look for in these settings (Box 3.4).

MUSIC THERAPY AND MUSIC EDUCATION

A true text on teaching students with differences and disabilities is not complete without a discussion of music therapy, including how music therapists address the needs of their clients and how this can directly relate to the music educator. The American Music Therapy Association defines music therapy as an established healthcare profession that uses music to address the individual needs (nonmusical) of its clientele. In this context, think of the clientele as music students in your classroom. The needs of the students in the music education classroom are the following: cognitive, communication, behavioral, emotional, physical, and sensory.

These needs are similar to those discussed in this text; however, music therapists are concerned with developing goals for their clients based on their individual needs. For example, when developing goals for a child who is nonverbal, one must think of the needs of that specific child. With just the knowledge that a child is nonverbal, what needs would be evident? It is possible that this child will have difficulty interacting with their peers; therefore, a social goal might be appropriate. Also, the child may attempt to be able to communicate with peers whether they are verbal or not. Therefore, a communication goal may be indicated. While these are not the only goals this child would need to work toward, this is the context in which goals are created.

Music therapists are more concerned with how music can assist in the development of nonmusical goals rather than skill sets. It is important for music educators and music therapists to collaborate and share knowledge of

Box 3.4 Fieldwork Protocols for Therapy Sessions

Student's name: ______________________

Age:_____

Therapist's name and contact information:

Type of Therapy (i.e. Speech; Occupational; Physical; Music; Other):

Therapy goals (articulated by the therapist):

How often does the child attend therapy?

Types of activities observed during therapy (including goals addressed):

Challenges observed:

Successes observed:

Potential uses in music education classrooms:

techniques used in each profession. It is also important for music teachers, whenever possible, to attend music therapy sessions to learn how to integrate individual developmental goals into a music lesson.

CREATING PRACTICUM EXPERIENCES WITH STUDENTS WITH DIFFERENCES AND DISABILITIES FOR PRESERVICE MUSIC EDUCATORS

Integrating topics such as teaching students with disabilities is a common theme in the teacher education literature (Peebles & Mendaglio, 2014). Often other program areas across campus are struggling with the same topics, and they may be open to collaborating to provide practica for preservice teachers. Vignette 3.4 is an example of how this can be achieved at the university level. This vignette will encourage ideas for further development of practica in music teacher education.

Vignette 3.4 An Example of a Collaborative Differences and Disabilities Field Experience at the University Level

The Ball State University Prism Project: An Immersive Learning Practicum Opportunity for Music, Theatre, Dance, and Special Education Majors

It is well known throughout the special education community that many students with differences and disabilities struggle in developing and maintaining social relationships with peers. Often, because of their disabilities, students with disabilities become isolated from society and have higher incidence of depression as well as other mental health challenges. Due to changing legislation, increasing diagnosis rates, and a continued focus on inclusion within many teaching and learning environments (including the public school system), schools and partner programs (such as arts programs) are seeing an increased population of students with differences and disabilities.

The Ball State Prism Project is a Saturday afternoon program using the performing arts as a medium to explore and develop social skills for children age 6–14 who are challenged with differences and disabilities. Annually, in the spring semester, the Prism Project presents a capstone performance of the music, theater, and dance scenes that were created during the semester by Ball State students and the students with differences and disabilities who are enrolled in the project. The Prism Project is a partnership between the School of Music, the Department of Theatre and Dance, Interlock: The East Central Indiana Autism Society of America, and Sibshops (a program for siblings of children with differences and disabilities). A music therapist is also on staff to provide assistance in integrating all of the disciplines and to provide insight into appropriate techniques for the performers.

Ball State University students are directly involved in the creation, implementation, organization, administration, and production of this project within an authentic teaching and learning environment. This project gives Ball State students a unique opportunity to test their skills as teaching artists within an authentic setting, serving as one-on-one assistants, coordinating programming and planning, and administrating this program. On a pragmatic level, each student is required to attend collaborative plenary meetings that will be chaired by the student leadership. At this time, lesson plans are developed, scenes are created, and music is composed based on the needs of the students who are enrolled in the project. This is an authentic environment that allows Ball State students to improve their skills. Ball State students receive a variety of academic

(continued)

Vignette 3.4 Continued

credits while being involved in the program (e.g., fieldwork hours and observation hours).

Many music education, music performance, theater education, and theater performance majors have had little or no experience in teaching students with differences and disabilities. Increased curricular and licensure requirements have left little time for training arts educators to teach students with differences and disabilities. This lack of experience may deter them from including students with disabilities in their own future programs.

The Prism Project serves to enhance the lifelong learning for three groups of people who will be involved in this project. First, the students with differences and disabilities who enroll in the project are, through engagement with the arts, developing enhanced potential for lifelong learning. The Ball State students have more experience with children with disabilities and therefore possess tools necessary to include them within their future programs. Finally, the parents not only get a few hours of much-needed respite but also have an opportunity to see their children perform.

Visit us on the web at: http://prismprojectbsu.org. This website includes show clips, interviews of participants, and interviews with performers.

CONCLUSION

Practicum experiences are the cornerstone for provision of near-authentic practice teaching to inexperienced educators, and for educators seeking to increase their effectiveness when working with students with differences and disabilities. Research has shown that practica with students in diverse learning environments increase confidence, understanding, and reflective thinking ability among preservice and in-service educators (Gerrity, Hourigan, & Horton, 2013; VanWeelden & Whipple, 2005). Current in-service music educators, music teacher educators, and preservice music educators will benefit from opportunities to incorporate understandings and materials provided in this chapter. Further, music educators may find their overall goals and philosophy changing because of working with students who overcome challenges to learn music. Music has many access points for all students. A team approach that encourages dialogue and the sharing of strategies and information through engagement will enhance music teaching and learning in music classrooms.

DISCUSSION QUESTIONS

1. What are the advantages and disadvantages of practicum in a differences and disabilities setting?
2. How does effective practicum take place? Please describe the steps to this type of practicum and how you see them working in your school or future school (observing, assisting, discussing, planning).
3. Discuss your experiences (if you have had them) serving as a one-on-one assistant to a student with differences and disabilities.
4. How does the concept of Continuum of Placement change your views regarding the least restrictive environment?
5. How could you implement a Prism Project, or other inclusive opportunities, for students with differences and disabilities?

Chapter 4

A Resourceful and Pedagogical Approach to Teaching Students with Differences and Disabilities

CHAPTER OVERVIEW

- Participation in the Process and Gathering Support
- Speaking with Special Education Professionals and Staff
- Parent and Caregiver Partnerships
- Individualized Education Programs and 504 Plans
- Transition Plans
- 504 Plans
- Attending IEP or 504 Meetings
- Understanding Accommodations, Adaptations, and Modifications (Winding)
- Incorporating the Six Domains Into Classroom Accommodations
- Teaching Music to Students with Cognitive Challenges
- Teaching Music to Students with Communication Challenges
- Teaching Music to Students with Behavioral Challenges
- Teaching Music to Students with Emotional Challenges
- Teaching Music to Students with Sensory Challenges
- Teaching Music to Students with Physical and Medical Conditions
- Intersections
- Putting It All Together
- Discussion Questions

PARTICIPATION IN THE PROCESS AND GATHERING SUPPORT

Vignette 4.1 regarding Gregory introduces an approach to teaching students with differences and disabilities that may be new for many music educators (and music education students). Collegiate students are not always given the opportunity to think critically and constructively about adaptations and

Teaching Music to Students with Differences and Disabilities. Third Edition. Alice M. Hammel, and Ryan M. Hourigan, Oxford University Press. © Oxford University Press 2025. DOI: 10.1093/9780197689356.003.0004

Vignette 4.1 Gregory

Gregory Smith is a second grader, age 8. Gregory attended Head Start at age 4. He adjusted well to school and liked it. Gregory loved the gross motor activities both in and outside, like swings, climbers, and big blocks. He enjoyed water play, the sand table, and listening to music. He showed age-appropriate social development. Gregory's health screening revealed he suffered from frequent ear infections and colds. His speech screening showed mispronunciations of *w*, *s*, *th*, and *l* in all positions. The speech teacher also noted that Gregory did not focus visually on her during assessment. He did not seem to pick up on subtleties in language such as plurals and possessives. His teachers reported that he had difficulty following directions, attending to stories, and answering questions. He also had trouble with tool control and generally did not choose centers that involved fine-motor control.

Gregory's kindergarten teacher reported that Gregory was a sociable youngster who enjoyed school. He was good at singing and seemed to learn the alphabet and other things through music. His math skills were age-appropriate. He exhibited great difficulty with concentration on rhyming activities and associating sounds with alphabet letters. In oral language, Gregory often used incorrect noun-verb agreement and he often had trouble selecting the correct word when speaking. His lack of progress in pre-reading and writing prompted his teacher to refer him to the Child Study Team.

Music is Gregory's favorite class. He looks forward to seeing Mrs. Fletcher each week. He waits for Thursdays all week long! He seems to veer away from Orff Instruments when given a choice in the classroom. He has trouble focusing on Mrs. Fletcher during group instruction. He can, at times, be a distraction to other students. Gregory also has difficulty waiting his turn because he is so excited about being in his favorite class. He wants to answer all the questions and pick his instrument first—perhaps to avoid instruments requiring fine motor skills. Mrs. Fletcher finds this lack of attention confusing because he likes music class so much. Gregory has difficulty relating to peers, who often tease him because of his differences.

Now, consider the following questions:

- What is the dilemma? Briefly outline the issues to be addressed.
- Who are the stakeholders in this scenario? Who will be most affected by the actions to be taken?
- Draft a brief solution. Are there alternate solutions available?

modifications for students with differences and disabilities prior to graduation from undergraduate school (Hammel, 1999; Hourigan, 2009). Skills developed while brainstorming ideas for students via vignettes may assist music educators as they derive strategies for students with differences and disabilities in music classrooms. This skill preparation also introduces the idea of a "team approach" when interacting with faculty, administration, students, and families. For these reasons, vignettes are included within the text to encourage this process when preparing to teach students with differences and disabilities.

The most effective approach when working within a school and school system is to become a part of the existing team of professionals. Teachers often become compartmentalized when teaching music in another part of the building or when traveling from building to building. Successful child-centered schools function as teams, and active participation is important for each individual teacher and for the overall success of the school (Adamek & Darrow, 2018). Being proactive and positive can assist teachers as they become involved as integral "team members" within a school. In addition, maintaining a positive and inclusive attitude will increase the view that the music program is an important and necessary component of school life for all students (Adamek & Darrow, 2018).

Being aware of the students in the music classroom, as well as their academic and behavioral needs, is a critical initial strategy in developing an inclusive scope and sequence for classrooms and ensembles (Hammel, Hickox, & Hourigan, 2016). Knowing that we teach students, with music as a catalyst, and that students come to the music classroom with a variety of independent and individualized needs, is important to inclusive-oriented music educators.

Another crucial initial technique in this process is to review class lists with a guidance counselor, special education teacher/staff member, or administrator to determine the students in music classes with differences and disabilities. Many of these students will have an Individualized Education Program (IEP) or 504 Plan on file at the school. These documents are critical as strategies, adaptations, and modifications are developed to include all students in the music classroom. More strategies concerning these documents will be discussed later in this chapter.

SPEAKING WITH SPECIAL EDUCATION PROFESSIONALS AND STAFF

Special education faculty members will be able to provide a great deal of information about effective inclusion practices for a particular student (Stronge, 2007). Welcoming them into the music classroom and asking for assistance is a way to begin this process. When other faculty members know you are actively seeking strategies, it increases the sense of teamwork in your school (Weiss & Pasley, 2004). Individual special education teachers have areas of strength, just as we all do, and it is appropriate to ask for their input regarding behavior strategies, adaptive equipment, understanding special education paperwork, and other issues that may arise as inclusion strategies are designed. Each of us brings a unique skill set to the educational environment, and we all appreciate being recognized for our contributions (Shellard & Protheroe, 2000). Reaching out to colleagues and being gracious in accepting assistance are powerful pieces to the team-building process.

A very important, and sometimes overlooked, member of the team is the paraprofessional (or aide). These professionals are employed by the school system to work with a specific student, or small group of students, during the school day. They sometimes travel with a student on the bus to school and may stay with the student for the entire day and the trip home. Paraprofessionals assist the student with daily tasks, mobility within the school, and behavior management, and they can be a great resource (Adamek & Darrow 2018). They know the student very well, but unfortunately, they are sometimes not included or considered as full members of the school team. It is critical that music educators develop relationships with paraprofessionals. This advocacy skill is imperative when requesting that paraprofessionals work with students in music classrooms, particularly when music educators perceive this will increase the appropriateness of an educational setting for a student with differences and disabilities (Pressley, Raphael, Gallagher, & DiBella, 2004).

Music teachers are a part of the "child study," or IEP, team, and your input is vital in the process. Music teachers are considered general education teachers and are authorized to serve on these teams. Once music educators are aware of the needs of students in the music classroom through studying student documents and speaking with classroom teachers and special education teachers, the true preparation of instruction that will reach all students can begin. While teaching, take data (notes, charts, brief notations) regarding the academic and behavioral struggles and successes of students with differences and disabilities. This preparation will be very beneficial as it enhances the sense of teamwork with other members of the IEP team (see observation protocols in Chapter 1).

PARENT PARTNERSHIPS

A recurring theme in this text is the goal of creating a channel of communication with parents of students with disabilities. Music teachers need to understand that this may be difficult. Parents may be under financial hardship or even in denial about their child's disability. Attempt to keep these conversations about music teaching and learning. The following questions are examples of how you may choose to approach a parent: (a) How might I assist Jennifer in my class? (b) Jennifer is having trouble sitting in her seat during class. What strategies do you use at home in this situation? (c) Jennifer sometimes becomes anxious and upset when we do movement activities in music class. Is there a way I can make this experience more comfortable for her?

It is often helpful to not mention knowledge regarding a difference or disability. Let the parent begin this discussion (unless both persons involved in the discussion have been in the same IEP or 504 meeting). Once the parent does begin to discuss the difference or disability, the music educator may then acknowledge an awareness. This recommendation is made because, in many ways, students with differences and disabilities are just like students without differences and disabilities. There are times when their behaviors and academic challenges are the result of being children who are learning, rather than students with disabilities. Remember, students with differences and disabilities have often experienced failure in many areas. The last thing a parent wants to hear is that music class is next on the list of things their child cannot do. Keep conversations positive and maintain a problem-solving attitude when communicating with parents. It is also important to begin and end conversations by relating successes and areas of strength noticed during music instruction.

INDIVIDUALIZED EDUCATION PROGRAMS AND 504 PLANS

All IEPs and/or 504 Plans follow a similar structure; however, different states, and school systems, are given the latitude to create their own template for these plans based on general guidelines presented in the law. All IEPs contain: (a) a statement of the child's present levels of academic achievement and functional performance; (b) measurable goals statements (academic and functional); (c) benchmarks and short-term objectives for students who take alternate assessments; (d) how progress will be measured and when reports will be provided (reports must be provided at least as often as reports for students without disabilities are provided); (e) for students participating in alternate assessments, a statement as to why and which assessment will be included; (f) an initial evaluation that is conducted within 60 days of parental consent for evaluation (or within the time frame chosen by a state); (g) transition services for children 16 years of age or older; and (h) a stipulation that the child must be present when postsecondary goals and transitions are considered—or the child's interests must be considered.

Figure 4.1 is a portion of an actual IEP. The section represented is Joshua's present level of academic achievement narrative that was written by his primary teacher of record. This particular statement was completed at the end of his kindergarten year.

Purposes of Case Conference

Transition, Annual

Case Conference Meeting Scheduled

Date: 04/28/2016 **Time:** 11:15 a.m. **Place:** Muncie Central High School

Evaluation Information and Student Data

Strengths of the student:
Joshua has made a wonderful transition to high school. He participates independently in Theatre and Japanese using his accommodations and has earned a GPA of 3.4 for the first semester. Mrs. Babb shared that Joshua's oral reading is a strength.

Progress Monitoring Data:

Teacher Observation, Comprehensive Progress Reports on Information Now, Grades, ISTEP assessment data. Joshua has maintained a 85-100% rate of assignment completion to earn the following grades for the

1st semester: 3rd Nine Weeks:

Earth Science: 99A 92A

Basic Skills: 100A 98A

Algebra I: 82B 96A

Math Lab: 90A 92A

Japanese: 86B 85B

Tech Theatre: 93% 95A

English 9: 88B 90A

Present level of academic and functional performance:

Joshua is a 16 year old young man who began his freshman year at Muncie Central this year. His educational diagnosis is Autism Spectrum disorder and Language Impairment and he has utilized support from extra adults in some

Joshua Ryan Hourigan Page 1

Figure 4.1. IEP present level of academic functioning statement.

classes and the accommodations included in his IEP. Doing so, Joshua has progressed very well to earn 7 credits for first semester plus an additional 2 credits he earned in 8th grade for his French class. His current GPA is 3.4 as he has earned all A's and B's so far this year. His team discussed continuing his supports and revised them accordingly.

Joshua's teachers have enjoyed having him in their classes. Mr. Babb reported that Josh currently has a 91%A for Algebra and makes a very good class effort, though he needs some guidance to complete assignments and usually has the assistance of Mrs. Gross for that. He further stated that Joshua sets a good example for behavior in that class and that his hard work has shown in the progress he has made. Mrs. Gross shared that when she works with Joshua, he is staying caught up. Mrs. Thompson has Joshua for Math Lab and has done some tutoring with him after school. She stated that it helps having an additional adult in the class and that remembering his algebra concepts for the year until he is assessed with the ISTEP may be an issue. The team discussed ways to maintain those skills including, using an app such as the Kahn Academy to review on a regular basis, having weekly tutoring through the summer or retaking at least the first semester of Algebra or the Math Lab for no credit next fall. The team resolved to offer the summer tutoring and Josh will take Math Lab I-1 class in the fall with an extra adult in the room. Mrs. Beckman assists in the Math Lab class and provides support to Joshua during his Earth Science and English 9 classes. She shared that he is doing well but may need some more structure for his iPad use. An accommodation will be added for that. Mr. Wafer is Joshua's Earth Science teacher and he reported that Joshua does a "top notch job in class" with "Great manners!" Mr. Wafer is glad that Joshua has an instructional assistant to help him stay on task with his assignments. Mr. Kidd provided a report and invited the Hourigans to visit his class after the conference. He shared that Joshua is a very willing participant in Japanese class and that he frequently raises his hand to respond to verbal questions or write things on the board. He included that Joshua's iPad has not been a distraction in that class. Mr. Kidd suggested that Joshua's homework is not done to the same level of accuracy as his in class work and that Joshua needs to use his notes, charts and sentence formulas when completing his homework. Also, Mr. Kidd encourages his students to correct and re-submit their homework for FULL credit. He stated that Joshua does not take full advantage of that. So, since Joshua wants to continue in Japanese, a Japanese Homework goal will be included for him.

Mrs. Babb, the special education teacher in Josh's co-taught English class, reported that "Josh is a great studen. During the class time, he has a personal aide that is there with him for the majority of class. His current grade is an 81% B-. He currently has 3 missing assignments and one not graded. His is missing the questions for Romeo and Juliet for Acts 1, 2, and 3. We worked on these assignments as we were reading the play and I believe he has worked on them, however, since he leaves with Mrs. Beckman 5 minutes early, I think he places them in his folder and walks off with them." The team discussed the issue of leaving early for the bus and decided that Joshua does not need the extra time to get to his locker and bus. That accommodation will be removed.

Mrs. Babb and Mrs. Ryder (the general education teacher for Joshua's co-taught English 9 class) agree that Josh's strength is in his oral reading. "He is not shy about reading out loud in front of the class (as well as doing a little bit of acting!). He may stumble over a few words, but he keeps trying until he says it correctly. Josh's weaknesses are in comprehension. He is so fixed on trying to have the right answer without fully understanding the question that he tends to blurt out any answer. He also has a difficult time understanding ambiguity in stories. A goal was created to assist Joshua in expanding his reading comprehension in written expression because Mrs. Babb shared that written expression is a related weakness. "In his writings in class, he is too focused on trying to write to please us instead of digging a little bit deeper. He has found a few graphic organizers online (readwritethink.org) that he likes a lot and that have helped him organize his writing. If he can continue to use these organizers, he will continue to grow in his writing." It would be beneficial if he could have a print out of a blank organizer of his choice to use on the ISTEP writing portion next year. The team will explore if such an accommodation is allowed. When Joshua did not use an organizer for his writing, he tended to go off topic or off focus and out of order. Therefore, an accommodation for use of a wipe off graphic organizer for written work in any of his classes will be added.

The case conference committee has determined that there is sufficient data to plan appropriately for the student. Therefore, reevaluation is not required at this time for the purposes of considering eligibility or providing additional information regarding the student's special education and related service needs. The school must consider reevaluation for each student receiving special education and related services at least once every three (3) years unless the parent and the school agree that it is unnecessary. In addition, the school must consider reevaluation if the school determines at any time during the three (3) year cycle that additional information is needed to address the special education or related services needs of the student, or if the student's parent or teacher requests an evaluation.

Joshua Ryan Hourigan Page 2

Figure 4.1. Continued

Figure 4.2 represents a goals page in an actual IEP for the same student, Joshua. The challenges a student encounters, his or her basic needs, and his or her goals are clearly represented in the present level of academic functioning narrative. As is apparent when viewing this IEP, music educators can get a great deal of information about students prior to having a student with differences and disabilities in music class. There are clear, measurable goals set forth by the members of the team. Goals can be set in each academic area

Data Used to Determine Present Level of Academic Achievement and Functional Performance

Present Level of Performance Data: Josh's expressive language was characterized by reduced vocabulary, pronoun confussion and deletion of verb markers.

Annual Goal:

To improve expressive language

Short-Term Objectives (at least two per goal)	Evaluation	Criterion	Schedule
1. J. will name pictures within categories describing their similarities as "fruits, clothes"	S	On 4 out of 5 trials	G
2. J. will a. appropriately use personal pronouns (he, she, you, I) b. produce a noun-verb-object sentence incorporating the auxiliary verb "is" when shown a picture stimulus	S	On 4 out of 5 trials	G
3. J. will produce pronoun-verb-object sentences when shown a picture stimulus	S	On 4 out of 5 trials	G

Date	Status Obj. 1	Status Obj. 2	Status Obj. 3	Comments/Data On Progress
3/17/06	4	2	4	
6/16/06	2	2	2	

Evaluation	Criterion %	Schedule	Status of Progress on Objectives
S Student's Daily Work D Documented Observation R Rating Scale T Standardized Test O Other (specify above)	Accuracy of Rate Achievement Level Other (specify above)	W Weekly D Daily M Monthly G Grading Period O Other (specify above)	1 Achieve/Maintained 2 Progressing at a rate sufficient to meet the annual goal for this objectives 3 Progressing below a rate sufficient to meet the annual goal for this objective (explain above) 4 Not applicable during this reporting period 5 Other (specify above)

Reporting Progress

The parents will be regularly informed in writing of progress on goals objectives of this IEP at the regular reporting periods applicable to general education students. Additional reporting:

How:		When:	

Figure 4.2. Academic goals page (from an IEP).

and in each therapy domain (e.g., speech, physical, occupational, etc.). The team evaluates each goal annually.

An imperative consideration to note from this specific page (Figure 4.2) is Joshua's unique language skills. He can receive much more than he can express. This may require a music educator to observe Joshua in other classes to see how teachers communicate with him. In addition, it is clear in Figure 4.2 that Joshua has difficulty with peer relationships. This might mean careful consideration for turn taking, group interaction, partner songs, and other such interactive lessons in the music classroom. Finding a student to place next to him that will model good peer relationships would benefit Joshua.

Notice the key at the bottom of the page. This details how, when, and what criteria will be used to determine whether a student has reached a particular goal. This particular goal area is speech. Many speech and language goals can be addressed in music, and often students experience similar challenges in music. In Joshua's case, simplified language in music class with visual reinforcement would be an excellent accommodation to add after viewing this page of his IEP. Music educators should also consider that Joshua has a reduced vocabulary. Using a simplified vocabulary that includes fewer words in music class will help Joshua succeed.

The next section of the IEP (Figure 4.3) represents how a school district fulfills the least restrictive environment (LRE) of the Individuals with Disabilities Education Act (IDEA). Notice this page is distinctly concerned with placing Joshua in a learning environment that is best for him, his teacher, and the other students. This includes the number of hours Joshua will attend regular education and special education classes per week, extracurricular activities, and support services.

Music educators looking at Figure 4.3 should consider how these accommodations will enhance Joshua's experience in music class. It is clear that a picture schedule (see later in this chapter) would assist with his anxiety about transitions. Based on Figure 4.3, music educators should modify tests and assignments. Also, it is clear from this page that Joshua needs one-on-one support during music class. Joshua also needs very frequent repetition

x 22

Least Restrictive Environment

This student will:

Fully participate with students who are nondisabled in the general education setting except for the time spent in separate special education programs/services provided outside of the general education classroom as specified in this IEP.

☒ Yes ☐ No (Explain):

Be fully involved in and make progress in the general education curriculum.

☐ Yes ☒ No (Explain): student participates with accomodations, some of his day is spent in special education classroom.

Have the same opportunity as general education students to participate in nonacademic and extracurricular activities

☒ Yes ☐ No (Explain):

Programs and Services

Supplementary Aids/Services/Personnel Support

Supplementary Aids/Services/Support	Time/Frequency/Conditions	Beginning Mo/Day/Yr.	*Ending Mo/Day/Yr.	Setting
1. visual schedules / supports 2. ASD coordinator	1. daily 2. daily	6-14-06 First day of school 06-07 year	6-17-06 6-14-07	Elementary School
3. pre-teaching of material / concepts	3. daily	6-14-06 First day of school 06-07 year	6-17-06 6-14-07	Elementary School
4. general education setting 5. Modified assignments / tests (multiple choice, paraphrasing questions)	4. 27.85-29.85 hours/week 5. daily	6-14-06 First day of school 06-07 year	6-17-06 6-14-07	Elementary School
6. additional adult support during general education settings for safety, social interactions, academics, personal care	6. daily	6-14-06 First day of school 06-07 year	6-17-06 6-14-07	Elementary School
7. Repetition of directions / check for comprehension of directions given 8. Priority seating	7. daily 8. daily	6-14-06 First day of school 06-07 year	6-17-06 6-14-07	Elementary School

All supplementary aids, services, and supports listed above will begin on the initiation date of the IEP as indicated on the signature page, following the approved school district calendar. ☒ Yes or ☐ No. If no, comment: ______

Special Education Programs/Related Services
Is there a need for a teacher with a particular endorsement? ☒ No ☐ Yes, specify:

Resource Program Only:
Is a Teacher Consultant with endorsement matching the student's disability needed? ☒ No ☐ Yes

Departmentalized Program (R 340.1749c) ☒ No ☐ Yes

Figure 4.3. Least restrictive environment page (from an IEP).

and simplification of directions. Therefore, simple classroom routines in music class need reinforcement (e.g., redirecting or repetition from aide).

The statement on the present level of academic functioning, along with goals pages in other areas, is an important piece of information for music educators.

It would be ideal for the music educator to gain access and review the IEP prior to instruction. Typically, IEPs are on file in the school or district office. Members of the special education team (and the music educator is part of the team) are required to have access to these files.

TRANSITION PLANS

As students begin their teenage years, the team begins to focus on their post-secondary lives. The IEP meetings and documents begin to consider what the student will do for work or school after high school completion or graduation. These parts of the IEP documents are useful to view because they give a glimpse of where the student is heading and what they will be expected to accomplish during their life. Some students will work assiduously in order to live in a supervised group home while earning money in a sheltered and supervised work environment. Other students are on a path that will lead them to college or technical school degrees. By viewing the plans, music educators can align their expectations and prepare the student to include music in their post-secondary school life in the way most appropriate. Figure 4.4 and Box 4.1 illustrate the differences between two students who have transition plans in place. One student will receive a certificate of completion of school and will spend most of his secondary school time in a classroom that has a focus on life skills. The other student will receive a high school diploma and may go on to post-secondary schooling of some type. This information is found in a section of the IEP called the Summary of Findings from Age-Appropriate Transition. For example, some students will work assiduously in order to live in a supervised group home while earning money in a sheltered and supervised work environment. Other students are on a path that will lead them to college or technical school degrees. By reviewing the plans, music educators can align their expectations and prepare students to include music in their post-secondary school life in ways most appropriate for their interests, needs, and plans.

THE 504 PLANS

Students who have a disability that is included in IDEA but whose severity does not require them to have the level of services of an IEP, as well as students who have a disability not included in IDEA, may participate in instruction under a 504 Plan rather than an IEP. The 504 Plans are derived from Section 504 of the 1973 Health and Rehabilitation Act. A 504 Plan is put in place to "level the playing field" for a student so they receive equal access to educational opportunities. A 504 Plan includes adaptations to the general classroom environment for a student with differences and disabilities. These plans do not require staff members to monitor progress and do not include supplementary aids and services (personnel) to achieve equal access to education. Some common 504 accommodations include an extra set of books at home, extra time on classroom assignments and assessments, separate or quiet areas when participating in assessments, preferential seating, frequent progress reports,

Jane Doe
Student ID:
FTE Number:
Date of Birth:

Somerset Public Schools
111 Elm St.
Somerset VA 11111
111-111-1111

Virginia's Standards of Learning Assessments

Student's Name: Jane Doe

Date:

Student ID Number: 1111111

Participation In The SOL Assessments

For the student who will be (1) in a grade level for which the student is eligible to participate in the SOL Assessment; (2) enrolled in a course for which there is an SOL end-of-course test; (3) participating in a remediation recovery program or (4) needs to take a SOL Assessment as a requirement to earn a Modified Standard Diploma, Standard Diploma, or Advanced Studies Diploma, list each test below. Next determine if the student will participate in the SOL test and then list the accommodation(s) and/or modification(s) that will be made based upon those the student generally uses during classroom instruction and assessment. For the accommodations and/or modifications that may be considered, refer to "Accommodations/Modifications" page of the 504 Plan and the Virginia Board of Education's guidelines.

- ■ State Assessments
  - ■ SOL Assessments and retake (SOL)
  - ☐ Virginia Grade Level Alternative (VGLA)*
  - ☐ Virginia Substitute Evaluation Program (VSEP)*
  - ☐ Other State Approved Substitute(s)

* Refer to Procedures for Determining Participation in the Assessment Component of Virginia's Accountability System and the Procedural Manuals for VGLA and VSEP.

SOL Tests	**Participation**	**Accommodations Modifications**	**If YES, List Accommodation(s) and/or Modification(s) by Test**
SOL ALGEBRA I	■Yes ☐ No	■Yes ☐ No	Extended time to take test. Use of calculator/multiplication chart. Write answers in test booklet for all tests including SOL test.
SOL EARTH SCIENCE	■Yes ☐ No	■Yes ☐ No	Extended time to take test. Write answers in test booklet for all test s including SOL test.
SOL GRADE 8 CIVICS & ECONOMICS	■Yes ☐ No	■Yes ☐ No	Extended time to take test. Write answers in test booklet for all test including SOL test.
SOL GRADE 8 READING	■Yes ☐ No	■Yes ☐ No	Extended time to take test. Write answers in test booklet for all tests including SOL test.

Mark any nonstandard administration with an asterisk*. These test scores will be reported as scores that result from a nonstandard administration. A student with a disability who has passed an SOL assessment utilizing any accommodation including a nonstandard accommodation has passed for all purposes.

Explanation For Non-Participation And How The Student Will Be Assessed:

If no is checked for any test, explain in the space below why the student will not participate in this test, the impact relative to promotion or graduation, and how the student will be assessed in these areas.

504 Plan Page

Somerset Public Schools Exceptional Education Dept.

Figure 4.4. 504 Plan

Jane Doe
Student ID:
FTE Number:
Date of Birth:

Somerset Public Schools
111 Elm St.
Somerset VA 11111
111-111-1111

Accommodations/Modifications

Student's Name: Jane Doe

Date:

Student ID Number: 1111111

This student will be provided access to the general education, special education, other school services and activities including non-academic activities and extracurricular activities, and education related settings:

with no accommodations/modifications

X with the following accommodations/modifications

Accommodations/modifications provided as part of the instructional and testing/assessment process will allow the student equal opportunity to access the curriculum and demonstrate achievement. Accommodations/modifications will provide access to non-academic and extracurricular activities and educationally related settings. Accommodations/modifications based solely on the potential to enhance performance beyond providing equal access are inappropriate.

Accommodations may be in, but not limited to, the areas of time, scheduling, setting, presentation, and response. The impact of any modifications listed should be discussed. This includes the earning of credits for graduation.

Accommodations/Modifications (please list, as appropriate):

Accommodation(s)/Modification(s)	Frequency	Location	Duration m/d/y to m/d/y
Content Area			
Copies of notes from teachers.	As needed.	SPS	01/01/0000 - 01/01/0000
Extended time to complete all classroom assignments.	Always	SPS	
Use of classroom computer when lengthy assignments are given	As needed	SPS	
Environmental			
Preferential seating near teacher	As needed	SPS	
General			
Extra set of books at home for all subjects.	During school year	SPS	
Organization			
Study guides should be provided.	Prior to testing	SPS	
Testing Accommodation			
Extended time to take test.	As needed	SPS	
Use of calculator/multiplication chart.	During math class when related to instruction	SPS	
Write answers in test booklet for all test including SOL test	As Needed	SPS	

504 Plan

Page

Somerset Public Schools Exceptional Education Dept.

Figure 4.4. Continued

use of a calculator or spell checker, use of a computer or keyboard for written assignments, reduction in amount of assignments or homework, and behavior plans. These plans are legal documents, as are IEPs, and it is both the right and responsibility of all music educators to follow all accommodations and adaptations listed on 504 Plans (U.S. Department of Education, 2023).

An example of a 504 Plan for a middle school student is listed in Figure 4.4. The template for the document varies by school district and state. The information included in a 504 Plan, however, is fairly consistent throughout the United States. The 504 Plan will list the strengths and challenges a student experiences, the accommodations required for state-level testing procedures, classroom accommodations and modifications, and any other specific information necessary for the equal inclusion of that student in the classroom. These accommodations will not be music specific, and it is the responsibility of the music educator to transfer these strategies to the music classroom.

Listed next are the accommodations listed in the example 504 Plan for a middle school student. Underneath the general accommodations list of the 504 Plan for Jane Doe, we have created a list of strategies for the music classroom based on the 504 accommodations for Jane Doe. These are included in italics. Almost every accommodation listed on a 504 Plan can be implemented in the music classroom. The following are examples of accommodations and music-specific accommodations:

1. Copies of notes from teachers

This student will need notes from the teacher of anything written on the chalkboard, whiteboard, or Smart Board. She may be unable to take adequate notes while attending to instruction in a music class or ensemble situation. Anything stated during class should be written or copied for the student to include in her materials for music class.

2. Extended time to complete all classroom assignments

This student may have great difficulty completing assignments in the standard amount of time. This may include composition or improvisation assignments, timed playing or scales testing, writing in phrases, breath marks, or noting dynamic markings, numbering measures, learning drills for marching band, memorizing music, creating rhythms or melody patterns in elementary music, or studying sight-reading material prior to singing or playing.

3. Use of classroom computer when lengthy assignments are given

This student may need accommodations when asked to write papers about composers or other music topics. She may not be able to adequately express herself during short-answer, description, or essay responses (in writing) and may need to respond orally instead. She may need to use a keyboard to organize her thoughts prior to speaking. This may affect a music classroom that includes music theory, history, or extensive long-form responses regarding performance practice or compositional styles. This accommodation sometimes indicates a challenge in the area of fine motor control that can also lead to difficulties in using mallets and rhythm percussion instruments and in the fine motor control necessary to play an instrument.

4. Preferential seating by teacher

Transferring this accommodation to the music classroom or ensemble can be difficult. In elementary music, this can be accomplished by seating a student near instruction (the instruments being played, the book shown during a lesson, or the board where rhythmic and tonal patterns will be presented). In the secondary ensemble classroom, students with this accommodation often need to be seated near the conductor, piano, or front of the classroom to increase attention and focus during instruction. If a student has earned a "chair" in an ensemble, the first placement should be the one he or she has earned. Other placements may be considered as needed and in consultation with the student, parents, and other teachers.

5. Extra set of books at home for all subjects

Students in music classes are often asked to have materials in class and then to use those materials at home as they prepare for class. The transfers of this accommodation to the music classroom include recorders, music, octavos, instruments, music stands, lyres, and method books. If no additional materials are available and these are clearly needed by the student, the special education department may have funding to assist with providing these additional materials for a student.

6. Study guides should be provided

A student with this accommodation may have great difficulty inferring possible test questions and performance expectations and may not be able to comprehend the information a teacher relays prior to an assessment. Before engaging in any assessment, it will be very important for this student to be aware of the exact knowledge, skills, and information she needs to succeed. This includes the exact scales (including the rhythm expected for the scale) or passages of music she will be asked to perform, a detailed outline of each subject to be included on a written assessment, and the type of questions on the test. This outline can include the way a question will be presented–for example, will the key signatures be listed and the student asked to name them, or will a blank staff be listed and the student asked to write the key signature? This is a critical distinction for a student who needs this type of accommodation.

7. Extended time to take tests

Timed tests can be unfair for students who are not able to recall information quickly. When we ask students to do this, we are measuring the amount of time required to display their knowledge, rather than the knowledge itself. Students who need extended time to take tests may need untimed scale tests, more time to complete singing or playing tests, and more opportunities to respond to a rhythm or singing assessment in elementary music, and may need to perform the test in an adjacent room or bring the completed test back to class after finishing it by using an electronic file or recording it on a phone.

8. Use of calculator or multiplication chart

This accommodation can signify a challenge in the area of memorization of facts and other information. Students who have this accommodation listed on their 504 Plan may have difficulty recalling note names and patterns quickly (an example would be note names or the circle of fifths). They may need to use mnemonic aids or outlines of information as they respond to classroom activities and assessments.

9. Write answers in booklet for all tests including the state standardized tests

This accommodation sometimes indicates difficulty with transferring information to other forms. A student may not be able to accurately complete an assessment on a blank piece of staff paper. She may need a template of staff paper to fill in the missing information. She may also do well if the format used for practice during class is exactly the same as the format used for assessment.

ATTENDING IEP OR 504 MEETINGS

As music educators prepare to attend IEP and 504 meetings for students with differences and disabilities, a review of existing paperwork, discussion with colleagues, and review of data/notes taken during class provide excellent groundwork. This level of preparation may increase the perceptions that other team members, and the school community at large, have of the individual music educator and of the overall music program at school. It also will be greatly appreciated by students with differences and disabilities and their parents/guardians. Moreover, music educators will have then created the opportunity to be better teachers to students with differences and disabilities by being prepared to teach *all* students.

Another very helpful step to take as a meaningful member of the child study or IEP team is to attend the meetings. It can sometimes be difficult to ascertain when these meetings will be held. Information about students with disabilities is held in the strictest of confidence, and meeting times and so forth are not posted where the general school community may read them. A good strategy is to discuss concerns with a lead special education teacher or the IEP case manager and request to be involved in the IEP meeting. If release time cannot be scheduled during the meeting, it is certainly appropriate to send a letter or list describing the areas of strength and challenge observed during music instruction. It is recommended that this list begin with the strengths a student brings to a situation and the successes (even if they are small) the student has experienced in class.

The possibility exists that music is an area of strength and success for a student with differences and disabilities. It is important for the team, including the parents of the student, to be aware of this. It is helpful to state, in a positive tone, the challenges a student is having and some suggestions of adaptive materials, alternate settings, or additional personnel that may make the experience a more appropriate learning environment for the student (Adamek & Darrow, 2018). There are times when a student with differences and disabilities may still struggle in a music classroom. In these situations, a positive attitude and emphasis on being a valued member of the special education team will assist communication and the establishment of an appropriate LRE for students with differences and disabilities (Rozalski, Stewart, & Miller, 2010). The data taken during class and active participation in IEP and 504 meetings (via written communication or personal presence) can now be of assistance as the problem-solving process begins for a student who is still struggling. It may be possible that the student has been placed in an environment that is not "least restrictive" and that a change in placement may be necessary. This change may be as simple as having the student come to music at a different time of day or with a different group of students. A student's medication titration schedule (the levels of medication in a student's system sometimes change during the day) may be considered an issue for discussion. Sometimes a particular group of students will be better suited to a student with differences and disabilities. A student may need to be part of a smaller class, or in a self-contained class, rather than in a general classroom. It may also be necessary for a student to have a paraprofessional during music, or additional adaptive equipment. These considerations are part of a possible change in placement for a student with differences and disabilities.

An initial strategy in this process is to discuss the struggles a student may be having in class. Meeting with the team may be necessary to discuss changes to the services a student receives in music. It is also important to make contact, either directly or through the special/general education teacher, with the parents or guardians of a student who is having difficulty in the music classroom. Creating short-term behavior or academic plans with frequent parental (and team) notification is often an effective way to either correct a situation in a brief amount of time or begin to pinpoint a more significant issue. Behavior plans will be discussed further in Chapter 5.

It is sobering yet empowering to know that the music educator, as a team member, has the right to ask for a full meeting of the team once all available procedures for identifying and ameliorating areas of academic and behavioral struggle for a student with differences and disabilities have been followed. If a meeting is requested, however, please be sure that appropriate data have been taken and all suggestions made during communication with other team members have been implemented. Music educators who follow these guidelines will be in a position of strength and will have the support of the school team. A change in the LRE can be made during the school year, and changes to the IEP or 504 Plan may be made at any time during the year by the team. The goal is to provide the most appropriate instruction for all students with differences and disabilities (Hammel, 2004).

UNDERSTANDING ADAPTATIONS, AND MODIFICATIONS (WINDING)

Once the inclusive music classroom has been prepared, IEP and 504 Plans have been reviewed, and relationships with members of the team have been established, music educators are ready to apply adaptations and modifications for students with differences and disabilities. It is a legal responsibility to apply these strategies in the music classroom. More importantly, it is good teaching to treat each student as an individual and to give everyone the tools they need to be successful in the music classroom (those with differences and disabilities and those without differences and disabilities). This is the essence of "fairness" in education. Fair is not equal. Fair is providing every student in your classroom with the tools they need for success (Turnbull, Turnbull, Shank, & Leal, 2002).

Appropriate adaptations and accommodations are critical to success in the music classroom (Box 4.1). Music educators are not limited to strategies listed in the special education paperwork. It is absolutely appropriate to find additional adaptations and modifications specific to your music classroom that will enhance the learning of your students. As music educators become more comfortable applying the adaptations and modifications listed and creating new strategies, the process becomes easier, and teachers may find that many of these strategies work for all students in the music classroom. *Universal design* is the term most often used to describe classrooms that are structured so everyone has equal access (Hourigan, 2023). That is one of the hallmarks of a truly successful inclusion classroom; all students can benefit from the strategies introduced to assist students with differences and disabilities (Van Garderen & Whittaker, 2006).

Box 4.1 Accommodations, adaptations, and modifications

Accommodations: Adaptations used when it is believed that a child can learn at the same level as the other students in the classroom.
Adaptations: Instructional tools and materials used to accommodate children based on their learning needs
Modifications: Adaptations used with different curricular goals in mind in order for the child to achieve at the highest possible level.

(Adamek & Darrow, 2018)

When reading IEPs and 504 plans, the term *accommodations* is often present. Accommodations are the overarching differences that teachers make to methods and materials. Students who need more or different from teachers will utilize accommodations created by the IEP and 504 teams. *Accommodations* is a broad term and can be used to reflect what we do to make learning more accessible for students with differences and disabilities.

Adaptations are employed when students will be able to meet the stated objective by the time students are assessed. Students who need these often require adjustments to the size, color, pacing, and modality (Chapter 6) of materials and methods. Adaptations are utilized with every student in the classroom and ensemble, even though not all students need them. This serves two functions. The first reason is that by utilizing the principles of adaptation with all students, we do not "other" students who are in need of these material and method differences. The second reason is that through the use of these principles, all students receive an enhanced and enriched experience that can assist the learning for everyone.

Modifications are used when students with differences and disabilities will not be able to meet the stated objective by the time students are assessed. Some students are not developmentally able to meet the objectives set for students who are neurotypical. These students will need modified objectives that wind back (Hammel et al., 2016) our literacy and experience sequences to find their current level of achievement. When we wind (modify) our objectives and assessments, every student in the room can have access to objectives that are meaningful and achievable every day. Winding is also very appropriate for students who have already met the objectives we have set for most of the class. Some students need for us to wind our literacy and experience sequences forward so those students may also have access to meaningful and achievable objectives every day. We use winding, rather than modifications, in our own practice because it encourages incremental sequencing through learning ladders and also provides the option to wind forward as well as backward. When seeing modifications listed, we encourage you to incrementally sequence and wind your way forward or backward to find the exact learning locus for each student.

INCORPORATING THE SIX DOMAINS INTO CLASSROOM ACCOMMODATIONS

In Chapter 1, six areas of challenge that affect students with differences and disabilities were introduced. These six areas are cognition, communication, behavioral, emotional, physical, and sensory. It is firmly believed that a classroom free of labels and designed to accommodate all students is the most respectful and successful environment for students with and without differences and disabilities. Many research-based and time-tested adaptations and modifications for students with differences and disabilities have been considered and chosen and are listed at the end of this chapter according to the areas of challenge a student may experience. Remember that a student may often experience challenges in more than one area.

Please also note that these strategies may be employed with all students in the music classroom or ensemble. The next section will offer specific strategies for the music classroom, as well as small vignettes of successful lessons and techniques designed for readers to gain insight and inferences for their own classrooms. In addition, music teacher educators are encouraged to use these vignettes as an introduction to discussions in the methods classroom. The vignettes are posted as written by students and some do not contain person-first language as the students were still learning to consistently use this when speaking about students with differences and disabilities.

TEACHING MUSIC TO STUDENTS WITH COGNITIVE CHALLENGES

Vignette 4.2 was written by a preservice music teacher who was struggling to plan a lesson for students with cognitive and physical challenges. Students with cognitive disabilities typically struggle in three areas of learning: input (the way in which they receive and process sensory information); retention (the ability of students to commit knowledge to memory); and output (the ways learners can demonstrate and express their understanding of knowledge and skills and generalize those concepts to other situations). Music educators who focus on cognition when teaching students with disabilities often consider enhancing the interactions between the learner and his or her environment (Wehmeyer, 2002). These learning strategies include the understanding that through this interaction "the learner is an active component who makes the learning occur" (Wehmeyer, 2002, p. 61). In addition, the learner is encouraged to construct new meaning from these experiences.

Vignette 4.2 Teaching Tempo to Students with Cognitive and Physical Disabilities

The Problem: The first class I see in the week are students in a mild cognitively impaired class. I needed to create a lesson that was visual based and involves movement in some manner for this group of students. This also brought to mind that the movement aspect of my lesson must either be obtainable for the severe class or must be modified to accommodate the needs of other students.

The Solution: When I thought about how I would make this lesson visual and movement based, a thought of a high school earth science lesson came to me. The lesson I was thinking of was one where the teacher stretched a slinky out across the floor and showed us the way different kinds of waves looked. He moved one end of the slinky back and forth. I thought that this could be easily adapted to a music lesson. I decided to use a rope instead of a slinky and have the students make the waves in the rope to the speed of the song being heard. This filled both criteria of approaches because the wave is a very visual representation of the speed and also by the students moving the rope back and forth it engaged them kinesthetically. I also picked a rope that was somewhat colorful and stimulating to try to engage them further. I also liked this because with the severe students could see it and hold on to one end of the rope and I can move the other to the appropriate speed so they can feel the change in tempo. I had all the students sit in a semicircle and I passed the rope end from student to student. With the severe class I just gave the students an end of the rope and they stayed in their wheelchairs. The paraprofessionals helped the students that needed assistance in holding onto the rope.

I felt that all three classes responded well to this exercise. They were able to demonstrate the difference between tempos by moving the rope accordingly. They also seemed to get excited about the music and participating in the activity. This activity was a very effective approach to assessing student knowledge. I utilized a visual and kinesthetic exercise, which I feel made this lesson as effective with these groups of students.

As discussed earlier in this chapter, before accommodating the learning needs of a student, it is very important that music educators read the IEP, 504 Plan, or other legal document created for the student. Once the documents have been reviewed, the accommodation process can begin. In the music classroom, a student with challenges in the area of cognition may need multiple opportunities and response modes when participating in classroom and ensemble activities and assessments. This may include many repetitions of the material, and their responses may be slower or uneven, and they need to have information presented in all three modalities (visual, aural, and kinesthetic). They may also receptively understand what is expected but not be able to reproduce it expressively. Once the music educator is aware of the preferred mode of learning, that modality can be stressed, although the others may still be included to strengthen receptive skills and increase the possibility that a student may begin to learn in more than one (or two) ways.

TEACHING MUSIC TO STUDENTS WITH COMMUNICATION CHALLENGES

Vignette 4.3 was written by a student teacher who was faced with teaching a lesson to students who either were nonverbal or had severe communication challenges. Valdes, Bunch, Snow, Lee, and Matos (2005) state: "All teachers, regardless of the language backgrounds of their students, are directly and intimately involved with language" (p. 126). It is valuable for music educators to understand that language development is critical to the success of students in the music classroom. If a student cannot understand instruction, their skills and understanding will not increase. It is imperative that music educators focus on language components when considering ways to deliver instruction to students with communication and language differences. As mentioned in the cognitive discussion, it is also important to observe the student, either in the music classroom or in other classes, to evaluate his or her receptive and expressive language skills as part of a formative data-gathering opportunity. A recurring theme in this book has been the importance of frequent consultation with the group of professionals who serve with the music educator on the team in various areas of special education services. In this instance, the speech pathologist or speech teacher would be an excellent resource. They will be able to recommend specific teaching and learning strategies such as communication systems that are needed to assist a student who is in the music classroom.

One particular communication tool that many special educators use is the Picture Exchange Communication System (PECS) (Figure 4.5).This system provides many students who have communication challenges with a visual and simplified way to communicate with teachers and other students. Many school districts already own the program Boardmaker. This program has many music icons available for use.

A PECS can be used in the music classroom to express needs and choices for students with disabilities who have difficulty in the area of communication. If students are choosing an activity or instrument, pictures of the choices can be presented to the student, who can then point, nod, or use a method of communication they are comfortable with to express a choice.

Vignette 4.3 Teaching "Fast and Slow" to Children with Cognitive and Communication Challenges

A Preservice Music Teacher's Perspective

I was working with a class of students who are cognitively and physically challenged, which involves mostly children in wheelchairs. The children for the most part do not show their understanding or recognition of the music or activities, so it's challenging to plan lessons with the class because it is the teacher's job to do everything and not expect much feedback from the students.

I was required to do a lesson based on fast and slow with the class. I made a CD of different pieces of music of varying tempos for them to listen to. I gave each student a maraca to shake when listening to the music. The students' aides were there to assist the students as needed. I wanted the students to shake the maracas fast when the music was fast and slow when it was slow. The aides had to help some of the students quite a lot in this activity, which I expected.

When the music was fast, it was easy to shake the maracas appropriately; however, when the music was slow, the maracas were not very useful. They did not represent a slower tempo very well. There was probably another instrument I could have used for the slower pieces; however, it would not have been wise to switch instruments for each piece with this class because it would have been too chaotic. In this situation, perhaps a different instrument in general would have been beneficial, but I was not aware this would be an issue until I experienced it.

Mrs. A, the cooperating teacher, assisted me in the lesson to help keep the students involved by having them move around, whether it be walking or being pushed in their wheelchairs. This gave them a different physical experience with the music, which is always beneficial in a special education class. In addition, we used PECS (Picture Exchange Communication System) to allow the students to choose fast or slow from a choice of icons. I learned that if something doesn't work as well as desired, then I should try to adapt my lesson as best as I can so that I keep each student involved.

A PECS is also helpful when students need to signify understanding or a lack of understanding, as well as when a student needs a break from instruction to rest or attend to personal care issues. Students can also indicate understanding of a concept. For example, if an early elementary class is working on the difference between beat and rhythm, a teacher can create a PECS with the two choices in picture form. The student can indicate whether the

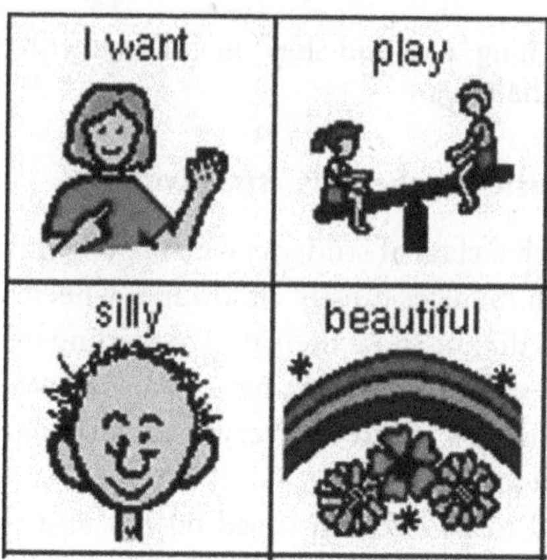

Figure 4.5. Picture Exchange Communication System (PECS).

beat or rhythm is being demonstrated during an activity. In addition to using Boardmaker, music educators often take pictures of choices and options available in their classrooms. These pictures can be laminated and presented as a PECS for students. Special education teachers and staff members are acquainted with these systems and may have many PECS options available for use in the music classroom.

It is also important to consider this information and the way it relates to a student's ability to receive, understand, and express music. There may or may not be a direct connection between the two. For example, a student with autism may be able to express themselves musically; however, they may have considerable communication challenges otherwise. Music educators must consider both instructional and musical language challenges that may arise in the classroom and how to modify the classroom in a way that will remove barriers for students. A student's language ability may help or enhance their musical ability, or vice versa. Working in tandem with the special education team may benefit the student in both language and music.

TEACHING MUSIC TO STUDENTS WITH BEHAVIORAL CHALLENGES

Student behavior can create unique obstacles for music educators. It is important to look at both positive and negative behavior. Specific adaptations, and modifications in the area of behavior and music will be discussed in Chapter 5. However, it is important (as it is with all areas discussed in this chapter) to determine whether the challenges associated with behavior warrant specific modifications to the way music is taught in a specific classroom.

The fundamental goal of these changes to daily lesson plans is to increase the occurrence of appropriate behavior, decrease the occurrence of negative behavior, and teach appropriate behavior that is absent from a student's repertoire (Lewis & Doorlag, 2006, p. 267). This will ensure the best possible opportunity for *all* students to learn in the music classroom.

One music educator in New York City used social stories to facilitate better management for two students with emotional and behavioral differences. Her story is in Vignette 4.4.

Vignette 4.4 Loud and Soft

Teaching "Loud and Soft" to Children with Emotional and Behavioral Challenges

When planning to teach a kindergarten music class for children with emotional and behavioral challenges, I reflected on the previous lesson when two of the children resisted transitioning into the music classroom and exhibited extreme behaviors when moving, performing, and experiencing loud compared to soft. As the class entered the music room the week before, Jacob had refused to come into the classroom and Jose ran into the music room screaming and showing aggressive behaviors toward his peers. When asked to find his carpet spot, Jose walked to the door of the classroom and sat next to Jacob in the hallway. After I was able to get both boys inside the music room, the students struggled to participate positively in the lesson activities, screaming or running anytime the class performed loud compared to soft.

After teaching this first lesson, it was necessary to observe and identify behavioral triggers and create supports to enable both Jose and Jacob to participate actively in the lesson. To help Jacob transition into the music room, I created a social story as a first step. Using pictures of Jacob walking in the hallway, waiting outside the door, walking into the music room, and sitting in his spot on the carpet, we created a story together that helped prepare him for the expectations of the next week. In addition, I pre-taught the lesson to Jacob so that he knew what activities, transitions, and expectations he would participate in after transitioning to music. Using the social story and pre-taught lesson plan, Jacob was able to practice before his class came back to music.

When reflecting on the lesson with Jose, I met with the occupational therapist and classroom teacher to assess whether the aggressive behavior related to sound was specific to music or seen in other settings. We noticed that loud sounds were a consistent trigger for his aggressive

(continued)

Vignette 4.4 Continued

behavior. To aid with his hypersensitivity to sound, the occupational therapist gave Jose noise-canceling headphones to wear during loud activities in the music room. I created a signal for Jose to communicate when an activity was coming that may be too loud. In addition, I asked the classroom teacher to transition him into the music room after the other kindergarten students were settled in the circle.

When the kindergarten class returned for the second week of the loud and soft unit, Jacob transitioned into the music room and checked in with the picture schedule on the board to remember the order of the activities. He took one break during the middle of the lesson after a challenging transition, but returned to the group once the activity started. Jose entered the room two minutes after the rest of his class and walked calmly to his carpet spot. The occupational therapist checked in with him throughout the music lesson and we practiced his special signal for when to put on the headphones. The second lesson of the loud and soft unit was more effective because of the behavioral supports put in place to aid in Jacob and Jose's learning.

(Taylor Walkup, VOICE Charter School, New York City)

TEACHING MUSIC TO STUDENTS WITH EMOTIONAL CHALLENGES

Students may also be diagnosed with severe emotional disturbance. When reflecting on an emotional disturbance, it is important for music educators to examine whether a student is internalizing or externalizing these emotions, and if adaptations can be made to assist with these issues. The music therapy field has made great strides in finding ways to use music to assist with emotional needs Sausser & Waller, 2005). Music educators can learn strategies by consulting or contracting a music therapist for issues regarding students with emotional disturbance.

In the music classroom, a student with behavioral and/or emotional challenges may have difficulty with structure, rules, and social cues. Music classes are active and student centered. Many students are initially not accustomed to this, and the perceived lack of structure can cause anxiety for a student with behavioral and/or emotional challenges. If the music classroom is structured so that each class begins and ends with the same song or activity, students may be able to self-calm, or redirect emotions, when they begin to feel angry, upset, or anxious. This also lets them know when a transition will occur.

Positive reinforcement is one of the most critical elements for success when working with students who are challenged by behavior and emotions. This includes musical reinforcers such as playing a drum or leading the group if those activities are, in fact, reinforcing for a particular student. The music educator who finds ways to positively reinforce good behavior, compliance, and academic success will be far more successful than a music educator who believes that all students should follow the same set number of rules to the same degree, every day of the school year (remember that fair is not equal). Social cues can be difficult for students with behavioral and emotional challenges. It is important for students to be seated near excellent role models who are able to serve as peer advocates and buddies. Consistent positive interactions and a stable, sequential environment will increase the academic and behavioral success rate for students with behavioral and emotional challenges. An example of a positive reinforcement plan appears in Box 4.2. These additive, rather than deficit, models are very effective with students who have challenges in this area.

Box 4.2 Positive Reinforcement Suggestions (choice time)

Sequence suggestion:

1. Find out what activity (e.g. leading the group) or material (e.g. a drum or a book) the student really enjoys and would like to do as part of music time.
2. Ask the student what he or she is willing to "work for" to earn that choice.
3. Spell out what needs to happen in music class that day in order for the student to be able to earn this choice time. Examples could but are not limited to either the behaviors that are causing learning interruptions or just the normal sequence of participation in the class.
4. Allow the student the structured choice time with the designated material or activity. It is very important that you provide the reward stated at the time promised. This will increase the possibility that the student will engage in this type of reinforcement activity again.

Please note: Positive reinforcement is about *earning* choices or privileges rather than taking these items away. Students either earn choice time or not. Therefore a checklist might need to be developed in order for the student to see exactly the choices he has made (either right or wrong). For example:

_____ Came into class and sat down without talking
_____ Participated without interruptions
_____ Treated others with respect and kept my hands to myself
_____ Did not interrupt the class or my teacher
_____ Choice time.

TEACHING MUSIC TO STUDENTS WITH SENSORY CHALLENGES

There are 5 + 2 senses (taste, touch, smell, hearing, seeing, and proprioceptive and vestibular. Students with sensory challenges may have a range of complications regarding language, communication, and behavior. The primary challenge in the area associated with sensory disorders is communication (Biel, 2017). The onset of the sensory challenge will often determine the type of system needed to facilitate communication with a student. For example, a student may be able to use speech reading (i.e., reading lips) and standard oral communication. A student may also use American Sign Language (ASL) in addition to or instead of speech reading and oral communication.

A person who has sensory differences may also have communication challenges. These communication challenges may be overcome by using aural forms of communication to reinforce visual experiences. There are two misconceptions about students who have visual impairments. First, many believe that because a person is visually impaired, his or her other senses are heightened. Research does not support this. The second misconception is that persons who have sensory challenges also have cognitive disabilities (Biel, 2017). Students with vision loss may struggle in the areas of mobility (i.e., getting from one place to another) and orientation (i.e., establishing one's position in relationship to others and the environment).

Students with vision challenges benefit from increased aural input during instruction and assessment. An increased (perhaps greatly increased) font size, enlarged music, bolder and darkened visual materials, and accompanying aural stimuli are excellent strategies. Some students may be interested in learning to read Braille music. A highly recommended source for information regarding reading Braille music and preparing music for use by students with challenges in the area of vision is Dancing Dots (http://www.dancingdots.com). While use of these adaptations requires music educators to learn to read Braille music, the benefits to students are lifelong, and programs like Dancing Dots create a gateway for this valuable information.

Students who have sensory challenges often need accommodations to be successful in the music classroom. Students who have challenges in the area of hearing may need very specific accommodations. A hearing difference can range from very slight to profound. It is important for music educators to be aware of the degree of hearing loss, the adaptive devices used by the student (auditory trainer, cochlear implant, etc.), and the signs or behaviors a student exhibits when he or she is becoming overwhelmed by sensory information. Again, this is why it is critical to consult special educators and to observe students with hearing loss in other settings.

Students with some hearing and students with cochlear implants often have difficulty with distortion of sound. Music can compound this, particularly in an ensemble setting. Music educators who speak with the audiologist associated with the student can often find the appropriate level of sound, the level to which a hearing aid may be adjusted during classroom music or an ensemble, and the degree of difficulty a student may have with other ambient sounds in the classroom.

Seating preferences are important for students with hearing challenges. If possible, these students should be seated near the music educator and in the center of the classroom so that visual cues, lip reading, and the use of visual materials (chalkboard, whiteboard, or Smart Board) can be optimized.

Instruments that readily carry vibrations (e.g., guitar or harp) can be good choices for students who have hearing challenges and wish to play instruments. Many students may also have excellent experiences with clarinet and saxophone because of the large frequency range and resonant capabilities. The most important consideration when choosing an instrument, however, is student interest. If a student has a sincere interest in an instrument, it is recommended that he or she be allowed to learn his or her instrument of choice.

The use of frequent visual cues during instruction and for academic and behavioral directions is valuable for students with these differences. It is helpful if the teacher and students learn some American Sign Language (or other method of signing used by the student) to assist with communication.

Students with sensory difficulties can also have challenges in the area of perceiving sensory information. These students are often overwhelmed by the amount of sensory information in the classroom and throughout their school day. Many are hypersensitive; however, some are hyposensitive to the same stimuli in the classroom. Caution in the use of colors, sounds, and textures in classroom materials, bulletin boards, and lesson planning can assist students who are challenged in this sensory area.

The senses of taste, touch, and smell are sometimes overlooked when speaking about sensory differences. Though we sometimes leap to hearing and sight, each sense is of equal importance and each sense can contribute to a classroom free from sensory disruptions. When a student experiences frustration and demonstrates a need for a change in sensory information, the first thing to consider is the overall classroom environment. Each classroom has its own unique smell. The amount of perfume or cologne we wear can be a disruptor to a student. The smell from the cafeteria, body odor from physical education class, dirty band uniforms, the teacher's lunch or coffee, or even rosin can create a sensory response from a student. By being aware of smell, we can begin to pinpoint possible areas of difficulty for our students.

Taste can be evident in a music setting as well. As we breathe, we gain information about the environment through our tongues. Some students can be greatly hypersensitive to the way the air tastes in a room. Plan to apply the same strategies to this area and communicate with colleagues to see if others are noticing similar responses from the student. Good teaching includes being an excellent detective.

There are two remaining senses to consider that were not part of our first-grade curriculum when we were in school. They are proprioception and vestibular senses. Proprioception is position sense. For appropriate proprioception, our cerebellum speaks to our arms and legs to let them know what position they should assume for any task. Proprioception is what helps us play our instruments well without thinking about each finger movement or watching our fingers to tell them what to do. If our proprioception is impaired, we may have difficulty walking, joining in games, and performing in an instrumental ensemble.

The vestibular sense works with our inner ear to let us know where our body is in space. It controls our balance and the way our eyes move. Students who have difficulty with the vestibular sense may often be dizzy and have trouble staying balanced. Students who struggle in this area are sometimes not sure whether they are upside down or right side up. This can affect their ability to play some singing games, learn show choir choreography, or remember how to move in a marching band show.

TEACHING MUSIC TO STUDENTS WITH PHYSICAL AND MEDICAL CONDITIONS

An important consideration when teaching a student with a physical or medical condition is that he or she may not have any other challenges. Teachers can often make mistakes in assuming when they meet a student with a physical disability that he or she also has a related cognitive challenge. It is very beneficial to conduct a complete assessment of a student's potential for success in music. Again, it is recommended that teachers observe students in other classes and that strategies be discussed with parents and other special educators. It is essential to focus on adaptations that will provide an opportunity for the student to make the most meaningful contribution, with dignity, in the music classroom.

Another caveat relevant to music educators that cannot be overstated is the importance of the awareness of the specific needs (physical and medical in particular) of students in the classroom. These students will also have specific needs that will require accommodation in the area of movement and accessibility to classroom instruments, stands, chairs, and risers. They may be absent from school for periods of time as health conditions necessitate, and it is the responsibility of the music educator to modify expectations and create appropriate accommodations. These accommodations may include a simplified part or partial participation in performances as the student may not be strong enough to perform an entire program or may have missed school and not been able to learn enough music well to be confident in playing all repertoire in a performance. When students with challenges in this area travel with musical ensembles, their needs and the possibility of intervention on the part of the music educator or other staff member who travels with the music ensemble could be critical. Creating accommodations that honor the student and his or her needs, as well as his or her musical strengths, is another example of "fair is not equal" and of considering the person rather than the disability.

INTERSECTIONS

Our identities make us who we are. None of us has just one identity, and we are all a combination of all of our life experiences and situations. Students with differences and disabilities have more than one identity as well. These identities include: gender identity, gender expression, race, ethnicity, class (past and present), religious beliefs, sexual identity, and sexual expression. In considering the needs of students with differences and disabilities, we must learn to acknowledge and consider their total identities and how the concomitant needs that accompany them present themselves in our classrooms and ensembles. None of us is monolithic and we all require an understanding of our full selves as we present ourselves to others.

PUTTING IT ALL TOGETHER

Successful teaching of students with differences and disabilities requires an extensive knowledge of the subject matter (in this case, music), a willingness to participate as a member of a team, a philosophy that places the students first, and a great deal of time and effort as we seek to provide each student with what they need in order to have the opportunity to succeed. It is an endeavor worth undertaking, and our students deserve nothing less. We encourage you to develop an inclusive philosophy as part of your overall philosophy of music education and to remember that music is for every child—not just for a few. Box 4.3 provides a compilation of many successful adaptations for use as examples in music classrooms and ensembles. It is organized according to the six domains discussed in this chapter. There are

Box 4.3 Examples of Accommodations, Modifications, and Adaptations for the Music Classroom

CG = Cognitive
CM = Communication
B/E = Behavioral/Emotional
P = Physical
S=Sensory

Accommodations and adaptations	**CG**	**CM**	**B/E**	**P**	**S**
Use an overhead projector or computer-enhanced image to enlarge materials (music, books, sheet music) as much as possible and provide written materials for all spoken instruction. A "picture" schedule is good for non-readers and students with autism.	X	X	X		X
Allow students a hands-on examination of all new materials, equipment and instruments during introduction of a concept. This kinesthetic approach combined with the visual and aural instructional elements will help students learn according to their modality.	X	X	X	X	X
Allow students to tape record rehearsals or lectures and tape record a test or assignment. Allow students to respond to tests or assignments on the tape, orally, or in writing.	X	X		X	X
Provide music or reading materials in advance to allow time for arrangements to be made for students with exceptionalities .	X	X	X		X
Use velcro strips to help students hold mallets or small instruments. Sticks can also be wrapped with tape or foam rubber to facilitate handling.			X	X	X
Jingle Bells, or cymbals can be sewn onto a band or ribbon and tied to the wrist. Straps and cords can be used to attach rhythm instruments to wheelchairs or walkers for students who may drop them during class.			X	X	X
Code music, or instruments with colors or symbols to help students remember notes, or rhythms. A highlighter or colored pens/chalk can be used to help a student focus on a specific part of the music or book.	X	X	X		X

A felt board, or other raised texture board can be used with heavy rope to demonstrate the concept of a staff to students who learn kinesthetically, or are visually impaired.	X	X		X	X
Provide a written rehearsal schedule for students to follow. These can be on the chalk or bulletin board or placed in folders.	X	X	X		X
Individualize some assignments for students who may not be able to complete the quantity of homework other students can. Check the IEP to make sure you are following the modifications listed.	X	X	X	X	
Make use of computers for students who need extra drill and practice.	X		X		X
Separate rhythmic and melodic assignments until students with exceptionalities can combine the two.	X			X	X
Limit the use of words not yet in the student's vocabulary and be consistent with the terminology you do use.	X				X
Allow students to help plan their own instructional accommodations and be a partner in the process.	X	X	X	X	X
When preparing music for use by students with exceptionalities, several adaptations can be made. The teacher can indicate tempo and meter, mark the student's part, allow students to highlight music, Write measure numbers and breath marks in the student's part, create visual aids for difficult words, and provide visual cues for score markings and phrase lengths.	X	X	X		X
When using written assessments with students with exceptionalities, provide accurate and complete study guides. Help focus study efforts on important events, ideas, and vocabulary. Use this tool to help students organize and sequence information.	X	X	X		

Box 4.3 Continued

Use short tests at frequent intervals to encourage students to work at an even pace rather than postponing the study of a large amount of material until just before a long exam. This also provides a student "some room" to perform poorly on a single test without significantly compromising the grade for the entire marking period.	X	X	X		
Allow students to use a word bank. They may remember concepts, but have difficulty recalling spelling.	X	X	X		
Vary the style of test items used. Using a variety of test items will prevent a student from being unduly penalized for having difficulty with a particular type of question.	X	X	X		
Place a rubber strip on the back of a ruler or use a magnetic ruler to help students measure or draw lines without slipping. Use adhesive-backed velcro to attach items to a desk or wheelchair laptray.	X			X	
Allow students to use pens (felt tip) or pencils (soft lead) that require less pressure or use a computer to complete assessments or assignments.		X	X	X	X
Wait to prompt students for verbal answers to questions after least 5 seconds have passed. They may need a longer period of time to process the question and determine an appropriate response. It may help to "call on" the student only when his/her hand is raised. This may lower any possible frustration level and prevent student embarrassment.	X	X	X		
If an accommodation or modification is listed in the IEP, it must be followed by all teachers.	X	X	X	X	X
Create a special seat or seating area so that a student knows and can expect where he will sit during class (chair, disc or carpet square, taped area, special mat).		X	X	X	X
Allow movement during class from one chair or special seating place to another.			X	X	X
Allow a student to participate for a small amount of time. Increase this time slowly as the student is acclimated to the classroom routine. This may begin with the start of class or the end of class depending on the student and her preferences.		X	X		X

many other adaptations and accommodations that may be used in the classroom. The strategies you find most successful will be the ones you develop and use when considering the needs of the individual students who are in your classrooms and ensembles.

DISCUSSION QUESTIONS

1. What are the seven senses, and how does each impact students in a music classroom or ensemble?
2. What are the similarities and differences between an IEP and a 504 Plan?
3. Please choose five accommodations and discuss how those may be beneficial for an entire music class or ensemble.
4. What are the differences between adaptations, and modifications?
5. How do winding intersections with race, class, sexuality, and gender affect students with differences and disabilities?

PART III

PRACTICAL CLASSROOM ADAPTATIONS, MODIFICATIONS, AND ASSESSMENT TECHNIQUES FOR TEACHING STUDENTS WITH DIFFERENCES AND DISABILITIES IN THE MUSIC CLASSROOM

Chapter 5

Developing a Student-Centered and Inclusive Music Classroom

CHAPTER OVERVIEW

- Classroom Management and Students with Differences and Disabilities: Four Important Considerations
  - Close Supervision and Monitoring
  - Classroom Rules
  - Opportunities to Respond
  - Contingent Praise
- Initial Preparation and Planning
- Continued Communication
- Physical Arrangement
- Parents and Classroom Behavior
- Anxiety
- Moderate Intervention Plans
- School-Wide Positive Behavior Supports System
- The Socialization of Students with Differences and Disabilities
  - Theoretical Framework for Socialization and Inclusion
  - Caring: A Feminine Approach to Ethics and Moral Education
  - Social Identity Processes in Organizational Contexts
  - Risks (Lessons Learned From Vygotsky)
- Practical Strategies for Music Educators
  - Be Aware of the Social Environment in Your School
  - Synergy
  - A Moral/Ethical Code
  - Be Proactive in Your Approach to Socialization
- Culturally Responsive Classroom Management
- Conclusion: Critical Issues for Students with Differences and Disabilities
- Discussion Questions

Teaching Music to Students with Differences and Disabilities. Third Edition. Alice M. Hammel, and Ryan M. Hourigan, Oxford University Press. © Oxford University Press 2025. DOI: 10.1093/9780197689356.003.0005

Classroom behavior is a common concern among many music educators. As seen in Vignette 5.1, this is particularly true for music educators who teach in inclusive settings. This chapter is designed to provide effective tools and strategies at the micro level (e.g., behavior and management techniques) and the macro level by informing the reader of philosophical underpinnings that encompass a successful inclusive classroom. The socialization and lasting relationships that all students develop in school are also of considerable importance. Therefore, it is imperative for music educators to strive for a caring, inclusive environment that is conducive for all students to learn. The practical strategies suggested at the end of this chapter are presented to encourage music educators to create a tolerant, caring classroom that is conducive for music teaching and learning. Many of the techniques discussed in this chapter are just examples of good teaching, regardless of what population of students you are teaching.

Vignette 5.1 Know Your Student

Carson is a second grader who transferred to Riverside Elementary School about halfway through the school year. His class meets for music at the end of the day for 40 minutes once a week. His daily routine is coming into the classroom and taking his shoes off because the material sometimes irritates him. His teacher encourages him to leave them on at all times, but we have an agreement that he leaves them near the door in case he needs to put them on quickly. We have also discussed that if he chooses to slide around the room in his socks, he will have to put his shoes back on.

When Carson first joined my class, he would plug his ears while in line to self-soothe when the other students were talking. He has become more acclimated to the noise of lining up and no longer plugs his ears as often. Upon coming into class, he will sit down and then almost immediately get back up and walk over to my Take a Break station to play with the glitter bottles, walk around the room to an area of his choice, or go toward the piano and other instruments to explore. This is different from when Carson will stand up and walk around my instrument carpet while the students are sitting at the dot carpet because he's still listening and comprehending. For example, "How many beats were in that song?" He can answer immediately with the correct answer of 16, while other students may guess 100 or count 13, 14, or 15.

Like his music teacher, Carson loves routine and knowing details. One day during second grade specials, our school had a guest artist in art so all of our second graders went to the art room. About halfway through, he was playing with a wooden dowel and a piece of paper given to him by our art teacher, and tracing shapes. When the art teacher went to take the things away at the end of class, he started growling and his anxiety escalated, so while our art teacher was with the other students, I took him into the hallway subtly. He was upset because he was going to have the materials taken away from him, so I eased his mind by letting him borrow another piece of paper and a pencil to take home, which was the same size as the wooden dowel. I showed him that the pencil and wooden dowel would make the same shape when traced. He agreed and then started drumming with his pencil and dowel and would not let me take them away. I told him that he could come up with an eight-beat rhythmic pattern and then hand the materials over to me ("1, 2, ready, go," he played, and then passed the materials back with no problem).

Carson and I work out simple agreements during class and outside of class. I give him incentives to work toward because he loves instruments and the piano. At the end of class, he gets a chance to play a short improvisation on the piano for his classmates, and during class, he gets to be a volunteer for each of our activities if he follows the directions of sitting in a circle with us and keeping his motions and sounds to a minimum. His class last year was very welcoming of him and understood that he learns differently and helped him in ways that they could, whether it be directing him to the circle carpet or in line at the end of class.

Carson loves knowing when his teachers care about his well-being and because of that, follows my agreements and understands when he does not follow what I expect of him. Visual (playing with the glitter bottles or stuffed animals at the end of class) and aural/physical (playing the instruments) incentives, as well as leadership roles (early to go in a game, helper with the board, etc.), are great for him.

(Morgan Robertson, Nelson County Public Schools, Virginia)

CLASSROOM MANAGEMENT AND STUDENTS WITH DIFFERENCES AND DISABILITIES: FOUR IMPORTANT CONSIDERATIONS

Effective classroom management begins long before the students enter the music room. A well-prepared environment is essential for optimal instruction and is particularly important when teaching music to students with differences and disabilities. This groundwork can be time-consuming and requires a thoughtful approach to the classroom setting; however, it is well worth the planning when the classroom becomes an inclusive and student-centered environment.

Conroy, Sutherland, Snyder, and Marsh (2008) explain that specific teacher interventions can lead to improved student behavior. These interventions include (a) close supervision and monitoring, (b) classroom rules, (c) opportunities to respond, and (d) contingent praise. As music educators, we can apply these principles to music classrooms. The next section of this chapter is designed to relate these interventions to music teaching and learning and to provide strategies for music teachers.

Close Supervision and Monitoring

Conroy et al. (2008) found that close supervision and monitoring can be implemented in the music classroom in the following ways: (a) student proximity to the teacher, (b) a music teacher's ability to visually monitor all students, (c) active engagement with students, (d) student access to the teacher, and (e) ratio of adults to students that is conducive to close supervision.

It is also important to point out that using the words "good behavior" and "bad behavior" can be problematic. If a student hears that they are exhibiting "bad" behavior often, the student can develop self-esteem issues. Even worse, the student can start to build an identity that is centered around "bad" behavior as a way of gaining the attention of the teacher. Just refer to behaviors as what they are: behaviors.

The proximity of the student (especially one who has the potential to disrupt class) to the music teacher is an important first step in managing behavior. In the beginning, it is often helpful to place students with differences and disabilities near an excellent student who can model appropriate behaviors. These interactions can then be monitored by the music educator. In addition, ensuring that students with differences and disabilities are actively engaged with other students may lessen the severity or frequency of outbursts and other inappropriate behaviors. It is important for students to have access to teachers and for students to know they can communicate with the adults at school in a manner that is comfortable and appropriate for them. If peer support is not effective, it may be beneficial to place the student near you (the music teacher). It is also helpful for the music educator to be aware of the student-to-teacher ratio in classrooms and ensembles and to advocate for additional adult assistance when necessary.

Classroom Rules

Classroom rules should be developed in collaboration with students, schoolwide standards of conduct, and the behavior goals of the Individualized Education Program (IEP). As part of this collaboration, students should express their willingness and ability to comply with rules and standards.

Creating a classroom culture that includes a regular and efficient manner of communicating and enforcing rules is important.

Class and ensemble rules can be developed with students each year. This provides a sense of ownership in the classroom, and students are often more willing to comply with a system they created. In environments of mutual respect, students are more likely to create rules that are simple and easy to understand. Music educators should regularly review the rules (or have student leaders review the rules) and communicate their willingness to apply consequences when necessary. This includes a consistent application of consequences when rules are not followed. When students are aware that the application of behavioral consequences is consistent and fair (remembering that fair does not mean equal), they know they are in a classroom where their behavioral efforts are honored.

In addition to using plans that coordinate with a school-wide initiative and plans put in place by general classroom teachers, it is important to have a clear set of expectations for students. Some teachers create class rules that are too vague, ask too much or too little of students, or compile a lengthy list of rules that are difficult to remember, comply with, and enforce. Begin with a few rules that are general enough to be adapted to many situations and are easy to remember. If a student is having great difficulty following the class rules, write or draw a picture of the rule on a note card and have the student put the card in their pocket to assist in remembering that rule. Some students will only be able to follow a few rules (or one rule) at the outset. In this case, hold the student accountable for the agreed-upon rule and be consistent in enforcement of that rule (Marzano, Marzano, & Pickering, 2003).

At times, a student can exhibit a behavior that is distracting or counter to the classroom culture and not be aware this is occurring. In these cases, create a special signal or gesture to let this student know that their behavior is not appropriate. Many students who are less affected by their disabilities respond well to this quiet and specific reminder regarding the rules (Cotton, 2000). This honors the student, respects the place this student holds within the classroom environment, and allows instruction to continue without time spent redirecting the student during class time. If the quiet attempts to redirect the student are not successful, the teacher may then choose to create a more specific behavior plan (Shellard & Protheroe, 2000). This method is often successful and can also improve the relationship between student and teacher as respectful and student-centered strategies are put in place.

Students who are developmentally able and less affected by their disabilities often appreciate the opportunity to participate in the creation of their own behavior plans, expectations, and consequences. This honors the personhood of each student and creates a partnership between teacher and student that can strengthen the nature of a student-centered classroom and the relationships necessary for student success (Bambara & Kern, 2021). Students often are keenly aware of their own limitations and of what strategies will assist them to be more successful during instruction.

Opportunities to Respond

Allow opportunities to respond during instruction that include time allotted for visual, kinesthetic, and oral responses. In addition, use an instructional model that allows students to respond individually, in small groups or in large groups. Give students many opportunities to demonstrate their knowledge (academic and social) and allow them to respond in the method that is most comfortable for them (visual, kinesthetic, or oral). Assess students frequently and in a variety of environments to ensure that their learning and response modes are honored.

Contingent Praise

Students need regular praise for appropriate social and academic behaviors. Unfortunately, we can often find ourselves correcting behavior more often than praising great behavior. There needs to be a balance. Specific praise offered within a system that includes the previous three interventions is a powerful and empowering experience. Students know they have worked well and to the best of their ability. They are also aware that you are aware of their efforts. "Catch them being good" is the old adage. It is not only applicable but also an achievable goal in our music classrooms.

INITIAL PREPARATION AND PLANNING

Once a music teacher is aware of the students who will be in a specific class or ensemble, they should develop a preliminary strategy for managing behavior. Many students with differences and disabilities already have behavior plans and management systems in place (see the IEP). It is very effective to follow the same strategies used by other teachers and staff members. Consistency is important in that it lessens the number of transitions required during the school day. Music educators will find it very helpful to talk with other team members and colleagues to define a set of expectations and possible consequences prior to the first day of school.

CONTINUED COMMUNICATION

Once the student has begun participating in the music classroom, continued communication with special education teachers and staff members is essential. Many students with moderate to severe differences and disabilities will attend music class with a paraprofessional or aide. These staff members are key stakeholders in the educational process because they often know the student with differences and disabilities very well (Southwest Center for Teaching Quality [SECTQ], 2003). Paraprofessionals are with the student all day and are aware of any changes in schedule or activities that may upset or over-excite the student. They can also be great partners in instruction. Music educators should treat paraprofessionals as team members in classrooms and provide them with information prior to class time to allow them to learn the lesson and prepare to participate in instruction. This allows paraprofessionals the opportunity to share any additional information that may assist in the teaching and learning process and shows them that their participation in the process is valued.

Students with more moderate to severe disabilities may be coming to music from a self-contained classroom. Music educators may be assigned to teach students in a self-contained classroom, or students who come to music as a class. In either situation, the lead special education teacher is a valuable resource as he or she has important insights into classroom management and behavior that may be useful in music classrooms (Sokal, Smith, & Mowat, 2003).

PHYSICAL ARRANGEMENT

Students with differences and disabilities often benefit from a consistent place to sit (Shores, Gunther, & Jack, 2017). Seating charts can be useful when planning for effective classroom management. Planning for appropriate seating may include proximity to a paraprofessional or student helper, as well as any instruments and music used during class. In elementary general music settings, place students near the teacher and also near any instruments or materials that may be used during class to lessen the number of transitions required. In ensemble settings, the use of a paraprofessional or student helper can ease transitions and anxiety that may arise during rehearsal. To promote effective socialization, do not physically or socially isolate a student from peers: place students near positive models (behavioral and academic). Not only can these students be a great help, but also they often may be of assistance with a student who has challenges.

It is also important to place students with differences and disabilities away from extraneous visual materials that can be distracting (e.g., bulletin boards that are not needed during the current lesson, posters, or other colorful art) or areas of the room that can decrease student attention either through visual, kinesthetic, or aural stimuli (e.g., ventilation systems, lighting that is audible, areas of high glare). Careful planning regarding seating can demonstrably increase on-task behaviors (Walls, Nardi, von Minden, & Hoffman, 2002).

PARENTS AND CLASSROOM BEHAVIOR

Parent support and communication are valuable when creating a classroom environment that is positive and student-centered. At the beginning of the school year, or when the student first becomes a part of class, communication (written or oral) with the parents/guardians is essential. Speak with parents/guardians to discuss their goals and the goals you have for their child. Discuss the musical and social goals for the student in specific terms. Allow parents to share the ways they feel their child's disability may manifest itself in the music classroom (Hamre & Pianta, 2005). Create a notification system and timetable and ensure parents are aware that you, as the music educator, are truly vested in their child's success. This initial contact is also very important if behavioral or academic issues arise during the year (Boyle-Baise, 2005). With a clear communication system in place, parents can be a part of the process, and classroom management issues can be ameliorated in a time-efficient manner (Langer, 2000).

ANXIETY

Some classroom management issues can stem from anxiety. Many students with differences and disabilities are anxious during class because they are unsure about teacher expectations and what will be asked of them that day (Zeichner, 2003). It can be very helpful to have a written or pictorial schedule of activities or a rehearsal order for students to use as a guide. This alleviates anxiety regarding performance expectations. It also gives students an idea regarding the amount of time they will be asked to sit still, move about the classroom, pay close attention, or work in groups. Perry, Marston, Hinder, Munden, and Roy (2001) explain that the teacher should honor the time, attention span, and behavior limits of students and allow them to attempt to monitor their own anxiety during class. Special educators and paraprofessionals can assist with information regarding ways this strategy is implemented in other classes.

The music classroom or ensemble setting can be very exciting as students work together to create music. This type of environment, however, can be overstimulating for some students with differences and disabilities. Be alert to the sensory limits of students (see the special education team) and provide a quiet place in the classroom for students who need a break. Use hall passes for students who need to leave the classroom at various intervals to decrease anxiety or sensory overload. This pass can be used for the student to go to another teacher or to a guidance counselor, who signs the pass, and the student can then come back to class without other classmates being aware of the reason for the brief absence. Strategies that honor the personhood of students with disabilities can benefit the entire school community (Southwest Center for Teaching Quality [SECTQ], 2003).

Intent is also an important consideration when determining consequences for inappropriate behavior. It may not be the intent of a student to be disruptive. He or she may be trying to communicate their anxiety, overstimulation, or overall uneasiness with the class (Ozonoff, Dawson, & McPartland, 2002). The student may have had an experience earlier in the day that is coming to fruition, or they may not be feeling well. Many students with disabilities have communication delays. This leads them to act out to express dissatisfaction with their surroundings. That does not mean they should not face consequences; however, as mentioned earlier, teachers have been known to label a child as a "bad kid" when in fact there is a simple communication barrier or misunderstanding within the classroom. Again, when disruptive behavior occurs, it is important for the music educator to follow up with other team members (e.g., special education teachers, paraprofessionals, parents/guardians, etc.). They may have seen similar behaviors and be aware of the triggers that cause such disruptions. They also may have strategies for curtailing such behavior.

Ultimately, the goal of effective classroom management is to allow students and teachers to work together in a community free from anxiety, negative personal interactions, and detrimental language and behaviors that are counter to an inclusive and positive environment. In addition to the strategies previously discussed, one of the most important elements in developing classroom management skills is to make sure the students are aware that they are all of equal value to the class or ensemble. Everyone seeks to be of value, and students with differences and disabilities may feel they are of lesser value than their peers. Frequent reminders using multiple strategies will help create an environment where acceptance is prized, and all participation is appreciated.

MODERATE INTERVENTION PLANS

There are times when even the most prepared music educator can face behaviors that are more difficult than expected. There are times when more information and intervention are necessary. If we begin each year by becoming familiar with the student's educational paperwork and behavior plans, and by engaging in discussions with other colleagues, it will be easier to approach other members of the educational team to request assistance when needed (Adamek & Darrow, 2018). The first step to take when a student is demonstrating difficult behaviors in a music classroom is to collect data. Data can include very short statements as to what was happening in the classroom before the behavior occurred, what the specific behavior included, and what you did as a result of this behavior. This type of data collection is sometimes referred to as a functional behavioral analysis and the three steps may be called "ABC," or antecedent, behavior, and consequence (Barnhill, 2005).

Taking data is important and can be powerful when presented to colleagues. Having specific information regarding your classroom environment, what is happening, and how it is affecting the class is very useful. When case study or grade-level teams are able to read specific information, it is much easier to begin planning interventions (Horner, Strain, & Carr, 2002).

If a plan is put in place, there should be a definite beginning and ending date, as well as a method for notifying all team members (parents included) of the successes and challenges encountered. A specific date for evaluation of an intervention plan will assist the music educator in that he or she is no longer alone in data collection and interpretation regarding behaviors. If the plan is not successful, the team now has more information and can take the next step together in defining expectations and consequences for the behavior of a student with differences and disabilities (Barnhill, 2005).

SCHOOL-WIDE POSITIVE BEHAVIOR SUPPORTS SYSTEM

Another set of goals used often in schools is the school-wide positive behavior supports (SWPBS) system (Horner, Sugai, & Anderson, 2010). This system, noted by Sugai, Simonsen, and Horner (2008), involves initial, secondary, and tertiary interventions that apply to all students in the school, is monitored by all teachers and staff members, and is positive in nature. Parental involvement is critical in this system, and all stakeholders are invited to participate in the creation of and support for positive behaviors in school (Barnhill, 2005). With school-wide participation, all adults in the building are equal stakeholders in the behavior and interactions of all students. This positive and collegial process can create an environment where all persons in the school culture are seen as valuable and equally responsible to each other (Marzano, 2003).

Music educators are integral to the success of SWPBS as the continuity of behavioral expectations expands to music classrooms and ensembles. By being aware of the specific behavior expectations for all students, as well as specific students who have challenges in the area of behavior, music educators will increase the possibility that SWPBS goals are met. This type of collegial participation also increases the perception by school and administration personnel that the music educator and music program are supportive of school-wide efforts that reach beyond the music classroom.

THE SOCIALIZATION OF STUDENTS WITH DIFFERENCES AND DISABILITIES

Music is by nature a social, interactive subject. Unfortunately, students with differences and disabilities are typically delayed in social development and may not be equipped to make connections with other students. Students who are not challenged with disabilities may have difficulty understanding how to engage or interact with students who are new or have challenges. The result can be serious for students with differences and disabilities. As they get older, they may fall further into isolation. Research suggests that students who are challenged with differences and disabilities are more likely to suffer from social isolation, depression, and mental illness (Goldson, 2001). Inappropriate behavior, if left unchecked, can lead to students with differences and disabilities being abused and to serious life-changing events. As music educators, it is our responsibility to promote a positive social environment for all of our students, regardless of the challenges they face.

THEORETICAL FRAMEWORK FOR SOCIALIZATION AND INCLUSION

In working with music teachers regarding how best to approach the social integration of students with and without differences and disabilities into music classrooms, three basic theoretical frameworks have emerged. These frameworks are: (a) *Caring: A Feminine Approach to Ethics and Moral Education* (Noddings, 1984); (b) *Social Identity Processes in Organizational Contexts* (Hogg & Terry, 2001); and (c) the zone of proximal development (ZPD; Vygotsky, 1934/1978). Each theory provides assistance in understanding how students in grades K-12 interact socially and how best to approach problem situations at all levels of instruction.

Caring: A Feminine Approach to Ethics and Moral Education

In our current educational environment, teachers are often challenged to teach social morals and ethical responsibility. Slogans, acronyms, and themes that encourage appropriate ethical behavior are often found on the walls of many schools. It can be difficult, however, to teach students to care about their peers. According to Noddings (1984), "As humans we want to care and be cared for" (p. 7). She explains that while students instinctively care about their peers, this instinct may not be motivation enough to act in a caring way toward others. As teachers we must integrate the value of caring into our approach to music education, especially for students who are challenged with disabilities. Having compassion for those who are disadvantaged is a life lesson that students can carry with them throughout their lives and can be taught as part of an overall philosophy in the music classroom.

In the music classroom, this may include a very low tolerance threshold for negative behavior (e.g., teasing or tormenting). In addition, an intervention that is planned by the music teacher and the rest of the team may be needed to establish an atmosphere of compassion within the classroom. Students may need to be instructed on such things as person-first language, how to engage and help a student, or how to express their concerns. This also may include organizing an intervention when negative behaviors persist. Box 5.1 is an example of how this might work in a music classroom.

Box 5.1 Steps to Organizing a Classroom Intervention for Positive Behavioral Support in an Inclusion Classroom

1. Identify behaviors that you would like to change and the student that you would like to support.
2. Speak with Special Education staff about appropriate terminology to use in describing the students challenges
3. Plan a day when the student in question can be diverted to another class or activity during this time (if needed).
4. Have special educators, parents, and your students sit together in an uninterrupted environment and make this the topic of the day.
5. Ask the students for help including what specifically they can do to assist you in teaching music.
6. Re-establish rules for conduct and what you expect.
7. Establish a clear conduit of communication for when adjustments need to be made.

Social Identity Processes in Organizational Contexts

Social identity theory is one theoretical underpinning by which researchers examine relationships and power within social groups. This theory specifically addresses how social structures can have a negative effect on individuals. The fundamental understanding of social identity theory is that a person's self-perceived value to a group can directly affect their overall self-worth and self-identity. Hogg and Terry (2001) explain that "a social category within which one falls, and to which one belongs, provides a definition of who one is" (p. 7). Music students can construct a social identity based on their experience within their music classroom in several ways. This identity can manifest itself within a social group, in a section within a performing ensemble, or in ways their self-perceived success relates to the overall goals or class expectations. Because a student's self-worth is a critical part of this identity, particular attention needs to be paid to those who are challenged, and how the student and the rest of the class perceive those challenges.

One coauthor recently worked with a student who was challenged by traumatic brain injury and played trumpet in a band. Because he struggled in band socially and academically, he had difficulty understanding that these challenges did not make him a bad musician or, more important, a bad person. It was just as much work for a teacher to convince him otherwise as it was to get him ready for a concert. At times he wanted to give up. His parents and the coauthor worked very hard to separate the academic, personal, and social challenges in his instruction and to encourage him to improve in all areas. This can be very challenging for music teachers. However, it is critical for a student with differences and disabilities to understand that their academic and social challenges do not make them "stupid" or "bad." It is obvious how these implications can snowball into larger mental health concerns.

Risks (Lessons Learned From Vygotsky)

Even as adults, forming relationships in a group setting requires risk. We must take chances not only to reach out and form a relationship, but also to foster and continue a relationship. This can be uncomfortable for all students, especially students with differences and disabilities. In our classrooms, a student may have tried to initiate and reinitiate contact and failed. Other students may have attempted to initiate conversation with a student who has a communication challenge and also failed. The combination of both behaviors can result in a "downgrade" of a student's place within a group (see social identity theory earlier). In addition, these events may discourage a student from attempting to connect in the future.

The zone of proximal development (ZPD) developed by L. S. Vygotsky is often used to explain the benefits of group learning within a social context. The basic premise is that students often learn more from capable peers than they would learn if left alone. Cooperative learning, peer tutoring, and modeling are all examples where the ZPD can be applied. The most important part of this theory regarding students with differences and disabilities is to understand their need for a "comfort zone." Students with disabilities often struggle with many aspects of everyday life that cause them to retreat into their comfort zone. Students can have a social, physical, sensory, or academic comfort zone. It is apparent that students with certain disabilities at an early age already demonstrate a lack of interest in engaging with their teacher or with their peers. It is important for teachers, therapists, and parents to keep students with disabilities interested in existing and learning with their peers.

Students who are not challenged by differences and disabilities also have a comfort zone. It is often easier for them to retreat into their established social network than to take the risk to reach out to a student who may appear to be different. The key is to encourage students (with or without disabilities) to take risks to make a connection with other students. As music educators, it is vital to encourage both groups to take the risk to interact.

Music teachers may ask: How do we encourage students to take risks in socializing with students? Ice breakers at the beginning of the year are great for this. For example, have students choose a number. Have them sit according to this prescribed number (to mix them up and not allow students to sit by their friends). Have your students interview the person sitting to their right. Questions could include items like: What is your favorite food? What kind of music is on your phone? Students will then realize that they have more in common than they think. There are also other ways of encouraging positive socialization, such as pre-assigning group projects (with students that you think would work well together), pre-assigned seating (as mentioned before), and mentoring (older students with younger students). Box 5.2 provides a list of print resources for music teachers to develop a deeper understanding of this phenomenon.

PRACTICAL STRATEGIES FOR MUSIC EDUCATORS

This section is designed to offer pragmatic suggestions for music educators in creating an inclusive social structure within their classrooms. These suggestions will be presented in a broad sense to be generalizable to as many situations within music education and music teacher education as possible. It is hoped that both preservice and in-service music educators, as well as music teacher educators, will develop a "toolbox" of techniques to promote a

Box 5.2 Resources for understanding student socialization

Baxter, M. (2007). Global music making a difference: themes of exploration, action, and justice. *Music Education Research, 9*(1), 267-279.

Colorose, B. (2004). *The Bully, the Bullied, and the Bystander: From Preschool to High School–How Parents and Teachers Can Help Break the Cycle of Violence.* New York: Harper Collins.

Emmer, E. T., Evertson, C. M., & Worsham, M. E. (2003). *Classroom management for secondary teachers.* Boston: Allyn and Bacon.

Hammel, A. M. (2004). Inclusion Strategies that Work. *Music Educators Journal, 90*(5), 33–37.

Hourigan, R. M. (2008). Teaching Music to Performers with Special Needs. *Teach ing Music, 15*(6), 26–29.

Hourigan, R. M. (2009). The Invisible Student: Understanding Social Identity Within Performing Ensembles. *Music Educators Journal, 95*(4), 34–38.

Kozulin, B., Gindis, V., Ageyev, V & Miller, S. (2003). *Vygotsky's Educational Theory in Cultural Context.* Cambridge, UK: Cambridge University Press.

Rawlings, J. R. (2017). The effect of middle school music ensemble participation on the relationship between perceived school connectedness, self-reported bullying behaviors, \and peer victimization. *Bulleting for the Coulcil of Research in Music Education, 213,* 53-72.

Rawlings, J. R. & Stoddard, S. A. (2017). Peer connectedness in the middle school band program. *Research studies in Music Education, 39*(3), 121-135.

positive social atmosphere in music classrooms. This is essential to provide a pedagogically sound, inclusive learning environment for all students.

Be Aware of the Social Environment in Your School

Music educators tend to be isolated within public schools. They are often the only teacher or one of the few music teachers within a school building. Many travel between buildings. This can be a disadvantage in understanding the social structure within a school. Create opportunities to get out of classrooms and offices and visit other parts of the school to get a sense of the social conditions that exist. The hallway, the lunchroom, the playground, sporting events, and other school-related social activities are all places to gather such information. In addition, just talking with students and parents/guardians at these events will provide a sense of which students are friends, which students seem isolated, and which students may be more likely to assist in establishing a positive social atmosphere in the music classroom.

It is important to know the social groups among students in a school. These groups may be created according to geographical boundaries (neighborhoods or portions of neighborhoods), socioeconomic status, academic standing, sports teams, extracurricular activities, and clubs. Unfortunately, sometimes race and gender can be factors in these groups as well. Having an awareness of the social strata within a school can be powerful information when creating groups within a music classroom or ensemble. An empowered music educator can use this information to create an inclusive and "clique-free" classroom environment.

Eckert (1989) explains that the atmosphere students create can be encouraged by the school environment, and sometimes by teachers themselves. She explains: "Adults do not impose their class system and ideologies on adolescents; they provide the means by which adolescents can do it themselves" (p. 6). Music educators can unintentionally encourage unhealthy social structures with their students. Music educators should self-evaluate and look at the big picture regarding how social groups in music classrooms function and how they relate to the overall school environment.

In your own self-evaluation, it may be helpful to examine how you may contribute to an unhealthy atmosphere. Questions may include:

- Do I (intentionally or not) play favorites?
- Do I gossip with students?
- Is my classroom an inviting place (from both the students' and the teacher's perspective)?
- Are there "cliques" in my classroom?
- Are they positive or negative in nature?

Other questions may come to mind. The goal is to be critical and objective in understanding the nature of the social atmosphere within the music classroom and ensemble setting.

Music educators play an important role in the lives of music students, and teacher attitudes and actions are powerful indicators of who we are. They also provide a great deal of insight into the behaviors our students may wish to emulate. If music educators model inclusiveness, acceptance, and kindness, students will demonstrate these qualities as well. Because teachers allow all students to participate equally in classrooms and posit a "fair is not always equal" philosophy, students are taught that everyone deserves to be treated fairly within a community (Stainback & Stainback, 1990). This may mean that some students get extra turns or get to choose more often. Some students may receive preferred seating in class. All of this may appear to other students to be preferential treatment. This may be a moment to teach students that these accommodations are a part of the overall teaching and learning process for everyone, and that some students need these accommodations in order to be successful. It is also helpful to state that if any student in the class or ensemble ever needs something new or more to learn, the music educator will ensure that student receives what he or she needs. It is important to assure students that true equity and fairness permeate the learning environment.

Synergy

Students often make choices in groups that they would not necessarily make on their own. These choices can be positive or negative. Students with differences and disabilities may not understand these social situations and are then unable to protect themselves from the malicious scrutiny of their peers (Dewey, 1991; Gustein, 2000). We have found that students with high-functioning skills who have differences and disabilities can fall victim to such situations without understanding the larger implications. Often students with differences and disabilities can unintentionally perpetuate the unwanted scrutiny (Marriage, Gordon, & Brand, 1995). Students who lack understanding about students with differences and disabilities may think they are having harmless fun without understanding the larger picture. Moreover, inappropriate behavior within a crowd can be a protective structure for a dominant leader within the group. If the group displays such inappropriate behavior, it is more difficult to "pin down" the individual to correct the situation.

Based on recent events in today's society, the implications can be critical. Bullying or hazing of individuals, if left unchecked, can lead to abuse and retribution. In these cases, students with disabilities need to be protected. It is important to be proactive in these situations (Ozonoff & Miller, 1995).

A Moral/Ethical Code

Hogg and Terry (2001) explain that the longer a teacher waits to provide information and model appropriate social behavior, the more vulnerable the group is to forming an unhealthy social hierarchy. In other words, "cliques" begin to form where students demonstrate power over those who don't belong within a self-identified group. This may seem a little extreme; however, the social dynamic within a music class may be indicative of a larger school problem. A student's music classroom can be a safe haven where everyone feels as though they belong.

When the synergy of a classroom or ensemble is structured to promote acceptance and inclusiveness, reflection among students can be quickly channeled to a positive course, even when students make errors in judgment. It is our consistent cultural mores and code of ethics that eventually envelop even the largest of music programs. If those mores and ethics are positive and inclusive, the resultant actions of our students will be positive and inclusive as well.

Establish a code of ethics and moral behavior within your classroom rules. This may be in a guidelines and procedures handout or a handbook. Send a copy home to parents to be signed. This sends a message that inappropriate behavior will not be tolerated. Most important, follow through with the guidelines established. This will make the message very clear that such behavior is not acceptable. Consistency is crucial in this area as students are not only learning from what we tell them, but also learning from what we do (Colvin, Ainge, & Nelson, 1997). Having a clear and consistent set of guidelines for behaviors and interactions is important for students with and without differences and disabilities. Even more important is to monitor and act on these guidelines. Students will honor these actions more readily than a vague listing of behavioral outcomes and procedures that are stated once at the beginning of a school year.

Be Proactive in Your Approach to Socialization

For a student with differences and disabilities, creating and maintaining relationships with other students can be a challenge. Students with disabilities may be coming to music from a self-contained classroom or even another school. The following suggestions are intended to encourage music educators to be proactive in their approach to create a positive social environment in the classroom.

As mentioned in Part I, in the days and weeks prior to the start of a new school year, it is critical that teachers take the time to read and comprehend the IEP and 504 Plans or Summaries for their students. As we know, this is a legal responsibility. However, more important, it is part of an inclusive philosophy to know the students in our classrooms. Taking the time to read the paperwork regarding a student with differences and disabilities is a helpful first step in integrating students (with and without differences and disabilities) in the music classroom. After reading the paperwork, it is also advisable to talk to the teachers closely involved in the educational planning for students with differences and disabilities.

If some students follow a specific behavior plan (see Part I), it is very helpful to make that plan a part of daily, or weekly, interactions with them. Consistency is imperative when defining parameters for classroom expectations and behaviors. These conversations are also important as they set the tone with other professionals regarding attitudes and levels of participation in the overall inclusive culture of schools. When colleagues are aware that music educators are prepared and willing to actively include all students in instruction, they will often be willing to assist with creating strategies to educate students with differences and disabilities (Hobbs & Westing, 1998).

In planning for the first few days, assist students in breaking down social barriers. Often, students simply do not know each other. Students can tend to separate from those who are different. In this instance, being proactive is the best approach. Take class time to allow students to reveal information about themselves to their peers. This may require assistance for a student with differences and disabilities. In some cases, it is advisable to involve a special educator or parent to explain the challenges a student faces. Try to move the focus away from a disability and to the common interests among students. For example, Andrew may have autism. With the appropriate permission and support, it may be acceptable to reveal the diagnosis and the challenges involved. Do this without dwelling on the diagnosis. Move to the fact that Andrew likes to play basketball or guitar. Students will attach themselves to those commonalities when they attempt to interact. Other techniques that are often used include icebreakers, wearing of name tags, and other techniques to initiate contact. Remember, information will promote acceptance.

In elementary music classroom settings, playing partner games and dances early in the school year will assist in introducing students to others they may not know. It also reminds students that we all have relative strengths and weaknesses. For example, Bruce may not be able to read notes on the staff quickly; however, he is one of the first to remember all the steps to a new folk dance. It is also important to choose partners carefully for students and to allow them to practice choosing partners themselves. A common approach is to have a student ask, "Will you please be my partner?" The other student then will say one of two things: (a) "Yes, I would be happy to be your partner," or (b) "I'm sorry–I already have a partner. Maybe next time?" This simple set of steps, taught early in the school year and reinforced throughout the year, may lead to increased positive interaction in the music classroom.

Seating for Socialization

As mentioned in Part I, strategic seating is essential for effective classroom management. Seating is also an easy, nonthreatening way to encourage students to interact. It is effective, even in performing ensembles, to vary seating arrangements. Another strategy is to create opportunities to encourage students to work together. Music educators can also be strategic in placing gregarious students with students who are reserved, or placing students who are farther along academically with those who need assistance. All of these seating approaches, if well considered, can make a meaningful difference in encouraging students to work together.

When planning classroom instruction, consider placement of students with differences and disabilities near students who are good academic and behavioral models. These students may serve as formal or informal "buddies" for students with differences and disabilities. A small caveat to this strategy is to not use the same students for each class meeting. "Buddy burnout" can be a negative factor among students who are consistently asked to partner with students with differences and disabilities. Also, consider only using a student helper for the portion of class when a student with differences and disabilities will need assistance. Another successful strategy is to ask a student with differences and disabilities to assist someone else. This has been a powerful reminder to all students that those with differences and disabilities have areas of strengths as well.

When placing students in semi-permanent seating, such as a secondary ensemble, consider the needs of the student and the ensemble, as well as the recommendations on the IEP or 504 Plan. Often, creative thinking can lead to finding a place for all students that fits their academic, emotional, and social needs. It is hoped that the suggestions mentioned will assist in providing a learning environment that is conducive to learning for all of your students.

Travel

Whether it is a field trip to an orchestra concert, a trip to a local festival, a day trip to perform at an amusement park, or a trip across the country, music groups often travel. Trips can often be times when students with social challenges have difficulty. Trips can also provide an environment for inappropriate behavior such as bullying or abuse. It is our job as responsible educators to curtail these behaviors and protect those who are vulnerable.

Allen (2004) explains that an unsupervised group in certain situations can attempt to exert group control over an individual. A familiar example of this type of situation is hazing. As mentioned earlier, the synergy of a group can outweigh the logical and caring judgment of the individual. Again, this may seem extreme. However, with the excitement of the trip, students can find themselves in a situation they will regret.

Be careful of such things as rooming lists and bus lists when traveling. Students with social challenges will struggle (if they attend at all) in these circumstances. Travel often requires students to take initiative to find people to room with or sit on the bus with during the trip. Signing up for a bus list or a rooming list often reminds them of the fact that they do not have friends within the ensemble with whom they feel comfortable.

Consider the following rules for such occasions: (a) assign bus and rooming lists yourself; (b) if you want students to sign up themselves, require students to have representatives from different groups (sections, classes, etc.); or (c) if you are on a longer trip, have a different rooming list every night. Some of these suggestions require more work and attention by the music teacher. These strategies can limit the possibilities of isolation and force students to ask other students to be a part of their travel plans. Again, model acceptance and zero tolerance of inappropriate behavior. This includes the willingness to accept anyone into a group. Students can learn valuable life lessons from situations where positive behaviors are modeled.

Free time at a festival, park, or museum is an optimum time for students with differences and disabilities to become isolated. Students who are socially challenged may attempt to stay with the adults instead of exploring with other students. It is easier to remain with adults instead of attempting to make a connection to a peer group. Remaining with adults on a trip defeats the purpose of experiencing such opportunities with peers. When this occurs, consider having a "buddy system" rule and require students to travel in groups. If someone is left out of a group, hold the "buddy" accountable. Students can learn the life lesson of caring about the well-being of *everyone* in a group by abiding by this system. Sometimes by adhering to these rules, students can connect with others whom they would not otherwise know. Again, establishing rules, such as the ones suggested, allows you to model acceptance and community building among your students.

Leadership

Leadership opportunities can be considered out of reach for students with differences and disabilities. It can often be challenging enough to be in class and participate. In secondary programs, leadership positions often go to students who are chosen, at least in part, by their peers. Students who are coming into music programs from self-contained classrooms or even from other schools may not, for whatever reason, be chosen. In elementary general music classrooms, music teachers can find themselves in a bad habit of choosing the most outgoing students for leading the class or passing out instruments.

Music may be a subject where a student with differences and disabilities can demonstrate and develop leadership skills. One coauthor recently met a young man named Sam who was diagnosed with autism and was elected president of his high school band. This was due in part to some assistance from his band director. His director nominated him. Sam probably would not have been nominated otherwise. Because of this nomination, Sam gained confidence, gave a good "pitch" to his peers, and won the position. In fact, his band director has expressed that Sam was the most organized and dedicated leader he has ever had. The students were so inspired by him that they had one of the most productive years in recent memory. In addition, his classmates nominated him for "student of the year" at a local television station.

The point of this example is that Sam needed some help in the initial nomination process. By nominating him, Sam's band director instilled a dose of confidence in Sam that allowed him to shine. In other words, Sam's band director forced his hand to integrate him into the social structure of the band by setting up a positive scenario for Sam to succeed. It is also important to point out that this required risk-taking by all parties involved.

We would caution that Sam was ready for this. Some students are not. The same sort of situation could have happened on a smaller scale. For example, Sam could have been elected to a position of less responsibility (e.g., section leader). It is up to the teacher to know the student well enough to understand what he or she can handle.

Collaborative Performance Opportunities

Performance opportunities can be an excellent way to encourage interaction among a group of students. Music can be the catalyst to encourage communication between students who would not ordinarily collaborate. Examples include collaborative performances between classes (e.g., self-contained classroom and general education classroom), group composition projects, and chamber music. The challenge is to not always group these performances by ability level. It is sometimes useful to group students together based on other outcomes. For example, you may place a student who is challenged in a chamber group with a student who is exceptional to achieve an instructional goal. Another example is to have a combined performance with a self-contained classroom (with students assisting each other) so that the outcome is more about teaching or building personal relationships. A student from another culture may have unique insights to share as an ensemble prepares a piece of music or a lesson from their culture. These students, who have often recently immigrated, sometimes have limited means to express themselves to their classmates. As music *educators*, it is important to step out of usual routines and take a look at the larger picture of what a performance could mean.

CULTURALLY RESPONSIVE CLASSROOM MANAGEMENT

It is again important to point out that students of color, poverty, and disability share many of the same challenges in our schools (Hammel & Hourigan, 2022). Therefore, it is also important that we consider how responsive we are, as educators, to these challenges. Weinstein, Tomlinson-Clarke, and Curran (2004) state: "We need to ask whether diversity requires different approaches to classroom management" (p. 27). Weinstein et al. go on to provide key components of cultural responsiveness in the classroom.

First, we must recognize our own ethnicity and biases. We could unwillingly make assumptions about a student's culture or even disability that could be unfounded. It is important to recognize these biases and do our best to keep an open mind regarding all of our students, regardless of how they present themselves. Weinstein et al. state: "Multicultural competence is directly related to an understanding of one's own motives, beliefs, biases, values, and assumptions about human behavior" (p. 29).

Second, we must become as knowledgeable as possible of students' cultural backgrounds. Weinstein and colleagues throw a caveat here. It is important that when learning about a particular group that it should not be assumed that a characteristic be generalized to all of the people in that group. For example, you may learn that in a particular culture a student in question is used to being corrected or disciplined by the female head of the household. That may not be true for a different student of the same group. They may be raised by their father.

Next, it is important to also understand that the American educational system as an institution already poses biases and political structures that we are forced to navigate. Weinstein and colleagues examine at length the plight of the African American male in our public school system. They (Weinstein et al.) portray a story about an African American male who was given a 10-day suspension for wearing the straps of his overalls un-snapped, which was a fashion trend at the time. Conversely, the same year a white student was not even reprimanded for wearing jeans with holes in them, which was a violation of the dress code. There are many other challenges that put certain groups institutionally at a disadvantage (Hammel & Hourigan, 2022). As educators, we need to acknowledge these challenges and do our best to not accept the norms and to attempt to effect change. Finally, it is important to be willing to change and adapt our strategies to be more inclusive, with the goal of creating a caring classroom community for all students involved.

CONCLUSION: CRITICAL ISSUES FOR STUDENTS WITH DIFFERENCES AND DISABILITIES

There is more at stake in assisting students with differences and disabilities than just creating an atmosphere of acceptance. Thompson and Cohen (2005) state: "Victims of chronic harassment are at serious risk for poor mental and physical health, as well as academic achievement" (p. 16). In the current school environment, it is important for teachers to set forth expectations in music classrooms that abusive behavior will not be tolerated.

Report any suspected behavior and immediately inquire about any potential abuse. Do not hesitate to bring in outside help from school counselors, social workers, and parents (i.e., a team approach). As mentioned earlier, the music educator is the model of appropriate behavior. If the model is zero tolerance, the students will follow this lead. The positive steps taken, however small, can have a lasting effect on a student's well-being.

It should be every music educator's goal to establish an inclusive, compassionate, safe, and productive teaching and learning environment. This includes strategies that allow all students to learn, including those with differences and disabilities. Understanding how the accommodations in this chapter may assist a student with differences and disabilities is a great beginning. It is also imperative for a music educator to know when and how to advocate for support when negative behavior is hindering the ability of students to learn (i.e., intervention plans). Finally, music educators must consider how students develop their personal identity through socialization.

Music can be the catalyst for students to develop healthy self-concepts and establish positive relationships throughout their time in public school. These concepts and relationships continue with students (with and without differences and disabilities) as they leave public school settings and continue their lives as adults.

DISCUSSION QUESTIONS

1. How will you, or do you, model compassion in the music classroom? What specific steps are necessary to achieve this goal?
2. What are some practical ways to develop positive relationships with students? What are some practical ways to develop positive relationships with colleagues?
3. How can you promote behavior inclusiveness among all students in your music classroom?
4. What are some creative ways to promote leadership within the music classroom or ensemble?
5. In what ways have you attempted to be culturally responsive in your classroom?

Chapter 6

Curriculum and Assessment for Students with Differences and Disabilities

CHAPTER OVERVIEW

- Fundamentals of Curriculum Design and Students with Differences and Disabilities (A Quick Review)
- Constructivism as a Curricular Model to Assist with Inclusion
- Four Primary Teaching Practices to Consider When Teaching Students with Disabilities in a Modified or Adapted Curriculum
  - Modality
  - Pacing
  - Size
  - Color
- Curricular Modifications in Music Education for Students with Disabilities
- Winding in Music Classrooms and Ensembles
- Parallel Curricula
- Incorporating Important Elements of Music Therapy Into the Music Education Curriculum (Contributed by Amy M. Hourigan, MT-BC)
  - Creating
  - Performing
  - Responding
  - Connecting
- Assessment and Students with Differences and Disabilities
- Measurement, Assessment, and Evaluation for Students with Disabilities
- Formative Assessments for Students with Differences and Disabilities
- Establishing a Baseline of Understanding
  - Elementary
  - Beginning Band

Teaching Music to Students with Differences and Disabilities. Third Edition. Alice M. Hammel and Ryan M. Hourigan, Oxford University Press. © Oxford University Press 2025. DOI: 10.1093/9780197689356.003.0006

- Beginning Choir
- Beginning Orchestra
- Secondary Instrumental
- Secondary Choral Music
- Writing Clear, Attainable Objectives for Students with Differences and Disabilities
  - Seventh-Grade Choir
- Assessing Nonmusical Goals
  - High School Orchestra
- Alternative Assessments for Students with Differences and Disabilities
- Summative Assessments and Students with Differences and Disabilities
- Conclusion
- Discussion Questions

Every successful music educator has a curriculum that contains a scope (overarching goals) and sequence (how we will achieve our goals and in what order) that are critical to reaching meaningful educational goals within the music classroom. Walker and Soltis (2004) state: "Working with the curriculum is an integral part of all teachers' daily lives" (p. 1). When specific curricula are not mandated (by the state or federal government), most music educators use a set of standards or guidelines to devise a scope and sequence for classroom teaching (i.e., the NAfME National Standards).

It is important to consider curricula when preparing to teach all students, not just students with learning challenges. This is one thing that separates an educator from a therapist or a service provider. The questions we will address in this chapter include: How do music educators maintain a focus on their own curricular goals while adapting that same curriculum to the individual needs of students? And how do we assess and reflect on these goals to make adjustments in our curricula?

These are difficult questions to answer. In fact, this has been a challenge for teachers since the inclusion of students with differences and disabilities began following the passage of P.L. 94-142 50 years ago. Walker and Soltis (2004) explain, "While many teachers supported the goal, many were offended that rigid regulations were imposed on them without their consent" (p. 84).

These issues require a thoughtful and sequential approach when preparing, presenting, and assessing instruction in the music classroom. However, the stronger the underlying curricular focus, the easier it will be to adapt and modify existing curricula to individualize instruction for students who have learning differences.

Specific curricula, if not mandated by a state or school system, will be a result of your philosophy of music education. Even when utilizing prescribed curricula, your choices in scope and sequence will reflect your values in the classroom. These same values will be reflected in the choices made in modifying curricula for students with differences and disabilities.

FUNDAMENTALS OF CURRICULUM DESIGN AND STUDENTS WITH DIFFERENCES AND DISABILITIES (A QUICK REVIEW)

The first priority in addressing the curricular needs of a student with differences and disabilities is to, once again, examine the Individualized Education Program (IEP) or 504 Plan. These documents will include all mandated curricular goals and assessments for determining curricular outcomes. Many inferences can be made through examining the choices of other teachers as they adapt their curriculum for a specific student or group of students. Speaking with other teachers who work with the same students with differences and disabilities is also a valuable strategy. Next, re-evaluate the fundamental model of your curriculum design at the school level and in your classroom. Consider the needs of your students and the goals stated in their special education documents, as you adapt curricula and expectations for a student with differences and disabilities. Your modifications can include musical, extramusical, and social elements that can be observed and assessed in your classroom.

To situate our discussion, we offer a quick review of basic curriculum strategy. There are many ways to design curricula. The four different types described offer suggestions for adaptations and modifications within the music classroom. This discussion is designed to allow teachers to make connections with the curricular focus of a specific classroom.

A materials-centered curriculum is centered on the selection of a basic set of materials (e.g., a general music textbook series or a method book series) and the design of lesson plans around this material (Labuta & Smith, 1997). Many general music classrooms and performance-based music education classrooms use the materials approach. These curricula often include a guide to a scope and sequence that teachers may follow throughout the year.

A content-centered music curriculum stems from music literature. Many performance-based classrooms use a content-centered approach. Teachers who use this approach choose a piece of music, a style of music, or a composer and build their curriculum accordingly. This type of curriculum usually requires a music educator to consider the skills necessary as prerequisites to learning or performing the material chosen. It is important to note that content considerations include representation (diversity, equity, inclusion, gender, LGBTQIA) to widen the experiences our students have and the number of times, and ways, they are represented in the music they perform.

An approach philosophy in music education stems from an established method or ideology (e.g., Orff, Kodály, Music Learning Theory, Dalcroze). Each approach leads music educators to create a scope and sequence for students. There are ways to adapt or modify methods for teaching music to students with disabilities within each approach while maintaining the basic tenets of the curriculum. These approaches are also enriched when we consider an equity lens in the repertoire used with students.

An experience-based curriculum, or constructivism, is another approach to music teaching and learning. This approach is centered on the learning experiences of our students. The teacher acts as a facilitator, concentrating on knowledge acquisition, in an active and engaged environment.

CONSTRUCTIVISM AS A CURRICULAR MODEL TO ASSIST WITH INCLUSION

While practical and fundamental modifications to curricula are important (e.g., the four primary teaching practices, discussed later), the musical meaning and aesthetic experiences of a musical education are also essential. There has been much written and discussed in music education regarding a constructivist approach to teaching and learning (Shively, 2015). A constructivist approach to curriculum can be defined as a learning theory that emphasizes learning as a social process in which students construct meaning through their own experiences (Dewey, 1929).

The constructivist philosophy of teaching is not always considered when working with students with differences and disabilities. Often this approach is reserved for students who are at grade level or above. It is important for music teachers to consider the musical experiences from a student perspective when working with a modified constructivist curriculum. Moreover, a fundamental value of constructivism is that "learning is a social act where students interpret new understandings of their worlds in relation to previous knowledge and experience" (Scott, 2006, p. 19).

Music enhances the quality of life of all people. Many adults with differences and disabilities find social and spiritual identity and purposeful experiences in the arts that they cannot find through other experiences. Therefore, enhancing their understanding will widen their ability to consume and participate in musical activities as adults. Due to delays in social development, many people with differences and disabilities require practice in interpreting their own understandings of music and its relationship to the world. Music can be the vehicle that will assist them as they make lasting relationships with peers, social groups, and the community.

Teacher-directed learning (the opposite of constructivism) approaches a musical topic or concept from one learning perspective at a time (e.g., aural or visual). Conversely, music educators who explore constructivism may uncover techniques that enhance the ability of students with differences and disabilities to engage with musical material and concepts within a curriculum. This multimodal effort vastly increases the possibility that students will access and achieve the standard, or modified, curriculum in your classroom or ensemble.

Constructivism allows teachers to create experiences for students as they enter a learning community from various levels of previous knowledge. Within the concept of constructivism, music teachers are seen as facilitators, collaborators, and co-learners in the music classroom. The experience is crucial to a successful lesson that allows students to discover knowledge through social experiences while they share inquiry into a topic with their peers. This is an effective approach for students with differences and disabilities. Table 6.1 offers two examples of the same lesson. One is conceived via a traditional approach and the other within a constructivist approach.

FOUR PRIMARY TEACHING PRACTICES TO CONSIDER WHEN TEACHING STUDENTS WITH DISABILITIES IN A MODIFIED OR ADAPTED CURRICULUM

Any of the aforementioned approaches to curricula can be adapted for students with differences and disabilities. However, there are certain overarching teaching techniques to consider when adapting curricula. These four techniques are modality, pacing, size, and color. By considering these techniques in the way we adapt or modify our curriculum and instruction with students with differences and disabilities (with obvious consultation with the special education documents and personnel), we give students more opportunities to learn in our classrooms. We realize that each of the four is also considered a teaching and accommodation technique; however, in teaching students with differences and disabilities, *these practices* should be considered when adapting or modifying curriculum.

Modality

When teaching any students, particularly students with differences and disabilities, it is critical to introduce each concept and skill through all

Table 6.1 An Example of Constructivist-based lesson for Students with Differences and Disabilities 6th Grade Composition

Teacher-directed or traditional approach	Constructivist or student-centered approach with modifications for a student with differences and disabilities
Objectives: 1-Students will demonstrate their understanding of notation by composing a piece of music within the guidelines provided.	Objectives: 1- Groups of students will demonstrate their understanding of notation by composing a piece of music within the guidelines provided
Procedures: 1-Students will work individually (with teacher assistance) in class. 2- Students will be required to finish their work at home.	Procedures: 1-Groups of 3 will be established and asked to contribute equally to the composition. **Modification:** Tim (student with differences and disabilities) will contribute based on his skill set. Students in his group will be informed of a potential role for Tim in the group. 2- Student groups will perform their composition and field comments from the class in order for them to reflect, revise, and re-submit their composition. 3- The instructor will also ask reflective and guiding questions (including questions directed at Tim's portion of the assignment) in order to probe deeper into the potential of the assignment.
Assessments: Instructor will grade each assignment with an established rubric	Assessments: 1- Students will perform their compositions for the class. 2- Peer feedback forms 3- Student-constructed rubrics will be used. 4- Modified rubric for Tim will be used based on his skills and progress

modalities (aural, visual, kinesthetic; Box 6.1). Everyone learns differently, and students with differences and disabilities sometimes have great preferences, or limited options, for the modality they use to process information. In preparing to adapt a curriculum for students with differences

Box 6.1 Modality Examples for Music Teachers

- Use raised textured board (perhaps a rope on a board to show a five line staff) for students to touch as they are introduced to the concept of lines and spaces. This adds a kinesthetic element to a primarily visual concept.
- Use movement activities to accompany some listening experiences. Many students learn best when their bodies are in motion and concepts such as tempo, style, dynamics, and genre can be practiced through movement. Using this to accompany the aural experience of listening can be very effective. These activities are enjoyed by students of all ages and do not need to be considered elementary in nature.
- Have students track measures in their parts or a score (possibly via a projected image) while listening to a recording. We often do this with beginning performance groups and with elementary students; however, this is still a useful activity with more experienced students as well. Score study is a complex, yet extremely useful skill, and a multi-modal approach can be an enriching experience for all students.
- Create three-dimensional figures to represent abstract concepts (notes, rhythms, solfege, dynamic and artistic markings). Some students must touch a three-dimensional object to grasp the meaning of some higher-level concepts.
- A picture or written schedule to accompany the aural directions and procedures in class can ease student frustration.

Students may excel when given the choice of modality for response to a quiz or performance test. They may also perform best when given the choice to respond in two or more ways to a question or task.

and disabilities, an effective strategy is to brainstorm the number of ways a concept can be taught. This list is universal, meaning it can be used for all students in a classroom, and all students will benefit from being introduced to material through multiple modalities. This strategy closely models Universal Design for Learning in that the lesson is created to be inclusive from the very beginning. Adaptations then do not seem to be added onto the lesson. The lesson is designed so that all learners can participate without barriers to access.

Whether a material-, content-, experience-, or method-centered approach is utilized, lesson planning can be enhanced using multimodal approaches.

It may be helpful to list the modality choices aural (A), visual (V), and kinesthetic (K) on scope and sequence charts and lesson plans to guide the use of multiple modalities in teaching.

Pacing

Our lives as music educators move very quickly. We often speak, walk, and teach at a rapid pace because we have a great deal of material to teach, have numerous performance deadlines, and want to give students the very best (both in quality and quantity) we have to offer. For some of our students, our pacing will still be considered too slow! Many of our students will be able to follow the pacing of our scope and sequence well. Conversely, some students will not be able to learn the amount of music studied in a class or ensemble and may become frustrated by the pace of instruction, amount of materials, performance expectations, and sheer sensory overload (visual, aural, and kinesthetic). Pacing in this context means the amount of material a student is responsible for at any one time. We can achieve this through part adaptations, and changing the expectations in the moment. This works very well for students who will be able to meet our objectives by the end of the unit or by the concert; however, they need information spaced differently when acquiring the skills and understandings necessary for success.

For students who need adjustments to the pace of materials, instruction, and overall curriculum, consider adaptations to pacing (Box 6.2). These adaptations require careful consideration, as it is important that the needs of all students in classes and ensembles are honored and that the alternative pacing procedures put in place are effective and appropriate for everyone.

Box 6.2 Pacing Examples for Music Teachers

- Part revisions may be necessary. Some students will be unable to read a part as written by the composer. It may be necessary to simplify a part (use bass line, chord outlines, first note of each measure, etc.) to meet the musical needs of a student. As the student improves, these modified parts may be adapted.
- A student may need to begin with a 'blank score' that is filled in slowly as his abilities increase. For some students, the amount of ancillary information on a page (title, composer, tempo and dynamic markings, pictures) can be distracting and frustrating. Placing only the amount of information a student actually needs to perform successfully may be very effective.

- Some students may need to learn less material than others. For example, learning the A section of a piece, memorizing the chorus rather than the verses, practicing the rhythm only rather than the rhythm combined with the melody, or mastering one movement instead of four may be the most beneficial way to begin with a student.
- For students who have sensory issues, partial participation in class or a performance may be necessary. If the pace of a class becomes too fast or the amount of sounds, sights, and textures overloads a sensory system, a student may need to participate in music for a shorter amount of time, or learn less material for the concert and only perform the portions of music learned.
- Student assistants (buddies) can be valuable in the pacing process as they can repeat directions, refocus attention, and answer questions a student may have if the pace of class/rehearsal is too fast. We suggest having several buddies take turns working with a student to avoid 'buddy burnout' among our assistants.
- Wait time is another important element of pacing. Some students take up to 10 times the amount of time we need to process a question or a piece of information. When asking a question of a student, wait at least 5 seconds before re-prompting or redirecting. If a student has difficulty with aural questions, try a modality and pacing accommodation and write the question on a piece of paper or draw a picture of the question or information. This combined with a longer wait time honors the student, and the process of teaching and learning.

Size

The size of materials can compromise processing time and effectiveness. When students with differences and disabilities are working very hard to process information, the relatively small size, faint font, and large amount of material on one page can be frustrating. When material is made larger and bolder, and when information not essential at the moment is removed, students often find they are more able to understand and respond to instruction (Box 6.3). Size can also be adapted by making musical materials smaller. This can be very helpful when reading multiple lines of a score as some students need the information to be spaced closer together. Size can also refer to any materials you utilize in classrooms or ensembles.

Box 6.3 Size Adaptations for Students with Learning Differences

Remove all extraneous material from a page and create a large space for the staff and musical notation.

- Use a large and bold font. You may also wish to use a card or piece of paper to cover the words or notes not needed at that moment. The card or paper may move along the page to assist the student as she reads the notation or words.
- Project material onto an overhead or lcd projector and allow students to stand near the projected image or touch the information as you are teaching.
- Use a font that is simple and has no decorative elements.

Color

It can be very difficult for some students to read music or books with a font that is black and white. These two colors are very stark, and the contrast can create issues within the eyes that cause the processing of information to slow. Color softens this difference and can drastically improve the ability of a student with differences and disabilities to read music. Color is also an excellent adaptation to draw student attention to details and items of importance. Finally, the use of color in photographs, diagrams, and pictures can improve student understanding of concepts presented during instruction (Box 6.4).

CURRICULAR MODIFICATIONS IN MUSIC EDUCATION FOR STUDENTS WITH DISABILITIES

Modifications are utilized when students will not be able to meet the stated goals and objectives for students who are neurotypical. Some students respond well to adaptations (size, color, pacing, modality) and are eventually able to meet the objectives set for the class or ensemble. Other students will need modifications. Modifications are adjusted goals, objectives, content presentations, and assessments to meet the needs of students who are not ready to achieve at the level of other students in the class.

WINDING IN MUSIC CLASSES AND ENSEMBLES

Modification is a very common term when working with students who have differences and disabilities. These are created for students who are not ready to meet the goals and objectives we set for approximately 80% of our

Box 6.4 Color Adaptations for Students with Exceptionalities

- Colored transparencies placed over music or written pages may assist students in reading. Another option is to cut strips of colored transparencies for students to use as they track their reading.
- Music and text can be highlighted for ease in score and staff reading. For students who are learning to play band and orchestra instruments, specific notes may be highlighted for practice. For example, a beginning flutist who is learning to play D, Eb and F may only be able to finger D at first. Highlighting all the Ds in a line can help her track and play the note she is practicing. Some highlighters have erasers at the opposite end. These can be used to erase notes and highlight new notes if needed, or to erase highlighted lines for use by other students who do not need highlighted materials.

For students who have difficulty remembering the note name, fingering, and playing procedure in the amount of time allowed in an ensemble setting, notes may be color coded at first to remove some of the steps required for this type of reading. For example, a beginning recorder student may be learning B, A, and G. B may be highlighted in blue, A may be highlighted in red, and G may be highlighted in green. As a student learns to read the notes, the colorcoding may become less frequent and then be phased out altogether. A teacher may further this modification by adding paper hole reinforcers around the holes. The reinforcers can then be color coded to match the highlighted notes in case a student needs to remember the color that matches the fingering.

students. While very helpful, modifications are also limiting as they only apply to students who are not ready. They do not apply to students who have already mastered our goals and objectives and need more. Winding forward and backward is much more flexible and can serve all our students, rather than only students who are not meeting our stated goals.

When winding for students, we must hyper-sequence the steps in the process. For example, if our class is working on syncopated patterns involving eighth and quarter notes in 4/4, some students may still be mastering paired eighth notes while other students are ready to learn syncopated patterns involving sixteenth and eighth notes. Through winding our content, we can create classroom activities where all students are experiencing all the patterns; however, students are assessed at their current level of achievement. In this example, we would need three separate objectives to note each level of achievement and three levels of assessment to evaluate our students where they are in our overall scope and sequence.

PARALLEL CURRICULA

Often special educators consider different curricular models when defining the least restrictive learning environment (LRE) for students with differences and disabilities. More often this includes constructing a parallel curriculum to the existing general education curriculum. A parallel curriculum follows the path of the existing grade level or subject matter of a student's regular education counterpart with modifications (winding) as needed. In a sense, the IEP is also a curricular document in itself. However, it does not include the specificity of units and assessments, or a scope and sequence, necessary for a strong curriculum.

A parallel curriculum can be designed using two potential threads. First, a modified curriculum follows the subject and approach (see earlier) but does not have the same expectations (i.e., level of difficulty). This is where the use of modifications (winding) is essential as we seek to provide the same type of objective (e.g., rhythm), rather than having some students work on rhythm while others work on harmony. An adapted curriculum (size, color, pacing, modality) allows for the same expectations; however, issues such as time, size of assignments, and physical adaptations are made to accommodate the student or students. Modifications and adaptations to curricula work together throughout the preparation, presentation, and assessment cycles in a classroom. Box 6.5 and Table 6.2 are included to compare what different modified curricular expectations look like in an instrumental (Box 6.5) and a general music class (Table 6.2). It is hoped these will spark ideas for the music classroom.

Evaluating your curriculum and determining best practice (through modifications and/or adaptations) for students with differences and disabilities is really just good teaching. This process follows the same principles used with all students. The difference is that students with differences and disabilities require an intensification of good teaching practices (modality, pacing, size, and color).

INCORPORATING IMPORTANT ELEMENTS OF MUSIC THERAPY INTO THE MUSIC EDUCATION CURRICULUM (CONTRIBUTED BY AMY M. HOURIGAN, MT-BC)

Children have similar needs that are necessary to address for success in their everyday lives; they are communication, social, and cognitive needs. These areas are continually developing in our students and can be addressed in the music classroom.

Box 6.5 A Modified Parallel Curriculum for 8th Grade Band

A Hymnsong on Phillip Bliss, David Holsinger (Content-centered): 8 Weeks

Non-modified or adapted curricular goals	**Adapted Curricular Goals (for included individuals in the same band)**	**Modified Curricular Goals (for an included individual in the same band)**
• Students will be able to sing the Hymnsong in the key of E-flat (National Standard 1)	• Student will be able to buzz (on their mouthpiece) the Hymnsong in the key of E-flat (Modification for a student with normal cognitive function and vocal or speech disability).	• Student will be able to match pitch on an e-flat.
• Students will demonstrate their understanding of all musical terms in this piece.	• Student will demonstrate an understanding of all musical terms in this piece. However, student will be given as much time as he needs to complete the task.	• Student will be able to demonstrate their understanding of at least two musical terms from this piece
• Students will perform their part individually with good tone, pulse, and rhythm.	• Student will perform the part individually with good tone, pulse, and rhythm. However, student will be given as much time as he needs to complete the task and will be given a proctor to assist him during the playing exam.	• Student will perform a modified-rewritten part individually with good tone, pulse, and rhythm. (this could also be a portion of a piece of music)
• Students will understand all key relationships	• Student will be able to play, sing, write, or use any means possible to demonstrate an understanding of all key relationships.	• Student will demonstrate an understanding of the "home" key.
• Students will understand the significance of Phillip Bliss and his contribution to the arts and culture.	• Student will be given multiple means to demonstrate understanding of this topic (oral exam, paper, traditional test with more time, etc.)	• Student will be able to understand when and where Phillip Bliss lived.
• Students will attempt to improvise in the key of concert e-flat within the context provided by the instructor.	• Student will improvise rhythmic and tonal (separately) patterns in the key of e-flat.	• Student will improvise rhythmic patterns while playing an e-flat.

Table 6.2 A Modified Parallel Curriculum for a First Grade General Music Class
Sol-Mi Notation – Quarter-Eighth Notation (Presentation Stage) (Method-Centered) 4-weeks

Non-modified or adapted curricular goals	Adapted Curricular Goals	Modified Curricular Goals
• Students will sing sol-mi patterns using neutral syllables	• Student will sing sol-mi patterns using neutral syllables at a tempo of his choosing	• Student will approximate higher and lower pitches following individual prompt by teacher
• Students will derive quarter eighth patterns from chants that are well-known to them	• Student will derive quarter eighth patterns using popsicle sticks given as much time as necessary	• Student will tap the rhythm with words to chants that are well-known to him
• Students will show higher and lower with their hands and with the use of icons	• Student will demonstrate higher and lower using icons and/or body motions	• Student will show higher and lower through any modality he prefers
• Students will discover the two pitches (sol and mi) and their similarities as noted in several folk songs well-known to them	• Student will discover sol-mi in at least one folk song well-known to him	• Student will sing folk songs that contain sol-mi with other students
• Students will apply new rhythm syllables to chants well-known to them	• Student will chant using rhythm syllables at a tempo of his choosing	• Student will chant rhymes that contain quarter/eighth with other students
• Students will apply new solfege syllables to chants well-known to them	• Student will apply new solfege syllables to at least one chant well-known to him	

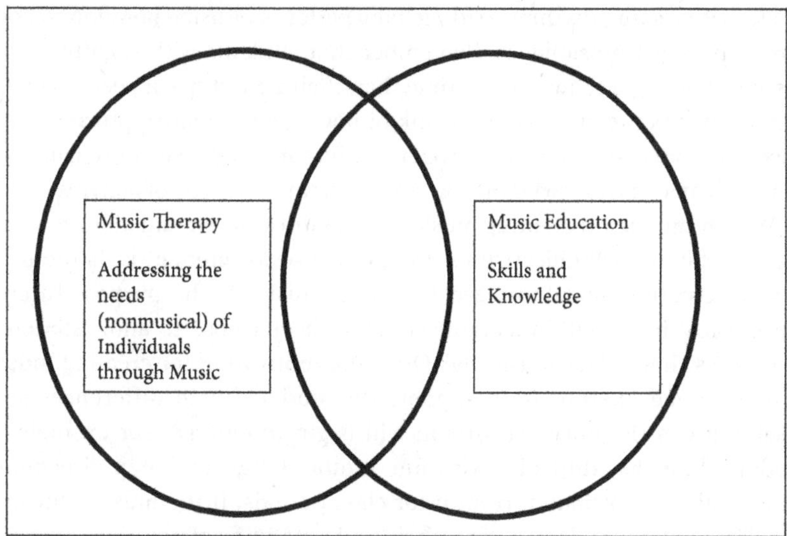

Figure 6.1. Music therapy and music education.

As mentioned in Chapter 3 (and shown in Figure 6.1), music therapists work to meet the nonmusical goals of their clients using music. Music therapists assess their clients by identifying strengths and challenges in the areas of communication, cognition, motor function, emotion, and socialization. While music educators are not music therapists, being able to assess the strengths and challenges of a student before planning lessons is a technique that can be adopted from the music therapy profession. The basis of music therapists' work is the use of music as the motivation for their clients. The next section is designed to shed light on how these disciplines can enhance each other. The National Association for Music Education (2014) standards will be used as a structure to discuss these theories and put these techniques into practice within the music classroom. These concepts are broad examples and offer a large framework of ideas. Because each child is different, music teachers are encouraged to modify these suggestions, as needed, within their own classroom. It is important to add that many other examples of lessons can be found in *Teaching Music to Students with Differences and Disabilities: A Practical Resource* (second edition).

Creating

Because there are numerous variables within the elements of music, creating music presents its own set of complications. There are multiple cognitive processes that must happen simultaneously to create music, whether the task is creating rhythmic and melodic patterns or using notation to document personal music ideas. Remember that students with cognitive processing challenges require more time than their neurotypical peers to make connections between concepts. Think of how many cognitive processes are necessary for creating music. A student with cognitive processing challenges can easily become overwhelmed when navigating this type of activity.

Within the area of creating music, music educators should identify what the specific musical objective for the project or assignment is. Is the purpose of creating music to learn to notate music? Is the purpose to create musical ideas within a framework? Is the purpose to allow students to express themselves musically? Once the motivation for creating music is determined, a strategy to support the students with differences and disabilities in the music classroom will begin to emerge. For example, a student, Luis, has difficulty with fine motor skills, multi-step directions, and recalling information from prior class periods. If the music educator requires students to demonstrate their understanding of notation of music, then the music teacher must consider accommodations that will support or streamline as many barriers to the student's learning as possible. Therefore, the teacher must be able to identify those challenging areas before creating accommodations. Luis's challenges with fine motor skills can be supported by eliminating his need to write by using technology, a scribe, or a set of rhythm cards; the barrier of not being able to accurately remember multi-step directions can be eliminated by providing him with written instructions; and the barrier of difficulty recalling information can be eliminated by providing him with choices rather than open-ended questions when asking him a question about material that has been covered in previous classes. Through the use of these and similar modifications, music educators can help Luis, and other students like him, develop his musicianship skills rather than focus on his limitations within the areas of fine motor skills and cognition, which most likely cause him to become frustrated and lose interest in the subject matter.

To motivate students to participate in music skill development, provide support for teaching composition and provide a limited number of choices. For example, offer students a pre-written composition that leaves out the last pitch in a phrase. Give the student three choices, which will help keep the student focused on the task, and then allow the student to choose a final pitch. Choosing just the last pitch not only will give students the opportunity to begin to make their own musical choices, but also will give insight into their musical understanding. Continue to use the same pre-written composition, adding additional phrases and leaving different sections of the phrase for the students to compose. This will give students the opportunity to create beginnings, middles, and ends of phrases.

Notating music will require more practice than composition. This is an especially difficult skill for students with differences and disabilities. Practice daily. Go slowly. Be patient. There is a great deal of cognitive processing required to notate music. Often, teachers use catchy mnemonic devices to teach the names of the lines and spaces on the staff. Be wary that these will require additional cognitive processing for students with differences and disabilities. Instead, try to use pre-written cards with rhythm and melodic patterns on them. The students can piece the cards together like a puzzle. The objective with notation is to visually represent what is heard. Pre-written material cuts out the middleman.

Improvisation is an area where students with differences and disabilities may excel. To provide a successful improvisation experience, support is necessary. At first, ask students to echo tonal and rhythm patterns. This provides the student an opportunity to play or sing what is heard and to perform alone. In the next stage, have students "pass" a given rhythm around the class (each student performs the rhythm given to him or her by the previous student). Next, combine a group playing the given rhythm with students performing their own rhythms. This type of improvisation provides scaffolded choices. Students are aware of how long they will improvise and when they are expected to start and stop. This will alleviate anxiety in some students and allow them the opportunity to be musically creative.

Performing

Similar to creating music, performing music also has its own set of challenges for students with differences and disabilities. Reading music often requires the rapid synthesis of identification, comprehension, and performance. This can provide a roadblock for students with differences and disabilities who want to perform but are not able to achieve this high level of cognitive processing. To provide all of our students the opportunity to perform music, whether it is on an instrument or singing, there are accommodations that can be put into place to streamline this undertaking. Music educators should be aware that students with disabilities need an access point in music class that matches their processing abilities.

When making literature choices, music educators should always consider the breadth of concepts being presented to students. Which musical concepts will be the focus of each piece of music that the students will be performing? Then, for the students who have difficulty with reading and receptive communication, the music teacher must find accommodations that allow these students to focus on the chosen goal, rather than decoding and pronunciation of the lyrics. For singing, this can be achieved in multiple ways, such as providing students with a recording of the song before the song is taught, using picture icons to accompany the lyrics, or dividing the class into parts and having each part only sing a section of the song. For instrument playing, music educators can also reduce the amount of information that students will be responsible to comprehend. Using iconic representation, visuals rather than notes and rests, can be helpful. Also, consider showing students the smallest amount of information possible. Cutting down on visual clutter, such as multiple staves of music, multiple lines of lyrics, and title information, increases students' focus.

Responding

Music educators should be aware that listening, analyzing, and describing are abstract concepts. And because the topics are abstract, music educators will need to think creatively in their approach. These skills will need to be practiced individually. Start small. To help students make more concrete connections with topics when analyzing and describing music, pair auditory concepts with visual and kinesthetic examples. For instance, play a recording of the *1812 Overture*. Give students instruments and a visual of a cannon to use while listening. While the students listen to the recording, they will play their instruments. Tell them when they hear the cannons to lift their picture in the air. When the cannons stop, the students will resume playing their instruments. These may be the first steps in the development of critical listening skills. Analysis in this case consists of two elements: cannons and no cannons. While this analysis is limited to two elements, using this template for analyzing music will produce a higher level of understanding for students with differences and disabilities.

To address the area of evaluating music, students must be able to comprehend the elements of music. Similar to analyzing music, this should start one element at a time. Allowing students to focus on one element will keep them more focused. In addition to limiting the focus of evaluations to one element at a time, music educators must think critically about the pieces being evaluated. Pieces with pronounced examples of the elements will work best. For example, allow students to listen to "Trepak Dance" from *The Nutcracker*. The first time through, just listen. For the second listening, use a parachute. Ask the students to demonstrate the rhythm of the piece of music by manipulating the parachute. Is it bouncy or smooth? Try listening to other pieces of music at the other end of the rhythmic spectrum to compare, such as "Aquarium" from *Carnival of the Animals*. This will lead to the class being able to demonstrate their ability to evaluate a piece of music.

Connecting

The best way to understand the relationship between music and the other arts is to experience them firsthand. For most of us, identifying artists willing to come to the music classroom may not be as difficult as expected. Be sure to plan a hands-on experience with the artist; this will be invaluable to your students, and you may learn something as well. If an artist is not available to come to class, technology may be a good alternative. Music educators can communicate via computer screen and get a glimpse of artists in other fields.

A music therapist can assist a music educator in accessing content, adapting, and accommodating material, and understanding the nuances and challenges of providing meaningful musical experiences for students with differences and disabilities. To summarize the discussion earlier (as shown in Figure 6.2), providing structure, pairing abstract with concrete concepts, and sequencing in small steps are all music therapy concepts that can be applied to music education. The most important consideration from the perspective of a music therapist is to think outside the box when teaching students with differences and disabilities. A music therapist can be an excellent partner when providing these types of suggestions within the music classroom.

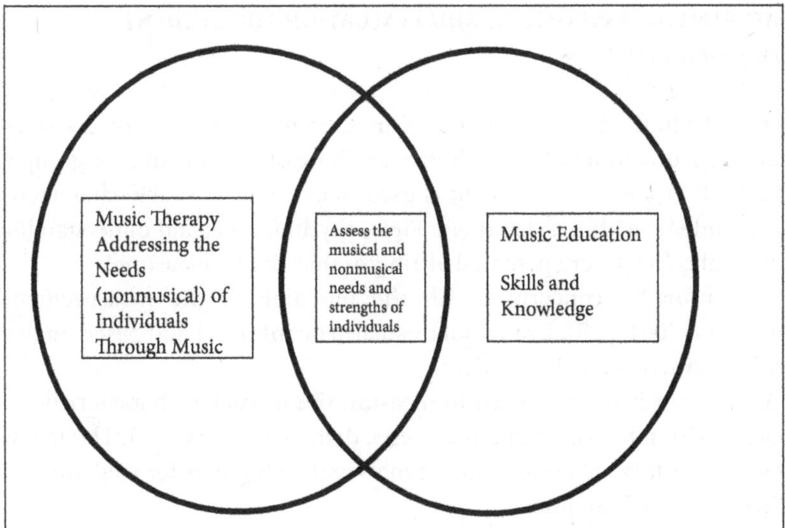

Figure 6.2. Combining music therapy concepts with music education.

ASSESSMENT AND STUDENTS WITH DIFFERENCES AND DISABILITIES

Assessment is the third essential principle (accompanying preparation and instruction) of an effective curriculum; it includes the self-evaluation of teaching practices and is a necessary aspect of teaching in public schools. By the time students finish high school, they have taken hours and hours of tests. Students with differences and disabilities sometimes take many tests just to determine eligibility for special education. For students to receive an IEP or 504 Plan, they are often given a series of tests to determine the degree of eligibility and disability. It is important to understand that assessment can sometimes be confused with testing. The assessments we conduct in the music education classroom, even with students who have differences and disabilities, center on the curriculum we teach and provide feedback for self-reflection and self-evaluation. Music educators are rarely asked to participate in the testing procedures as part of special education identification and classification. However, quality assessment based on music literacy and content goals (including the individualization of assessment) is one element that separates a music educator from a music therapist.

In the following section of this chapter, we review basic assessment techniques and how they can be modified or adapted for students with differences and disabilities. In addition, we provide examples for use in music classrooms.

MEASUREMENT, ASSESSMENT, AND EVALUATION FOR STUDENTS WITH DISABILITIES

Oosterhof (2001) defines educational measurement as "the process of determining a quantitative or qualitative attribute of an individual or group of individuals" (p. 6). Measurement is used to evaluate learnable characteristics of students within a classroom. Pitch, rhythm, tone, and understanding of musical concepts are potential attributes that can be measured.

Evaluation "is concerned with the outcome of the measurement" (Oosterhof, 2001, p. 5). Evaluations can also be informal and based on day-to-day interactions with a student.

Assessment is the tool used to measure the learnable characteristics of students within the classroom (e.g., tests, demonstrations, etc.). The following section is focused on assessment tools and techniques for students with differences and disabilities.

The reason for the previous review is to provide an opportunity to consider ways in which current terms are used. Are objectives established in the curriculum that can be adequately assessed (and that are attainable by students with differences and disabilities)? Are these objectives consistent with the curriculum and with the National Core Music Standards (or another set of standards put forth by your state or school district)? Do you regularly evaluate these objectives and determine their relevance to the individual needs of your students (including those with differences and disabilities)? Do these objectives need to be modified? These are important questions for consideration. They become especially important when deciding to modify or adapt a curriculum for students with differences and disabilities.

FORMATIVE ASSESSMENTS FOR STUDENTS WITH DIFFERENCES AND DISABILITIES

Formative assessment occurs as we are beginning instruction and is incorporated into teaching practice. Garrison and Ehringhaus (2009) explain that "when incorporated into classroom practice, it provides the information needed to adjust teaching and learning while they are happening" (p. 1). In classrooms, we find ourselves determining the current achievement levels of our students by assessing them in the moment. For example, a teacher may begin a lesson by singing a song. After this particular song is sung (depending on how well it is performed), the teacher may determine whether or not the song requires rehearsal or if the class will move on to another activity. This is part of formative assessment.

When teaching students with differences and disabilities in an inclusive setting, teachers may need to conduct many formative assessments to monitor the learning of an individual. This information is used to evaluate whether instruction should continue down a certain path, a student will be sent with an aide or helper to reaffirm the subject matter, or instruction will need to be wound forward or backward. These formative assessments are part of our daily teaching.

ESTABLISHING A BASELINE OF UNDERSTANDING

The first step in understanding assessments and whether adaptations and/or modifications (winding) will be used is to construct a baseline assessment. A baseline assessment occurs prior to instruction. This can be informal testing either with the entire group or with a small group of individuals. It can be done without causing anxiety or stress, which may exacerbate the possible skill deficit present in some students with differences and disabilities. However, it is also important to determine the specific skills and understandings a student brings to the classroom.

Some examples of formative assessments follow.

Elementary

Students are seated in a circle facing outward. The teacher sings a short pattern and students repeat the pattern. As the teacher walks around the outside of the circle, he or she can hear the students who are matching pitches and can note this on a chart as a formal formative assessment.

Beginning Band

Students play the "tag game" with each other. One student performs a rhythm on one of the notes the band has learned (e.g., Concert F). His or her partner then echoes the rhythm pattern (they will self-select for level of difficulty by choosing patterns comfortable for them). The teacher can walk among the partners, listening and noting the patterning successes and challenges of the students.

Beginning Choir

Students stand in a circle facing outward. The teacher has them improvise and sing known notes in a pentatonic scale (do-re-mi-so-la). The students show hand signs and improvise solfège they know well (they are self-selecting for level of difficulty by choosing patterns comfortable for them). The teacher walks around the circle noting students who are maintaining the tonal center, singing correct solfège syllables, and showing correct hand signs.

Beginning Orchestra

Students sit in sections with their instruments (no bows). The teacher calls or plays open strings. The students play the pattern indicated by the teacher. The teacher notes students who are playing the correct open-string patterns. Students may also do this in a circle as a section, taking turns calling and playing the open-string patterns.

Secondary Instrumental

Have a beginning-of-the-year basic playing exam (either on MakeMusic or in person). Try to be as positive as possible. Look for motor skills, embouchure issues, and music literacy challenges that may affect the student. This will assist in the creation of adaptations and modifications (winding).

Secondary Choral Music

Conduct a beginning-of-the-year vocal warm-up to establish parts (formative assessment). Check for things such as pitch-matching ability and music literacy. You can do these warm-ups in small groups to not embarrass the student you are assessing. In both secondary areas, good communication with previous music teachers is recommended. It is important to add that many other examples of lessons can be found in *Teaching Music to Students with Differences and Disabilities: A Practical Resource* (second edition) (available separately).

WRITING CLEAR, ATTAINABLE OBJECTIVES FOR STUDENTS WITH DIFFERENCES AND DISABILITIES

After establishing a baseline of skills and knowledge, it is time to write clear and attainable objectives for your students with differences and disabilities. It is recommended that music educators create very specific objectives that are observable and measurable. Examples of objectives that have been modified for students with differences and disabilities follow.

Seventh-Grade Choir

Objective: The students will solfège unfamiliar patterns using only notes in the diatonic major scale (steps–no skips); rhythms that include quarter, paired eighth, and half notes; and equivalent rests.

Many seventh-grade choir students will be able to achieve this goal. Students with excellent preparation in elementary school will find this objective easily attainable. Some students with differences and disabilities, however, may find this objective to be very difficult. When students are having particular difficulty with an objective, expectations can be modified (wound) while noting student progress toward the goal. These expectations are then charted for students with differences and disabilities, and the charts are used to document progress toward achieving the stated objective (Table 6.3). These micro-sequenced skill charts can be used with all students; however, they are particularly helpful to show small growth over time in students who are neurodivergent. An added benefit of creating alternative assessment charts is that it allows the music educator an opportunity to revisit the many steps required to perform a sometimes seemingly easy objective.

Music educators may prefer to use a different adapted assessment tool (winding) with students who have differences and disabilities to record incremental progress on a long-term objective. Many elementary school students learn to read quarter, paired eighth, half, four sixteenth, one eighth, two sixteenth, and four sixteenth-note patterns as part of their rhythm literacy objectives. Some students may be able to echo or pattern all these rhythms yet only be able to create or derive quarter- and eighth-note patterns. A chart that shows student progress over time can

Table 6.3 (7th grade Choir)

Pitch matching	
Sing major scale on neutral syllables, ascending	☐
Sing major scale on neutral syllables, descending	☐
Sing major scale with solfege, ascending	☐
Sing major scale with solfege, descending	☐
Sing pitches on a staff with solfege	☐
Find and sing "do" using a "do key"	☐
Reading	
Recognize staff	☐
Recognize treble and bass clefs	☐
Understand line and space notes	☐
Name the line in both clefs	☐
Name the space in both clefs	☐
Identify notes on lines and spaces in both clefs	☐
Recognize rhythms: half, quarter, eighth and equivalent rests	☐
Recognize bar lines and measures	☐
Recognize time signatures 2/4, 3/4, and 4/4	☐
Rhythm readiness	
Maintain steady beat	☐
Chant and clap	☐
Perform half notes and rests	☐
Perform quarter notes and rests	☐
Perform paired eighth notes	☐

be used as part of the overall documentation of learning in the music classroom. Some teachers attach these as ancillary data on report cards or share these with parents and classroom teachers during IEP and 504 meetings or at parent/teacher conferences. Figure 6.3 is an example of an adaptive assessment tool for a student with differences and disabilities in an elementary music classroom.

ASSESSING NONMUSICAL GOALS

Some students experience difficulty with transitioning to the music classroom or ensemble setting. It can be difficult to assess the progress of a student without creating a task analysis of all the elements necessary for that student to perform the stated objective. An example for a cellist in a high school orchestra follows.

Rhythm sequence	♩	♫	𝅗𝅥	𝅘𝅥𝅯𝅘𝅥𝅯𝅘𝅥𝅯𝅘𝅥𝅯	𝅘𝅥𝅮𝅘𝅥𝅯𝅘𝅥𝅯	𝅘𝅥𝅯𝅘𝅥𝅯𝅘𝅥𝅮
ECHO Neutral						
Syllable						
Transfer neutral to syllable						
IDENTIFY In a rhyme or song - aurally						
Visually						
DERIVE From a rhyme or song						
CREATE New rhythms that contain						
Anderson & Hammel (2007)						

Figure 6.3. Rhythm reading sequence: Elementary school rhythm reading (adapted sequence).

High School Orchestra

Objective: The students will perform Peter and the Wolf *expressively (with peers) as part of a varied repertoire of music.*

For a student with moderate communication and cognitive challenges, this typical high school orchestra objective requires many discrete skills that we may not notice unless we list the steps required to perform this task. For some students, the nonmusical skills required are equal in challenge to the musical skills. Table 6.4 provides a chart listing the steps in this process. These steps stop at the point the music begins to illustrate the nonmusical skills necessary for this student to be prepared for a downbeat or tuning note.

As you can imagine, it can be exhausting to complete all the steps necessary for success in a high school orchestra when you have moderate communication and cognitive challenges!

The next step is to begin the modification (winding) or adaptation process as the music educator creates an assessment to chart progress toward achievement of the musical objective. These modifications may include an audio/video file of the orchestra performing *Peter and the Wolf*, an individual

Table 6.4 High school orchestra objectives.

Finish task in previous classroom	☐
Put materials away and walk with aide to door	☐
Walk from classroom to orchestra room	☐
Walk into the orchestra room	☐
Go to the instrument storage room	☐
Find cello	☐
Take cello, bow, and resin from case	☐
Walk to folder cabinet	☐
Find folder	☐
Carry all materials (with assistance of aide) to collect chair and stand	☐
Place folder on stand	☐
Sit in chair	☐
Place endpin in chip on the floor	☐
Prepare bow with resin and tension	☐
Check space for arms	☐
Open folder	☐
Choose "Peter and the Wolf"	☐
Place music on stand	☐
Put pencil on stand	☐
All ready!	☐

recording of the cello part (or a modified cello part if the student needs this modification), color-coding, directions to assist the aide as they work with the student, and time spent on on-task (or time allowed for rest and quiet off-task) behaviors. Be sure to allow "brain breaks" and remember the skills the student is demonstrating just to be in the room with other students.

ALTERNATIVE ASSESSMENTS FOR STUDENTS WITH DIFFERENCES AND DISABILITIES

Often teachers focus on the product instead of the process. This can be a difficult quest for both the teacher of a student with differences and disabilities as well as the student. A student may exhibit an extraordinary amount of effort; however, because of their differences, they may not be able to demonstrate their understanding on the day of a test or an evening performance. Student portfolios are a way for students to demonstrate their work over a long period of time rather than a one-chance performance either on an exam, in a classroom evaluation, or at a concert. Student portfolios can also be adapted or modified (wound) for the student based on their ability to meet stated objectives. The portfolio can include the student's written work, photos of the student working toward objectives, results of playing tests, exam scores, recordings (made by the student), reflections, or any class material that can be archived within a portfolio.

SUMMATIVE ASSESSMENTS AND STUDENTS WITH DIFFERENCES AND DISABILITIES

After determining goals for an individual student, you must also determine how you will know if these goals are attained, and how the curriculum may be adapted or modified (wound) to enhance learning. We have discussed formative assessments, created a task analysis of elements required to perform an objective, and given examples of alternative assessments in the music classroom. The final type of assessment is summative assessment. This assessment takes place at the end of instruction when you are evaluating whether the students have met the goals set, based on your formative (or baseline) assessment.

Oosterhof (2001) explains that "summative evaluations follow instruction and typically involve unit tests, midterm and final exams, and projects, or other end of unit assignments" (p. 22). In music this may involve experiences that show mastery of content (curriculum mastery), music theory exams, music terms tests, singing or playing tests, district or mandated music skills testing, and other types of summative assessment. These are important to a successful curriculum and for an educationally successful classroom experience.

There are many questions a music teacher should ask before establishing a fair summative assessment for a student with differences and disabilities. These questions include:

- What can be gained by assessing this student?
- What am I looking for with this assessment?
- How will this assessment inform my teaching of this student with disabilities?

Music teachers must be aware of the ways a summative assessment may impact a student (academically, socially, and emotionally). Remember, a student with differences and disabilities has spent a great deal of time being tested. Whether it is to determine a diagnosis, determine eligibility, or establish a baseline in language or speech, they have been through batteries of exams. Many students with differences and disabilities understand what these tests are, and they are sensitive to the outcomes.

It is important for students with differences and disabilities to know they have done well and have learned. Through winding our content back, summative assessments can show the student has achieved the wound objectives set for them. This is demonstrated through a modified (wound) assessment. It is not useful for music educators to remind a student (again) that they are different or unable to complete an objective obtained by their classmates. By deriving and teaching achievable objectives, through winding content, every student can succeed at an individual level in a music class or ensemble. Remember that fair is not equal. Fair is ensuring that every student has the opportunity to succeed. By adapting and modifying your curriculum and assessment procedures, you are creating fairness for your students.

CONCLUSION

This chapter provides instructionally appropriate strategies for music teachers as they adapt and/or modify (wind) curricula and assess students with differences and disabilities. Students with differences and disabilities often engage in modified or adapted curricula in other subjects. In fact, the IEP itself is a document that contains these modifications. The opportunity for music educators is to create similar opportunities for students with differences and disabilities in the music classroom and ensemble. In addition, it is important to continue to assess students regardless of their age or stage of development. Students with differences and disabilities are sometimes omitted from assessments. This can create a false sense of your teaching ability, as well as an inaccurate portrayal of the learning capability of an individual who is neurodivergent. This, in turn, will inhibit the potential acquisition of skills and understanding for music students with disabilities. As music educators, we understand the different ways in which students learn music. It is up to each music teacher to create adaptations and/or modifications to curriculum design and assessment procedures to create the opportunity for every student, including students with disabilities, to be successful in music.

DISCUSSION QUESTIONS

1. A student with communication challenges has been included in your middle school orchestra program. She is having great difficulty remembering the exact placement of her fingers (even with the tape placed for the finger placements). A playing test is in two weeks that

will require her to know these placements without stopping to look at her fingers and move to the next note. Do you think this student would benefit more from modifications (winding) or adaptations to the objectives for the playing test? What can you do to modify (wind) or adapt her objectives to make the test "fair" for her and to give her an opportunity to succeed?

2. There is a new percussionist in your high school marching band. Previously, he has only played bass and snare drum. He is resistant to playing mallet percussion and absolutely refuses to play the cymbals because they are too loud. The student is currently not receiving services for a difference or disability. Your band curriculum specifies that all percussionists learn to play all instruments, and there are specific objectives for mallet percussion skills. What can you do to adapt or modify (wind) the curriculum for this student?
3. Your fifth-grade music class on Wednesday mornings includes a student with severe cognitive challenges. In reviewing your curriculum for fifth-grade music, you see that every student is to demonstrate mastery of sixteenth-note rhythms in all variations (duple and triple). You are sure this student, whom you have taught since kindergarten, is going to have a difficult time achieving this district-mandated objective. What can you do to modify (wind) or adapt the curriculum for this student?

Chapter 7

Teaching Strategies for Performers with Differences and Disabilities

CHAPTER OVERVIEW

- The Hidden Curriculum in Traditional Performing Ensembles (Equal Access)
- Participating in the Special Education Process
- Understanding the Disability (Seeking Resources)
- Adaptation of Instruction for Performers with Differences and Disabilities
- The Use of Technology
  Hammel, A. M., & Rathgeber, J. (2021). Living at the intersection of tablets, music, and disability. In F. Abraham (Ed.), *Creative music making at your fingertips: A mobile technology guide for music educators*. Oxford University Press.
  - Large Group Performing Ensembles: Are They the Appropriate Placement for Students with Differences and Disabilities?
  - Meaningful Participation
  - Alternative Models of Performance for Students with Exceptionalities
  - Conclusion
  - Discussion Questions

Because of previously discussed changes in philosophy and policy, the demographics of our performing ensembles are constantly changing. Many school districts have moved toward a policy of full inclusion of students with differences and disabilities. This has led to an increased number of students with differences and disabilities in performing ensembles and has challenged many conductors to find ways to include many students with disabilities who were not previously a part of performing ensembles. In addition, this has forced many conductors to re-examine their underlying philosophy of what it means to be a successful ensemble conductor.

Teaching Music to Students with Differences and Disabilities. Third Edition. Alice M. Hammel and Ryan M. Hourigan, Oxford University Press. © Oxford University Press 2025. DOI: 10.1093/9780197689356.003.0007

The purpose of this chapter is to offer techniques for choral and instrumental conductors who teach performers with differences and disabilities and to suggest ideas for consideration for those who are preparing to conduct performing ensembles. These strategies come from extensive work researching, consulting with ensemble conductors, and working with parents of performers with differences and disabilities. This chapter is designed to alleviate any anxieties that conductors and conducting students may have and to provide confidence when teaching students with disabilities.

THE HIDDEN CURRICULUM IN TRADITIONAL PERFORMING ENSEMBLES (EQUAL ACCESS)

Typically, the percentage of students with disabilities in performing ensembles is far less than the overall percentage of students with disabilities in a school. This is anecdotal data, however; the open challenge exists to those who teach performing ensembles to truly examine this phenomenon throughout their school system (pre-K through 12). Vignette 7.1 is an example of a supportive and inclusive learning environment.

Unfortunately, band, choir, and orchestra directors can inadvertently discourage participation of students with differences and disabilities in their ensembles in many ways. For example, many band and orchestra programs have an entry point in or around fifth grade, and after that point, students are not allowed to join. Unfortunately, many students with differences and disabilities are not developmentally ready to join an instrumental or choral ensemble in fifth grade. Many of these same students would be extremely successful if given another point of entry later in their school career. Small curricular nuances, such as a floating entry point to beginning band, choir, or orchestra, can make a meaningful difference in developing an inclusive performing ensemble program in a public school.

Another hidden discouragement is the fact that students, as a requirement for participation, are required to be "put on the spot" regularly. Auditions, playing tests, and informal demonstrations of achievement are common in the typical rehearsal. The authors have even seen conductors engage in these types of exercises on purpose to "weed" students out of their program. For some students with disabilities, this is just one more way to feel they are not as capable as their peers. It is easier for them to not participate and to choose something else.

Parents of students with disabilities can learn from other parents about how participation works in performing ensembles. In some communities, parents form subcultures through their work with support groups, similar participation in activities, and fundraising organizations. It is very easy for

Vignette 7.1 Henry, Part 1

We recognize that music is a valuable tool of communication for humans. We respond to music through how it makes us feel and think. Participating in musical activities is one of the most basic forms of human interaction and human development. Music makes us real.

I am fortunate in my school district to work with a team of special education instructors who recognize the value of music participation and inclusion of students with differences and disabilities into our music program. We have a positive working relationship, and they recognize that when students enter the band room, every accommodation possible will be made to enable successful participation in band.

Henry is a 14-year-old freshman at our school. He loves all things sports and can be found leading our football and basketball teams out onto the playing field with a school banner on his wheelchair. He frequently presents the officials with the game ball. Henry has bright blue eyes that gleam with contagious energy. His smile brings sunshine to an entire room, and his tears and moans of sadness, when heard in the hallway or around the building, can bring a crowd of students or adults immediately to his side, wondering how they can help.

An increasing need for Henry as he has now reached high school is for him to develop more skills for independence. The educational team has been working to provide ways for him to move around the building from room to room without the assistance of adults. This is done through signs on his wheelchair that indicate his destination. The goal is for him to be able to get to the nurse or to his classrooms without the aid of paraprofessionals. We are continually seeking ways to discover what he is capable of managing on his own and when he needs assistance from others.

In addition, Henry has an increased need to belong to groups inside the school. An innate part of what makes us human, what makes us driven with a sense of purpose, is to belong to something greater than ourselves. As educators we must recognize that all children, no matter what their gifts or abilities, have this need inside. It is our job to assist students in harnessing their potential and paving a pathway so that they can find this sense of purpose.

Discussion Questions:

1. How could Henry find a place in your current performance program (or future program)?
2. What would be your first step to include Henry?

a conductor to be known as an inclusive, accommodating teacher or a discouraging, non-inclusive teacher just by the way their program is designed and implemented.

For those music educators who are currently conducting ensembles in public or private schools, a further challenge is to look at the entire music education program objectively and consider whether the program is accepting of all students regardless of their abilities. For the music education student preparing to conduct ensembles, the challenge is to consider your philosophy and the way the changing demographics in schools may be reflected in performing groups in future music education programs.

PARTICIPATING IN THE SPECIAL EDUCATION PROCESS

Many music educators, including many conductors, do not understand their rights and responsibilities as teachers of students with differences and disabilities. This was discussed at length in Chapters 1 and 2. However, many also do not understand the Individualized Education Program (IEP) or 504 documents and the meetings that take place to meet the needs of an individual student (this process will be discussed later in this chapter). This section of the chapter is designed to give further understanding into the special education system as it relates to performing ensembles.

As mentioned earlier in this book, the first step in understanding a performer's disability is to contact or consult with members of a student's IEP or 504 Plan team. Attending these meetings as part of participation in the special education process is a valuable activity. Much can be learned about a student's talents and capabilities. Many conductors of school ensembles have stated anecdotally that they have never attended (or in some cases have never heard of or about) an IEP or 504 Plan meeting. The same directors also explain that they feel unsupported and misinformed about their students. These meetings are "ground zero" for information that leads to a better understanding of a student's capabilities.

If attending an IEP or 504 Plan meeting is not possible because of scheduling, seeking the document (that results from these meetings) is an acceptable replacement. It is also the law. There are a few areas in the document that are of particular importance and are critical to understanding a student's needs. The first is called the present level of academic function section (terminology varies by state). This statement is a narrative put together by the team regarding a student's capabilities. By reading this section, conductors can gain insight into the challenges the student may face when engaging in a performance setting.

The second area of the IEP or 504 Plan to consider is the set of academic goals established by other teachers. This will increase the level of understanding regarding the strengths and weaknesses of a performer with differences and disabilities. This becomes even more valuable when designing assessment opportunities for the same students (discussed later in this chapter). These portions of the legal documents are critical prior to the design of adaptations, or modifications for students with disabilities. Further ideas for adapting instruction will be presented later in this chapter.

UNDERSTANDING THE DISABILITY (SEEKING RESOURCES)

It is the responsibility of ensemble conductors to know the students in each ensemble. Yet, it is perplexing to hear of an ensemble director who spends hours and hours programming music, organizing trips, and preparing for contests, but who fails to seek background information regarding a student. It is also a legal obligation to be aware of, and implement, the adaptations, and modifications listed in the document. There are many publications in the music education literature that focus on students with disabilities (see Chapter 9). Seeking these resources (see Suggested Resources) and reading about the needs of a student take a small amount of time.

Suggested Resources

Hammel, A. M. (2004). Inclusion strategies that work. *Music Educators Journal, 90*(4), 33–37.

Hammel, A. M., Hickox, R. Y., & Hourigan, R. M. (2016). *Winding it back: Teaching to individual differences in music classroom & ensemble settings.* New York: Oxford University Press.

Hammel, A., & Hourigan, R. M. (2011). The fundamentals of special education policy: Implications for music teachers and music teacher education. *Arts Education Policy Review, 112*, 174–179.

Lapka, C. (2016). Students with disabilities in high school band: We can do it. *Music Educators Journal, 92*(4), 54–59. https://doi.org/10.2307/3401113.

Lewis, R. B., & Doorlag, D. H. (2011). *Teaching special students in general education classrooms* (8th ed.). Upper Saddle River, NJ: Prentice Hall.

Zdzinski, S. F. (2001). Instrumental music for special learners. *Music Educators Journal, 87*(4), 27–29.

The relatively small amount of time spent consulting with special educators, reading available articles in music education (or music therapy) regarding a certain disability, and talking with parents can make the difference. An important part of this consultation should be to determine whether the student is at grade level academically. Sometimes disabilities can be deceiving. If the student is not at grade level, find out if he or she is on track to receive a regular diploma at the end of high school. This will help determine some of the possibilities for this student.

Knowing the transition plan in place for a student (college, vocational school, supervised work training) is of value when considering the specific ensemble placement and set of accommodations that may be employed when teaching a student with differences and disabilities. This information is important because it lets us know the expectations that other team members have for the student. Conductors can use this information as they design adaptations and modifications for a student and a plan for inclusion in specific ensembles. For example, a student who will be placed in a supervised work training environment may not be able to participate in marching band or show choir because both activities may have responsibilities at a certain time of day, or after school. Students who are working toward supervised work employment will be required by the school (and their employer) to work a set number of hours at specific times of day. This may limit the ensemble choices, and consultation with the team (including the parents) is advisable.

Remember that most students with differences and disabilities will have a transition plan in place during their high school years. This is part of their IEP or 504 Plan. Knowing this information will take some time but is rewarding in the end. Remember, all students are different. Articles and books can provide a broad sense of a student's capabilities. Yet, it is the special educators and parents who can be of the most assistance in understanding the specific needs of a student with differences and disabilities who is part of an ensemble.

ADAPTATION OF INSTRUCTION FOR PERFORMERS WITH DIFFERENCES AND DISABILITIES

The previous information leads us to the question: How do I begin to teach a performer who has a disability? In general, most music educators are much more qualified than they realize. The following section is designed to remind ensemble conductors of techniques they may not have considered. Many of these ideas may have already been put in place without knowledge of the value for students with differences and disabilities.

The first priority for a music educator who is adapting instruction is to understand that they are the expert music educators (or future music educators). Be confident in your previous music experience and realize you do understand the many ways in which students learn music. It is surprising that music educators, especially ensemble directors, sometimes forget this premise when teaching a student with differences and disabilities. Even though the music educator is the expert, teaching a performer with differences and disabilities may require an examination of ideas about how students really learn music and a sincere effort to be creative when accommodating performers.

The next step in adapting instruction is to determine how a specific student learns best (see previous chapters in this text). The student may be an aural learner rather than a visual learner. This may require the student to

Box 7.1 Technology Suggestions for Performance-based Adaptations

Video Sharing Applications

Loom (loom.com)

Similar to Zoom, Microsoft Teams, etc.

Theory and Concept "Drill" Platforms

NinGenius Music App (https://www.ningenius.net)

Music Theory drill application for beginners. Works with most devices

Music Theory.net

Similar to NinGenius

Practice Support Applications that include Method Book Access (most include built-in rhythm tracks, metronomes, tuners, etc.)

Make Music (makemusic.com)

Music First (musicfirst.com)

Music Racer (musicracer.com)

Very good for reinforcing note names and fingerings

John McCallister Music (https://www.johnmcallistermusic.com)

Very highly recommended from former students and colleagues

Free to everyone

Contains warmups, exercises, video examples

Tonal Energy (tonalenergy.com)

Very good for tone quality work

Method Books that Contain their own Platforms

Essential Elements

Tradition of Excellence

learn music by ear first; therefore, they may need recordings of the music to help with practice. The student may struggle with the routine of a rehearsal. The music educator may need to provide a list of what will happen on a daily or weekly basis to aid this student. Just like many curricular decisions in music, all strategies are individualized for each student and may be defined as the result of trial and error during rehearsals. All students are different and require some individualized thought, and it is always acceptable to continue to try new ideas and techniques when others are not meeting the needs of students–those with and without differences and disabilities–in ensembles.

THE USE OF TECHNOLOGY

There are many ways technology can be used to assist students when practicing. Smartphones can easily be used to record a student (or a conductor) playing an individual part for a student. This can easily be text messaged to a student or a parent ahead of time. Technology, such as wix.com,[1] allows instrumental and vocal music teachers a place to gather and organize these clips, which can be watched for reference.

In addition, MakeMusic[2] is an excellent tool to extract parts, make recordings, and choose appropriate literature for a student with differences and disabilities. MakeMusic can also be used to modify assessments for students with differences and disabilities. MakeMusic allows students who have anxiety about performing in front of an instructor the opportunity to go home and complete the assessment in private online.

Notation programs (e.g., Finale) can be used in a variety of ways to extract, modify, and simplify parts for individual performers. In addition, these notation programs can be used to highlight or increase the font of passages for performers who will benefit from this adaptation. Many conductors overlook these devices as tools for accommodation when in fact they are very appropriate tools to enhance performance. Box 7.1 is a list of technology resources sourced by surveying music educators in the field who consistently work with performers with learning challenges. Annotations are provided as descriptions of the technology.

For further information regarding the use of technology, we have inserted a chapter here from another source. The source is:

Hammel, A. M., & Rathgeber, J. (2021). Living at the intersection of tablets, music, and disability. In F. Abraham (Ed.), *Creative music making at your fingertips: A mobile technology guide for music educators*. Oxford University Press, (pp. 29–42).

LIVING AT THE INTERSECTION OF TABLETS, MUSIC, AND DISABILITY

Alice Hammel and Jesse Rathgeber

INTRODUCTION

Some see tablets as a key to equity in many school and community spaces. Some may also assume that tablets are equalizers and that by having them in a learning space we are successfully embracing all learners, including disabled musicians or musicians with disabilities (DM/MwD)[1] in music making. Adam Goldberg, a New York City music teacher, discussed (in Bell, 2015) the assistive power of tablets in his work with DM/MwD, stating:

> I am able to use the iPad to create a highly accessible music-making environment for my students, whether individually, or as part of an ensemble. Because each iPad can be modified, via the huge variety of apps and the modifications that can be made within many apps, to suit each student's learning needs and abilities, I can optimally challenge each student so that they grow as musicians, both in an individual sense and as part of an ensemble. Regardless of student ability, each can find their own voice, expressed within a group of students of widely varying abilities. (p. 51)

Although this may be true, it is important to note that tablets, alone, will not create equity in a learning space. Tablets, and specifically the apps that empower them, may indeed provide potentially assistive technology that can level specific barriers to music learning and music making for specific DM/MwD, yet the barriers related to an app's purpose, layout, and accessibility, the curricular goals with which they intersect, and the personal desires of DM/MwD against which they may bump up can make them more or less equitable without careful consideration.

What are the primary barriers for DM/MwD? How do we organize this process to create spaces that represent all learners? One way to approach this process is to consider the principles of universal design for learning (UDL). The overarching ideas of UDL include creating a space for learners that provides multiple means of representation, multiple means of expression, and multiple means of engagement (CAST, 2018). When we consider these principles while examining the benefits and barriers of various tablets and apps, we may begin to organize our thoughts and music-making spaces.

Having multiple means of engagement involve recruiting the interest of our students. This means building our learning spaces around what they want to learn. When we engage our students in a variety of ways, we invite them to share their ideas and goals for themselves and their music. We also wind back or forward our learning goals to meet the current, and perhaps constantly changing, amount of effort and persistence our students are demonstrating. We recognize their needs and are able to alter the technology and our expectations so that we do not over- or underestimate what they can achieve in that moment. We also monitor and encourage the development of self-regulation by calibrating the technology they are using to fortify their efforts.

When we provide multiple means of representation in our learning spaces, we are able to perceive the musical intent of our learners, and program and use language and symbols familiar and meaningful for them, while we adjust the technology used to meet their level of comprehension. These considerations lead to multiple means of action and expression demonstrated by learners. They are then freed from possible disabling features of technology to physically control the tablet and app, express and communicate their musical needs in meaningful ways, and demonstrate their musical ideas without having those ideas weakened by the arduous use of technology not suited to their needs.

What procedures should be utilized when examining tablets and apps for use by DM/MwD? Can we use traditional adaptations when engaging with technology? One set of adaptations includes the considerations of size, color, pacing, and modality (visual, aural, and kinesthetic; Hammel & Hourigan, 2017) when adapting experiences to include all learners. We can certainly adjust the size, color, pacing, and modalities experienced in utilizing tablets and apps, but is this enough? How can we be sure that we are creating the equity we seek in our learning spaces? In this chapter, we discuss assistive technology and explore multiple apps and app types that, given the goal and specific DM/MwD, may act as powerful assistive technology to help learners find their own voice.

ASSISTIVE TECHNOLOGY

Assistive technology has been defined as "any device or system that allows an individual to perform a task that they would otherwise be unable to do, or increases the ease and safety with which the task can be performed" (Cowan & Turner-Smith, 1999, p. 325). The U.S.-based disability education legislation termed the Individuals with Disabilities Education Improvement Act (2004; also known by the acronym of its predecessor, IDEA) defines assistive technology as

> any item, piece of equipment, or product system, whether acquired commercially off the shelf, modified, or customized, that is used to increase, maintain, or improve functional capabilities of a child with a disability . . . [excluding] a medical device that is surgically implanted, or the replacement of such devices. (§602)

Music education scholars Watts, McCord, and Blair (2016) note that assistive technology "can range from simple items to sophisticated, multicomponent product systems" (p. 88). These systems can serve any number of functions, such as (a) speech communication support (e.g., text-to-speech and speech synthesis), (b) written communication support (e.g., pencil holders, dictation programs, and Braille readers), (c) computer use supports, (e.g., eye gaze or voice recognition devices), (d) reading support (e.g., screen readers, Braille, magnification, and audiobooks), (e) hearing support (e.g., hearing amplification and live-captioning services), (f) organizational support (e.g., planners, note-taking apps, and "remind me" programs), (g) creative supports (e.g., individually adaptive controllers and interfaces and computer applications such as Soundbeam that transfer one modality into musical expression), (h) daily living support (ergonomic instruments, alert devices, and dressing tools), (i) movement and transportation support (e.g., wheelchairs, canes, instrument mounts, and prosthetics), (j) recreational support (e.g., adaptive sports, musical, and cooking equipment along with dating applications and services), (k) environmental adaptation (e.g., ramps, curb cuts, and remote control devices), and (l) equipment adaptation (e.g., height-adjustable workstations, adapted furniture and body supports) (Watts, McCord, & Blair 2016; Thompson, Watts, Wokcik, & McCord, 2003).

Tablets and apps can act as assistive technologies in many ways if their purpose and use are intended to "increase, maintain, or improve functional capabilities of" DM/MwD (Individuals with Disabilities Education Improvement Act, 2004, §602). Yet it is important to note that technologies and individual pieces of equipment are not in and of themselves assistive unless they are intended for and used for the purpose of assisting a specific DM/MwD specifically engaged in an activity that addresses a specific need or desire of that person (e.g., a Kindle Fire tablet with an installed text-to-speech app exists only as a potential tool unless used by a learner in need of such an application in order to communicate). Below, we illustrate how some specific tablet-based applications or types of applications can be used as assistive technologies given the personal needs and desires of the learner as these interact with specific music learning and music making goals. For each app or app type, we include a brief vignette to center the learner in a real-world context and then discuss the context and technological uses, as well as potential pitfalls.

GARAGEBAND IOS

As the first semester begins at Thomas Shakespeare School, Anika enters the music room at a quick pace, her forearm crutches catching the light and sending it glimmering off the rows of guitars, orchestral percussion, and choral risers near the back of the room. "Mx. Titchkosky, Mx. Titchkosky! I signed up for Modern Band this semester and I'm so excited to rock out. I just can't wait to play drums and bass and sing and rap." The passing bell rings and Anika is out in a flash. The teacher sits finishing their oatmeal and thinking about how well Anika did in Exploratory Music last year, with the exception of her coordination differences on guitar. Anika has a lot of control over gross motor-friendly activities such as their drum circle project. She was really creative during their songwriting project. Guitar posed a lot of barriers to Anika, specifically when more than one finger was needed to fret a chord or note. so Mx. Titchkosky decided they would offer Anika an adapted three-string guitar that had worked with another student with cerebral palsy a few years ago.

The teacher planned an informal time to "explore the instruments and jam" for the first day of Modern Band and asked that Anika find them after she had a chance to play around a bit. Anika formed a small group in the back, playing drums in the group for a while, and then found her way to Mx. Titchkosky, who was playing guitar. "Anika, thanks for coming over. I wanted to chat about your thoughts on playing guitar this year, since each student plays multiple instruments through the semester. I remembered that the guitar provided some barriers to your playing the way you wanted to last year, so I wanted to see if you had an idea of how you'd like to learn and make music using guitar this year," Mx. Titchkosky said. "Oh, I don't care, I can just play bass, maybe," Anika replied, with some reservation. "You can play guitar, Anika. I don't want you to think I didn't want you to, I just want to make sure you are and feel as successful as you can," Mx. Tichowsky replied. "What about the three-string guitar?" "Well, I don't really want to play that guitar because I can't get it to sound like the sounds in my head, and the color stickers and missing string just make me feel like I have a sign on my head that says 'disabled kid.' I just want to be able to sound like the guitar goddess I am, you know," Anika responded. "I just want to make the sounds." "Okay, well, the goals for playing guitar are, first, to be able to accompany using different strum patterns on three-, four-, and five-chord songs, and second, play and improvise melodies over three-, four-, and five-chord songs using scale or riff patterns. You could do that without the physical guitar. What do you think about playing on a tablet using an app?" Mx. Tichowsky suggested. Anika replied, "I don't know, as long as it sounds right, maybe." "Okay, here, try this iPad and the apps in this 'Accompanying' folder. Try to find an app that has the guitar sound you're thinking about and that you'd want to use. If you don't like any, we'll look for something else," said Mx. Titchkosky.

After some exploration with headphones, Anika landed on GarageBand iOS because she could change the sounds by picking different guitars and adding effects. She could strum using the Smart Guitar screen, and Mx. Titchkosky even showed her how to remove chords from the screen using the Edit Chords option in the settings. She loved playing melody patterns on the Notes screen, and picking a scale helped her improvise more fluently. As she became confident with her instrument and with the help of an iPad stand, Anika could stand to play along with her friends when it was her time on guitar. Her face-melting tapping solo was a feature of the end-of-semester album.

GarageBand iOS, the mobile version of Apple's seemingly ubiquitous digital audio workstation, has garnered a great deal of attention on the part of music educators (e.g., Bell, 2015; Riley, 2018; Ruismäki, Juvonen, & Lehtonen, 2013; Williams, Chapter 7 in this book). Whereas the Mac OS version of GarageBand used on Apple desktop and laptop computers is a digital audio workstation (DAW) dedicated to multitrack recording, mixing, and mastering, the iOS mobile version is both a DAW and an instrument in its own right. Along with loops and recording capabilities, the app gives a user access to keyboard, drum, strings, bass, guitar, and world instrument interfaces that can be customized for key, mode, arpeggiation, and timbre, as well as automated using Smart Instrument settings. By tapping or swiping at the screen, users with different combinations of fine and gross motor control can use fingers and styli (pen-shaped, ergonomic, and guitar pick-style touchscreen tools) to make music along with others--including recording.

With all of the potential of GarageBand iOS there are, as with any app, pitfalls related to regular use and adaptation for individual needs. With all applications, it is important to know for whom and for what they were created. GarageBand iOS was created as a simplified version of the seminal Mac OS DAW with the addition of smart instruments to best make use of the touchscreen platform. As it has evolved, both the recording aspect and the live performance aspect of the app have become more complex and have offered an array of options that can clutter the visual field or be hard to find in the menus and options. Preset sounds may not be the sounds that DM/MwD are seeking, and they may have a difficult time finding their sound. Given the importance of timbre in performed and recorded music, providing DM/MwD with guidance, chances to explore, and time to develop their sound is important. In addition, the built-in Voiceover function in iPad's Accessibility controls can be a powerful screen reader, but it may have difficulty with some aspects of GarageBand iOS, limiting for accessibility for DM/MwD who may have visual impairments or are blind (Endarion, 2018). Another pitfall of this application, and a pitfall for all touchscreen devices, is the limited tactile response or feedback for users. Whereas the physical feel of guitar strings and frets may aid users to some extent, a touchscreen has no such textures. Teaching styles and approaches that may have been based on tactile response, therefore, need to be adjusted.

THUMBJAM, NODEBEAT, BLOOM AND AUXY

It is the middle of the school year and Dr. Oliver is excited for the upcoming soundscape project with the eighth-grade Exploratory Music classes. The project came about through numerous explorations with learners in all sections about how composers developed and communicated a sense of place in their music via melodic and rhythmic motives (e.g., Gandolfi's "The Garden of Cosmic Speculation"), lyrics (e.g., Jay Z's "Empire State"), and texture (e.g., Libby Larsen's "My Ántonia"). One day Belen, who was in the "self-contained" section of the class, shouted, "Grand Canyon," and began to make deep vocal scoops. Dr. Oliver and the paraprofessionals learned that Belen had recently been to the Grand Canyon and was making music to evoke the depth of the canyon. Throughout that week, Dr. Oliver spoke with other learners in these classes about their ideas for places and musics. Most learners were excited about the idea of creating their own soundscapes to evoke a place.

Dr. Oliver initially thought of acoustic instruments in the classroom as the basis for all the sounds in this project because he was familiar with these instruments (pitched and nonpitched percussion, guitars, ukuleles, keyboards, recorders, and some wind instruments) and they were easily available. Yet he wanted to provide additional sounds and choices for learners. Watching Najma use her Samsung Galaxy tablet to communicate to the paraprofessional working with her, Dr. Oliver noticed that she unintentionally opened an app that translated finger swipes to melodic content. Dr. Oliver asked Najma if she had any other music apps and she showed him apps such as NodeBeat, a music sequencer that uses circles, squares, and lines of various lengths to create music, and Bloom, an app that generates ambient textures based on app settings and user taps. Najma also used the text-to-speech feature on her Galaxy tablet to type/tell Dr. Oliver that at home she had an iPad with Figure, a beat-making app by Propellerhead Software AB, and Auxy, a mobile music studio app that she loved to play around with.

Surveying other learners in the classes, Dr. Oliver developed a list of apps to try for himself. After work he tinkered with many apps, finding out about their affordances and constraints and noting for whom they seemed to be designed. He used tutorials to learn how to use the apps beyond a basic level and created model pieces of music. In one tutorial he discovered another app called ThumbJam that seemed perfect for the melodic improvisations he envisioned as part of the learners' project. After his personal professional development, he selected some low-barrier, high-expressive-potential apps and then placed two apps into each folder based on possible uses for the project (e.g., texture, melody, or percussion) on the classroom Android devices and a few iPads borrowed from the computer lab.[2] *Dr. Oliver then set up the project with all the classes and encouraged them to explore all sounds in the classroom. Dr. Oliver provided assistance with all learners as they explored their sounds, including providing app demos as needed. Afterward, Dr. Oliver asked learners to choose to work solo or as a duo or trio as they chose a place, described the place, and sought out digital and acoustic sounds to evoke their place and place description. Learners selected sounds and controllers or instruments that not only fit the place on which they focused but also fit the ways their body-minds functioned (e.g., seeking out in a subconscious manner tools that posed minimal barriers to their engagement and expression). Dr. Oliver facilitated learners' work by asking questions to help them think in sound, consulting with them regarding adaptive approaches to using controllers or instruments, and providing them space to follow their own processes.*

At one point Dr. Oliver decided the groups would perform their works live for the school. When he shared this idea with the learners, most were unenthusiastic about the idea while others seemed outright resistant. After a few days of inner sulking about the rejection of the big performance, Dr. Oliver asked the learners how they wanted to share or preserve their work. Ash pointed to iMovie on their iPad, Johanna eagerly suggested a mini-performance, and Najma used her text-to-speech function to support the option of movies. Dr. Oliver worked with each group to create a unique way to share their works, some making videos and some performing live. The classes decided to share their works in conjunction with a PTO-sponsored family game night that would take place near the end of the semester. Learners would get to share their music and chat with parents, friends, and teachers in an informal atmosphere–and get to play some games and have refreshments together.

In this vignette, Dr. Oliver engaged in an adaptive type of curricular planning, one informed by the interests and needs of learners along with the particularities of time. He found new resources by being attentive to those used in and outside of class by learners and allowing learners to be teachers, themselves. Although he may have had a wealth of knowledge regarding acoustic classroom instruments, he continued his personal education regarding new controllers afforded by tablet apps and gave himself time to explore and learn them, even if they seemed strange to him. He found that apps such as Figure, Auxy, and NodeBeat might give the learners in his care access to sounds that, owing to the cost of controllers or instruments or barriers to play, might not otherwise be accessible to them. Such apps provide interesting synthesized timbres, and other apps such as Thumbjam provide synthesized sounds as well as sounds that replicate acoustic instruments.[3]

Although apps such as these offer multiple timbres and means of engagement and expression, they are tools designed with specific ends and for specific users. As such, they involve barriers and ableist assumptions that may be deeply hidden. Without inspection and personal professional development, these "hidden landmines" might go unnoticed and could be potentially damaging to learners and one's relationship with them. Much as a new piece of music for an ensemble requires score study, each new app requires careful study and critique in order to be prepared to share with learners and help them develop their musicianship beyond entry level. NodeBeat, for example, is a very engaging application, but without checking screen reader capability along with the timbral choices and setup of controls, one might either hand a learner a controller that can be used with the expressivity of a toy or provide a disabling experience that may induce mental and social trauma.

ABLEISM AND TABLET USE

Through living, we construct the social world for specific movers doing specific kinds of movements for particular thinkers thinking in particular kinds of ways, for certain accessors accessing the world in certain ways, and so on. In other words, certain ways of being and doing are privileged in social settings and via social creations such as tools (tablets and apps). People may not think about their privilege because often it is not a visible or tangible part of their daily thoughts and actions. This privilege is rooted in what disability scholars and disability rights advocates call "ableism." In this section we attempt to investigate the intersections of disability and tablet technology using ableism as a lens while we encourage readers to take an anti-ableist stance. We do this by means of the development of a critical heuristic for considering tool selection.

Ableism is similar in shape to other "isms" such as racism and sexism because it is used to label disability-based discrimination. Linton (1998) defined ableism as "the idea that a person's abilities or characteristics are determined by disability or that people with disabilities as a group are inferior to nondisabled persons" (p. 9). It arises from the centering of nondisabled mind-bodies, from which comes notions of what it means to be able, productive, normal, and right. Drawing on the work of Campbell (2009), (Rathgeber, 2019) noted that

> ableism is tacitly enacted through many existing cultural practices that separate people based on ableist categories: (a) architectural design that favors certain abilities over others (e.g., the use of stairs rather than ramps) separate people in physical space, and (b) educational practices that organize learners into categories for instruction and access to opportunities based on ability measures (e.g., using literacy measures to sort students into groupings in which some students lose access to other learning opportunities because of extended literacy instruction, or using physical measurements or characteristics to decide which musical instrument a learner is allowed to pursue). (p. 42)

Because of this, it is important that we become conscious of the "contours of ableism" (Campbell, 2009) in order to identify our own privilege. Our privilege can be manifest, even unintentionally, when we apply reasoning that is based in ableism in how we approach and conceive of learner goals and tools for music learning and music making. When we make assumptions regarding those who are different or who have disabilities, our ableist reasoning stands between ourselves and learners, blocking us from fully engaging with them and often silencing their autonomy. One way in which our ableism becomes manifest is via statements regarding universality or accessibility in apps or tablets. Stras (2009) has discussed how disability in music is typically associated with the physical body, the implication being that a person unable to "correctly" play an instrument is unjustly labeled as "disabled" when the socially constructed context is at fault. Goldberg lauds the iPad for inverting this paradigm because it can be modified, enabling music makers as opposed to disabling them by making possible "a highly accessible music-making environment" (Bell, 2015, p. 51). The "barriers" posed by other instruments and music-making contexts can be subverted with the versatile iPad.

All too often, DM/MwD are not consulted during the creation of technology that is then promoted as a universal design device. Although this is an apt marketing tool or selling point, there is no way to create a completely accessible technological device without knowing which person will be using the device. We can, however, come much closer to general accessibility by including persons with disabilities in the design process. Those involved in disability advocacy say, *Nothing about us without us!* (Charlton, 1998; Nielsen, 2012; Rembis, 2017).

HEURISTICS FOR ANTI-ABLEIST TABLET USAGE

In Chapter 4 of this book James Thomas Frankel discusses the model known as Substitution, Augmentation, Modification, and Redefinition, or SAMR (Puentedura, 2013). This model uses the ideas of substitution, augmentation, modification, and redefinition as tools to calibrate the ways technology is changing (and ultimately redefining) the ways in which we engage in musicking in classrooms and ensembles. Devices such as the Soundbeam, Skoog, Push, and O-Generator can assist in accessibility and, therefore, modify or redefine the way DM/MwD interact with music. They are not universal, however, in the way we may think of an adaptation or modification, until we know a student and the technology well enough to meet that person's individual needs. Evaluations are conducted within the SAMR model on an individual basis, and an app or device that may be a modification for one student can realistically be a redefinition of expressivity for another. The Skoog is an example of a device that can have multiple meanings within the SAMR model depending on the specific student and the needs of the moment. By calling a device accessible or promoting it as suitable for DM/

MwD, we may be engaging in othering in which we separate the abled from the disabled, the capable from the seemingly incapable, and the musician from the disabled musician.

Beyond the call for universality in designs, we might wonder if a single tool or design can be fully created with all in mind/body; perhaps it is useful to think about when the specific is preferable to the universal by seeking tools that may address specific needs and desires, rather than tools that purport to be one-size-fits-all. In thinking this way, we can begin from the end, almost, and utilize technology in the way best suited for students and their interests. One set of considerations for teachers to use when choosing which technology will best serve students in a particular instance is posited by Frankel in Chapter 4. They include the following:

1. How the technology supports their curricular goals
2. What specific technology is made available to them and their students by their school
3. How the technology facilitates powerful music-making and music-learning experiences
4. Offering a variety of ways for students of varying skill levels to be creative
5. How easy the software is to learn

If we examine these considerations from an anti-ableist (Rathgeber, 2019) perspective, we can see that these questions may be problematic when teaching learners who access the world differently.

1. Curricular goals vary widely and often are closely defined in the individualized education programs (IEPs) of learners with disabilities in K-12 settings. In addition, there are many learners who access the world differently who do not have IEPs or other paperwork to coordinate their learning needs. Those learners may also need varying curricular goals. Moreover, learners in schools often have their own curricular goals and ways they wish to music. By superimposing our goals, product ends, and performance expectations on them, we may be removing the primary reason why those learners came to be interested in musicking during school.
2. The specific technology available is another item with wide variance; special education funding may be available for learners with IEPs. Grant funding is another possibility, particularly when a teacher is seeking technology for learners who learn in different ways. It can take a great deal of planning and thought to identify and acquire the most accessible technology for learners with disabilities, but it is possible.

3. By defining what powerful music making and music learning experiences are, again, we are deciding for our learners what is important and valued. This can be considered ableist when we apply it to learners with disabilities. By developing relationships with our learners and working with them to choose what and how to proceed in making music with tablets, we multiply the possibility that the powerful experiences we imagined for them also belong to them.
4. This consideration is reminiscent of UDL with regard to providing multiple means of action and expression. When we provide these for our learners, they do not necessarily need to be attached to or as a result of a perceived lack of skill. Rather, some learners are skilled in ways not highlighted by the current classroom environment.
5. The ease of use of hardware or software is variable, and our presumptions about this ease can be considered ableist. When examining or choosing technology, considering barriers to access is an excellent first step. The most important step is to consider the individual student who will be interacting with the technology in your classroom or ensemble.

When reviewing these considerations for selection of technology, it may also be appropriate to examine the 5Ps model (Bell, 2015). This model likewise introduces five factors to think about when choosing technology for student use:

1. Presumptions: The DAW is no exception to the fact that all musical instruments presume that specific conditions must exist in order for them to be played.
2. Privileges: Computer programs privilege some actions over others by making them easier to do.
3. Provisions: When software steers the user toward an action it is masking the fact that other actions are provided that are not as immediately intuitive to the inexperienced user.
4. Protections: These are the capabilities of a program that are hidden from the user.
5. Preventions: Preventions, akin to "anti-affordances" (Norman 2013), are simply actions that the DAW does not permit.

When being actively anti-ableist in choosing technology, consideration of the 5Ps as well as the factors posited by Frankel are important. The presumptions, privileges, provisions, protections, and preventions available within technology can lead us to ask different questions of both the provider and ourselves. Understanding these frameworks can then lead to better-informed discussions with our learners as we work to remove barriers and increase accessibility in a more inclusive manner.

Following examination of the frameworks discussed above, the authors created a guide that may be useful when choosing technology that considers accessibility.

- Identify teacher (curricular) goals considering the individual needs of the student.
- Identify student (curricular) goals considering the interests of the student.
- Identify ableist assumptions about
- the final product
- performance goals
- ease of use
- accessibility and
- student needs and wants.
- Consult learners (see Chapter 1).
- Watch how they process.
- See what steps they take.
- Notice what features they use.
- Explore on your own.
- Look for accessibility features built in, or not, and contact others if needed.
- Seek customizability.
- Look for barriers.
- Evaluate with learners based on goals, learner desires and needs, and practicality.

When we consider the decisions we make on behalf of our learners, it is imperative that we actively include them in our choices. All learners need to be partners in their own education. If not, education becomes something that is done to learners rather than with them. They deserve the respect developed through engaging in choices that also help develop critical technological literacy skills. We sometimes assume that Generation Z is replete with learners who are almost born with technological literacy, so-called digital natives (Prensky, 2001). This is not universally true, and many learners benefit from carefully designed pedagogical discussions regarding the choice, use, and design of devices as well as apps.

When we create our learning and music making spaces, we must begin to include all our learners from the outset. By designing our teaching with universal processes, we invite our learners to join a space that is inherently inclusive. Learners are very aware when teachers are scrambling to change what they have planned, add apps to tablets at the last minute, and move seating to accommodate them. Although that may be what they are accustomed to experiencing, it is certainly not what they deserve. Of course, there will always be situations that require adaptations in the moment. It is in the intentions at the outset that we show our learners that they are all partners in the musicking experience with us and that learners deserve chances to develop self-adaptive strategies and use their personal agency (i.e., develop self-determination; Nota et al., 2007).

Because we do have ableist tendencies, it can be quite useful to examine these tendencies as we create more equitable practices in our classrooms. When we catch ourselves thinking in ableist ways we can use those moments to examine why we thought that way and how those thoughts may be used to strengthen our resolve to scrutinize the things we say and do to improve the experiences of those around us. We must use our ableist ideas to identify possible barriers to inclusive participation for our learners. This practice is not limited to learners who have identified disabilities, IEPs, and 504 plans in K-12 settings and who have obvious differences in accessing our learning spaces. A more universal set of delimitations can be powerful as we consider any possible interference with the process of making music.

In order to do so, it can be helpful to use either the heuristic above or to create your own to meet the individual and collective needs of learners sharing music experiences and spaces with you. Through careful consideration of the needs and desires of the learners, the technology in use, and your own limitations, it is possible to begin a course or project with everyone engaged. Preparation of the space helps build a culture that encourages diversity in musicking and ways to music. By winding back, forward, and sideways our assumptions regarding the processes learners will use to complete a task (Hammel, Hickox, & Hourigan, 2016), we continue to refine the experiences we share with our learners as we progress through our musical learning together.

When we truly create and maintain spaces that are equitable for all and continue to refine them as warranted, the successes of our learners can be in the forefront and can be celebrated. By becoming aware of specific areas of challenge that individual learners may encounter and ameliorating those areas by collaborative problem solving with learners, we begin to see more accurate demonstrations of their musical ideas and skills. We also develop relationships via music that can lead learners to be actively musical throughout their lifetimes.

NOTES

1. This complex formation places both person-first (i.e., musicians with a disability) and identify-first (i.e., disabled musicians) in parallel tension, opening ways in which persons may know and name themselves rather than closing possibilities. The use of this naming convention is further addressed in Rathgeber (2019) and bell and Rathgeber (2020).
2. Providing too many options can be far from freeing for learners.
3. Fuelberth and Todd (2017) note that for "alternative methods of communication, applications like Thumbjam provide opportunities to engage in improvisation. The app can be programmed to play a set of pitches, and learners can participate by improvising either with their singing voices or the app" (p. 42). Randles (2018) and Searle (2018) have also discussed ThumbJam, specifically, in depth in relation to music education and inclusivity.

SUGGESTED APPS

Nodebeat (iOS and Android) https://nodebeat.com
Bloom (iOS) http://www.generativemusic.com/bloom.html
Figure (iOS) https://apps.apple.com/us/app/figure-make-music-beats/id51126 9223?ct=phweb
Auxy mobile studio iOS and Android)- https://auxy.co
Beatbox (Android)https://play.google.com/store/apps/details?id=com.theagoliddell.beatboxapp&hl=en_US
Thumbjam (iOS) https://thumbjam.com
Bebot (iOS and Android) http://www.normalware.com

REFERENCES

Bell, A. P. (2015). Can we afford these affordances? GarageBand and the double-edged sword of the digital audio workstation. *Action, Criticism, and Theory for Music Education, 14*(1), 44–65.

Bell, A. P., & Rathgeber, J. (2020). Can the disabled musician sing? Songs, stories, and identities of disabled persons in/through/with social media. In J. Waldron, S. Horsely, & K. Veblen (Eds.), *Oxford handbook of social media and music learning.* New York: Oxford University Press.

Campbell, F. (2009). *Contours of ableism: The production of disability and abledness.* Berlin, Germany: Springer.

Charlton, J. I. (1998). *Nothing about us without us: Disability oppression and empowerment.* Berkeley, CA: University of California Press.

Cowan, D., & Turner-Smith, A. (1999). The role of assistive technology in alternative models of care for older people. *Royal Commission on Long Term Care, 2*(4), 325–346.

CAST [Center for Applied Special Technology] (2018). Universal design for learning guidelines, version 2.2. Retrieved from http://udlguidelines.cast.org

Endarion (2018, April 8). GarageBand on iOS: Accessibility case study and call to action. [Web log post]. Retrieved from https://www.applevis.com/forum/garageb and-ios-accessibility-case-study-and-call-action

Fuelberth, R., & Todd, C. (2017). "I Dream a World": Inclusivity in Choral Music Education. *Music Educators Journal, 104*(2), 38–44.

Hammel, A. M., Hickox, R. Y., & Hourigan, R. M. (Eds.). (2016). *Winding it back: Teaching to individual differences in music classroom and ensemble settings.* New York, NY: Oxford University Press.

Hammel, A. M., & Hourigan, R. M. (2017). *Teaching music to students with special needs: A label-free approach.* Oxford University Press.

Individuals with Disabilities Education Improvement Act of 2004, Pub. L. 108-446, 118 Stat. 2647. (2004).

Linton, S. (1998). *Claiming disability: Knowledge and identity.* New York, NY: New York University Press.

Nielsen, K. E. (2012). *A disability history of the United States.* Boston, MA: Beacon Press.

Norman, D. (2013). *The design of everyday things* (revised and expanded ed.). New York, NY: Basic Books.

Nota, L., Ferrari, L., Soresi, S., & Wehmeyer, M. (2007). Self-determination, social abilities and the quality of life of people with intellectual disability. *Journal of Intellectual Disability Research, 51*(11), 850–865.

Prensky, M. (2001). Digital natives, digital immigrants. Part 1. *On the horizon,* 9(5), 1–6.

Puentedura, R. (2013). SAMR and TPCK: An introduction. Retrieved from http://www.hippasus.com/rrpweblog/archives/2013/03/28/SAMRandTPCK_AnIntroduction.pdf

Randles, C. (2018). Abigail's story: The perspective of the professor/iPadist/teaching artist. In C. Christophersen & A. Kenny (Eds.), *Musician-teacher collaborations: Altering the chord* (pp. 146–155). New York, NY: Routledge.

Rathgeber, J. (2019). *Troubling disability: Experiences of disability in, through, and around music* (Doctoral dissertation). Arizona State University, Tempe, AZ.

Rembis, M. (2017). 11 disability studies. *The Year's Work in Critical and Cultural Theory, 25*(1), 211–230.

Riley, P. E. (2018). Music composition for iPad performance: Examining perspectives. *Journal of Music, Technology & Education, 11*(2), 183–195.

Ruismäki, H., Juvonen, A., & Lehtonen, K. (2013). The iPad and music in the new learning environment. *The European Journal of Social & Behavioural Sciences,* 6(3), 1084–1096.

Searle, O. I. (2018). Challenging creativity: Inclusive composition. *ÍMPAR: Online Journal for Artistic Research,* 2(1), 19–33.

Stras, L. (2009). Sing a song of difference: Connie Boswell and a discourse of disability in jazz. Popular Music, 28(3), 297–322.

Thompson, J. R., Watts, E. H., Wokcik, B. W., & McCord, K. (2003). The AT matching game (Unpublished manuscript). Illinois State University, Normal, IL.

Watts, E. H., McCord, K., & Blair, D. V. (2016). Assistive technology to support students in accessing the music curriculum. In D. V. Blair & K. A. McCord (Eds.), *Exceptional music pedagogies for children with exceptionalities: International perspectives* (pp. 85–104). New York, NY: Oxford University Press.

LARGE GROUP PERFORMING ENSEMBLES: ARE THEY THE APPROPRIATE PLACEMENT FOR STUDENTS WITH DIFFERENCES AND DISABILITIES?

It is often a surprise to music educators when the statement is made that large group music may not be for all students. Some specific students with differences and disabilities have a very difficult time with large groups and loud music. For those students, a smaller chamber group, sectional setting, or adaptive performance class may be more appropriate. Some parents have difficulty understanding this, and it is possible they are pushing the student to participate in a large ensemble rather than the student initiating participation. Many successful ensemble conductors begin by offering small group music experiences, such as lessons or chamber groups, in place of the large group setting for a student with differences and disabilities. If the student becomes interested (notice we said student), it may be helpful to slowly orient them to the large ensemble to determine whether this is the best current option for the student.

Making an appropriate placement in an ensemble is imperative for the success of a student with differences and disabilities. Select ensembles should be for select students who qualify. Again, this is often a surprise to many when stated directly. The authors are tireless advocates for students with differences and disabilities. However, with advocacy comes responsibility. As explained before, students with differences and disabilities should be placed in a situation that offers the most potential for success (a free appropriate public education in the least restrictive environment). As long as there is a place for all students in a music program (a second or third ensemble, as well as a select ensemble), it is okay for there to be a place for select students who may or may not have differences and disabilities. A teacher would never place a student in trigonometry if they could not understand algebra. Conversely, it is also worth noting that when a student has mastered the content and objectives of that second or third ensemble, he or she should be considered for a more select ensemble based on past performance and current skill level.

Our music classrooms give them this opportunity. When we include all children, no one sits on the outside looking in; rather, all students become partners in the musical journey and active participants in the full experience that music can bring into life.

MEANINGFUL PARTICIPATION

The key to participation by a student with differences and disabilities is that it must be meaningful. Each student should make a contribution to the ensemble. Recently, a university supervisor observed a student teacher in a junior high school band setting. The cooperating teacher had a student with differences and disabilities in his band class. The student was a percussionist who stood in the back corner of the room playing on a practice pad instead of a real drum. However, it was obvious (by the skill level demonstrated as the student played on the practice pad) that he could handle something expressive within the percussion section, such as a cymbal part or a "toy" part. His participation did not contribute musically to the ensemble, and it was obvious that he knew it. This was disheartening to watch. It was just laziness on the part of the conductor.

This highlights the fact that some ensemble conductors assume that students with differences and disabilities cannot contribute. Some conductors may not want to take the time to consider ways a student can contribute to the musical ensemble in a meaningful way, as the teachers in Vignette 7.2 did so well. Many students can be fully functioning members of an ensemble with the assistance of the music educator. This may include rewriting a part to reduce the complexity of their contribution, or limiting the number of pieces students may play in a concert. However, it is important that what they do perform represents an authentic contribution to the ensemble. The adaptations created to help students signal the beginning of their success in an ensemble. Remember, the music educator is the musician and, therefore, the expert in that performing genre. Ensemble conductors (through their own experience) can be very effective in creating adaptations and modifications for music ensembles.

Creating adaptations may also require a music educator to assist a student with practice techniques. For example, Jason has difficulty (because of his disability) with written material. His teachers realized that most of his music was learned by rote. In the beginning a music educator was videotaped playing the student part. The student then practiced with the videotape by copying what the music educator was doing. However, the ability to learn to read music was always a goal. After Jason learned his part aurally, the music was used as a guide for practice. Jason, like many other students, has the ability to learn basic music reading skills. Jason also learned a great deal from repeated viewing of the video. These can be powerful visual reminders of sitting (or standing) posture, breath support, and vowel placement for singers. These kinds of adaptations to practicing strategies are a necessity for early and continued success. As music educators know, students can leave programs out of frustration. Helping a student with differences and disabilities learn to practice can be of vital assistance as they find success in an ensemble situation.

Some students may have physical differences and disabilities that will require some accommodations. Again, be resourceful. Many music dealers are willing to make physical adaptations to instruments. In addition, federal law requires that all rehearsal spaces be accessible. Therefore, school districts should provide these accommodations.

Many ensemble conductors leave students with differences and disabilities out of the assessment process, assuming they are exempt. Holding students with differences and disabilities accountable is part of the teaching and learning process. This is where it is advised that the IEP or 504 Plan be reviewed again. Look at the goals in some of the other subject areas, such as math or English. See what kinds of adaptations or modifications a student receives in other classes. The student may be able to learn the same music and may need more time to complete an assignment. A music educator may need to simplify directions or ask for assistance in administering a singing or playing exam. Review the adaptations and modifications listed earlier in the text. Many of these are appropriate for an ensemble situation as well. Formative assessment strategies may need to include reading or writing help for students. These options will become clear after reading the IEP or 504 document and consulting with a special educator.

Vignette 7.2 Henry, Part 2

When Henry's mother Trisha was first approached by the special education team about course offerings for Henry, she was hesitant yet hopeful about how he could be involved in the band. He has a love for the band and at the ballgames would often look over at the band, mesmerized by the sound and what his classmates were doing. Trisha was uncertain that Henry would be able to participate. He would not be able to blow into an instrument; he couldn't hold an instrument. How could her child belong in band? Yet when the special education teacher suggested that she meet with me about the possibilities, she complied because she wants nothing more than Henry to be a part of activities and student life at school and to find friendship, acceptance, and belonging.

Immediately, I realized that there would certainly be technology available to make Henry a part of our percussion section. I assured Trisha and the team that we could easily find and use these tools so that Henry could join band. We also discussed the ways in which I would work with the family to accommodate at concerts and field trips away from campus. Communication between the special education team and his parents is an important component to his successful involvement in the band program.

Henry is already familiar with using an iPad for his school work, which tracks his eye movements to communicate. I was able to talk with someone about a program to use for band. In this program, a red line appears on the screen, and it is set to various percussion sounds. When Henry moves his head or eyes, the iPad picks up this movement and the sound is then produced electronically. I write out simple rhythmic parts for him to play, and his sound is played through a small speaker system so that he and the audience can hear it.

Henry has been thrilled to be part of the band. The goal of independence for him is being realized through his participation. I will never forget how hesitant Trisha was on the first night of pep band as she brought Henry over to his place to play in the group. I could tell that she wasn't sure she should walk away from him and leave him there, but she knew she must because he was growing up and could do things on his own with his group of friends. He was safe in the environment and cared for. Henry showed great happiness. The smile on his face was so broad as he began to play the percussion sounds. People would walk by and comment to him about how awesome he was at playing in the band, and his smile became even greater. It is impossible to capture on paper the brightness of Henry's eyes as he proudly wears his red bowtie and concert attire at our concerts, looking out at the crowd and seeming to say, "Look at me! I am part of the band! How awesome is this!?"

Henry is included in all aspects of our band program. When we went to the Indianapolis 500 to march in the Parade of Bands before the race, Henry was there right in the thick of the percussion section and playing with the band. Accommodations were made to have his parents along with the group to help him manage the accessible areas provided for those with disabilities. Of course, we had to be sure the school bus we were transported on was wheelchair accessible. These efforts and adjustments to make accommodations are worth the time and energy to ensure that Henry has a place in the band.

I have noticed over the years that it tends to be a characteristic of band students to find their way to the band room at all times of day whether class is meeting or not. It's a hangout and a safe spot for many. Henry is no exception. On several occasions, I have looked out my door to see Henry coming into the room with some of the other band students, smiling and laughing as he heads in to talk and practice. The students in the band program enjoy having Henry in the group and display a natural ability to include him and to help him when needed.

Educational and life goals for Henry are being met through his involvement in the band program at our school. He gains independence and has a sense of pride in the accomplishment of playing an instrument. His peers admire his determined nature and his jovial spirit. The band is better because Henry belongs in the band.

Life is richer and sweeter when we choose a path of inclusion of everyone into the joy of music making.

(Written by Michelle and James Byrn, Caston, Indiana)

ALTERNATIVE MODELS OF PERFORMANCE FOR STUDENTS WITH EXCEPTIONALITIES

Over the past few years there have been a number of models and nonprofit organizations centered around appropriate performance opportunities for students with differences and disabilities. One successful nationwide instrumental performance program is United Sound.[3] Founded by Julie Duty,

United Sound provides "musical performance experiences for students with differences and disabilities through peer mentorship" (http://www.unitedsound.org). United Sound has its own method book series designed specifically for performers with differences and disabilities, and provides after-school instruction where current high school or college band students provide peer instruction for students with differences and disabilities.

The second model of performance instruction is in the choral area. Partner choirs are choral groups that partner a student with disabilities with a peer in his or her school choral program. An example of this is the All Access Choir in Downers Grove, Illinois (Downers Grove North High School). A YouTube channel has been established with interviews and highlights of how this ensemble was established and how it exists within the framework of a public high school.[4] The good news about new models of instruction is that there is more opportunity for inclusion.

CONCLUSION

The suggestions provided in this chapter are designed to help ensemble conductors prepare to teach music to students with differences and disabilities. This process challenges music educators to participate in the special education system and to be resourceful in learning about their students with differences and disabilities from special educators, documents, and parents. It is hoped that the suggestions mentioned will help music educators understand performers with differences and disabilities and to be more confident in their attempt to provide a worthwhile performing experience for all students.

DISCUSSION QUESTIONS

1. How would you address the inclusion of students with differences and disabilities in your choral ensemble when recruiting students at a local elementary school? What strategies can you employ that will ensure every student knows they are welcome to join your program? How can those strategies be demonstrated during your recruiting performance?
2. Is there a way to appropriately include a student who struggles with loud sounds and large groups of students in a performing ensemble? Please list some strategies and rationale for discussion.
3. Would one of the alternative models for performance be a possibility in your school (or former school)?
4. What are three important strategies to remember when including a student with differences and disabilities in an instrumental ensemble setting?

Chapter 8

Teaching Music to Students Who Are Intellectually Gifted

CHAPTER OVERVIEW

- Intellectual Giftedness in the Music Classroom
- Understanding the Spectrum of Differences and Disabilities (Gifted and Talented)
- A Brief Background of How Students Are Identified as "Gifted"
- The Current Identification Process
- Individual IQ Testing and Other Identification Practices
- Categories of Giftedness
  - Highly/Profoundly Gifted
- A Discussion of Variant Needs and Services Provided to Students with Differences and Disabilities
- Elitism Versus Egalitarianism
- Characteristics of Students Who Are Gifted
  - Behavior
  - Learning
  - Creativity
  - Emotion
  - General Intellectual Ability
  - Specific Academic Aptitude
- Instructional Delivery/Pacing/Process/Modifications
  - Grouping Options
- Teacher Characteristics That Are Successful When Teaching Students Who Are Gifted
- Twice Exceptional
  - Including a reprint of: Hammel, A. M. (2016). Twice exceptional. In D. V. Blair & K. A. McCord (Eds.), *Exceptional music pedagogy for children with exceptionalities: International perspective*, 16–38. Oxford University Press.
- Putting It All Together
- Conclusion
- Discussion Questions

Teaching Music to Students with Differences and Disabilities. Third Edition. Alice M. Hammel and Ryan M. Hourigan, Oxford University Press. © Oxford University Press 2025. DOI: 10.1093/9780197689356.003.0008

INTELLECTUAL GIFTEDNESS IN THE MUSIC CLASSROOM

There are students like Hannah (Vignette 8.1) in our public schools. They are inquisitive, questioning, and exceptionally interested, and have a distinct look about them as they learn new information. They are the students who learn difficult concepts instantly and completely. They are the students who can comprehend an entire scope and sequence of a topic, seemingly in an instant. They are also at great risk in our classrooms, which are often designed for the average student and to offer accommodations for students with other types of differences and disabilities. The differences and disabilities of students who are intellectually gifted are often delayed, ignored, and denied. For these students, the promise of tomorrow and a teacher who will finally challenge them begins to fade. This reality often sets in during the late elementary and middle school years.

UNDERSTANDING THE SPECTRUM OF DIFFERENCES AND DISABILITIES (GIFTED AND TALENTED)

While the philosophy of this text has placed importance on encouraging "label-free learning" for students with differences and disabilities, there are times when a distinction is necessary. One of these distinctions is in the cognitive domain. Most often, music educators adapt teaching to accommodate students who learn at a slower rate; however, it is also essential to consider adapting our teaching for those students who learn faster than their peers. These students are often identified as being "gifted." The philosophical premise that students learn best and teachers are most prepared when a label-free environment is established remains a hallmark of this book. We consider the decision to briefly digress as we discuss students who are gifted as necessary to understanding the specific differences and disabilities of students whose cognition capabilities are vastly increased. At the end of the chapter, we will return to our label-free approach as we summarize the information gleaned from this area of students with differences and disabilities.

A BRIEF BACKGROUND OF HOW STUDENTS ARE IDENTIFIED AS "GIFTED"

The identification of students who are gifted has had a long and circuitous journey. Alfred Binet was the first to develop a measure for judgment of mental age to screen and provide educational barriers for children not considered intelligent enough for a formal education (Binet, 1894). He designed his intelligence test for these purposes, yet he did consider intelligence to be

Vignette 8.1 Hannah in Band

11-year-old Hannah was very excited when her mother told her that the band director at Blue Middle School had agreed to work with her after school on Wednesday. Hannah had begun middle school the month before and had been waiting to play her flute for the band director since the orientation night when she learned that the school had three bands (beginning, intermediate, and advanced). She had practiced very hard and was hoping to be told she was good enough to be placed in the advanced band, even though she was only in sixth grade. She wasn't able to be in the band class during school because she had been promoted to eighth grade academic work and was taking three high school credits this year. There was no room for band in her schedule.

On the day of the advanced band audition, Hannah practically ran to the band room with her flute in her hand after school. The band director had said she would meet with her and a few other students who wanted to audition. They all sat nervously on the front row waiting for Ms. Harvey to enter. While waiting, Hannah looked at all the shiny trophies that sat on shelves around the room. She counted them. There were twenty-seven in all. She thought they looked beautiful and really liked the shiny gold and other metal that designated the category of awards.

Finally, Ms. Harvey was ready to hear the students play. Hannah waited patiently while the other students played some scales and their chromatic scale for the band director. She knew they played pretty well, and she also knew she was better. When Ms. Harvey asked her to play, Hannah played the most difficult scales she knew, as many octaves as the fingering charts had shown in her flute book. She also played her chromatic scale very, very fast. The band director didn't seem to know what else to say to her except to tell her she did well. Ms. Harvey had never heard a sixth-grade student play a three-octave chromatic scale with sixteenth notes at MM = 120. That was a great performance level for a high school student. She was a little relieved that Hannah would not be in the band on a regular basis because she wasn't sure how she would be able to teach her much, let alone challenge her. Ms. Harvey then began working with the other students and told them that they all played well enough to play in the advanced band. Hannah looked at the clock and saw that she still had 30 minutes until her mom would be there to pick her up. She looked at the trophies again and suddenly realized that maybe they weren't metal at all. They might be made of plastic instead. Then, she began to count the pillars on them and created algebraic equations based on color, size, and shape. It would be a long 30 minutes.

educable and stated that intelligence can be improved and enhanced over time (Walker, 1991).

Lewis Terman standardized Binet's test at Stanford University. It then became known as the Stanford-Binet Intelligence Scale (Winner, 1996). Through the standardization process, Terman determined that intelligence is fixed and will not change over time (Terman, 1925). He was the first person to use the term *gifted* (Terman & Oden, 1959; Walker, 1991). Terman defined giftedness as the top 1% level in general intelligence ability, as measured by the Stanford-Binet Intelligence Scale or a comparable instrument (Terman & Oden, 1947).

Renzulli (1977) noted that superior intellectual ability alone does not necessarily identify a student with extraordinary capabilities. He posited that students who demonstrate above-average intellect, high task-commitment, and high creativity skills create the profile of a gifted student. Renzulli's model of giftedness has been widely used to identify students who may not otherwise receive gifted services (Webb, Meckstroth, & Tolan, 1994). He also distinguished two types of giftedness, termed *schoolhouse giftedness* and *creative-productive giftedness*. Renzulli spent much of his career encouraging schools to include more creative and artistic opportunities for students who were gifted (Renzulli, 1986).

THE CURRENT IDENTIFICATION PROCESS

Many students in elementary schools are given group IQ tests to identify those students who may be eligible for gifted education services. These tests are not as accurate as small group or private testing, particularly when identifying younger-age elementary students (Walker, 1991). School systems set their own benchmarks for IQ testing and services. Generally, the baseline IQ range for services is between 125 and 145. Some research has shown that students from diverse backgrounds and socioeconomic levels are disproportionately absent from gifted programs, particularly those programs that use group IQ testing as the primary assessment vehicle for acceptance (Webb et al., 1994; Winner, 1996).

Recently, schools have begun using portfolios, interviews with teachers and parents, and other authentic measures to identify intellectually gifted students who may not score in that range through an IQ test alone. These tests include some nonverbal testing that serves students who do not appear gifted according to their expressive language skills but who possess a high intelligence level. Through these multiple means of identification, the inclusion of students from diverse socioeconomic backgrounds has increased in gifted education programs. While the philosophy of this text has placed importance on encouraging "label-free learning" for students with differences and disabilities, there are times where a label can be helpful.

INDIVIDUAL IQ TESTING AND OTHER IDENTIFICATION PRACTICES

Individual IQ testing is much more expensive and time-consuming than group IQ testing. It is, however, much more accurate (Silverman, 1993). Some argue that IQ testing only measures academic aptitude within the dominant culture rather than a pure measure of intelligence (Walker, 1991). Again, this is why the inclusion of other measures has become increasingly important.

Additionally, gifted students are sometimes identified through Standard Achievement Testing (academic), teacher nominations, and parent nominations (VanTassel-Baska, 1998). In addition, teacher and parent (Kerr, 1994) input is seen as crucial, as their anecdotal information can be very accurate and sometimes augments data received through standard IQ testing (Winner, 1996). Creativity testing is also sometimes used to identify students with strong divergent thinking skills. Other ancillary identification methods include student-derived products and performances, the top percentile of honor roll listings, individual pupil motivation for learning, and peer nomination (Walker, 1991; Webb et al., 1994).

CATEGORIES OF GIFTEDNESS

Highly/Profoundly Gifted

Hollingsworth (1931) stated the following regarding students who are gifted:

> Where the gifted child drifts in the school unrecognized, held to the lockstep which is determined by the capacities of the average, he has little to do. He receives daily practice in habits of idleness and daydreaming. His abilities are never genuinely challenged, and the situation is contrived to build in him expectations of an effortless existence. Children up to about 140 IQ tolerate the ordinary school routine quite well, being usually a little young for the grade through an extra promotion or two, and achieving excellent marks without serious effort. But above this status, children become increasingly bored with school work, if kept in or nearly in the lockstep. Children at or above 180 IQ, for instance, are likely to regard school with indifference, or with positive distaste, for they find nothing to do there. (Winner, 1996, p. 401)

Box 8.1 Giftedness as measured by IQ Scores

Mildly (or basically) gifted	115-129
Moderately gifted	130-144
Highly gifted	145-159
Exceptionally gifted	160-179
Profoundly gifted	180+

Students who are highly gifted may find themselves waiting after assignments are completed for as much as 50% of their school day, and students who are profoundly gifted may "waste" 75% of their school day (Webb et al., 1994). Box 8.1 delineates the categories of giftedness as determined by IQ. These designations are often included in literature regarding students who are intellectually gifted.

A DISCUSSION OF VARIANT NEEDS AND SERVICES PROVIDED TO STUDENTS WITH DIFFERENCES AND DISABILITIES

When tested, most of the general population falls within one standard deviation of the norm (IQ 85-115). Figure 8.1 shows the standard deviation model as applied to IQ scores. Much of the energy, time, resources, and discussion regarding students with differences and disabilities focuses on students who perhaps have IQs less than 85. The lowest 2% to 3% of students, when viewed according to IQ scores, receive the bulk of services, personnel, and funding to facilitate their education (Winner, 1996). Students with IQs ranging in the top 2% to 3% often experience very little in the way of services and supplementary aides (Winner, 1996).

Students who have IQs that fall in the bottom two standard deviations are enrolled in special education programs and receive services, often extensive services. Students who possess IQs that fall in the top two standard deviations are often not provided services at all (VanTassel-Baska, 1998). If services are provided for students who are gifted, they are often not individualized to differentiate their respective level of giftedness (gifted, moderately gifted, highly gifted, profoundly gifted; Winner, 1996). Often, students with IQs of 130 are offered the same level of services as students with IQs of 180 (VanTassel-Baska, 1998). If we look at the other end of the bell curve, we see that students with IQs of 70 receive a vastly different educational experience than students with IQs of 20 (Winner, 1996).

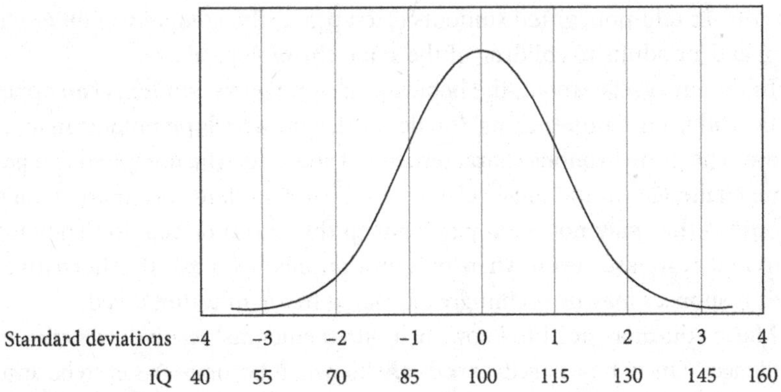

Figure 8.1. Sample universal bell curve.

ELITISM VERSUS EGALITARIANISM

The discussion of elitism versus egalitarianism is one often repeated when discussing appropriate services for students who are gifted. The concept that giftedness is an elitist value is as absurd as proposing that teaching students with intellectual disabilities is not worth serious discussion within the educational community. Some gifted education experts call for the same level of individualized education and changes in the least restrictive environment (LRE) for students who test at three and four standard deviations above the norm as for those who test at three and four standard deviations below the norm (VanTassel-Baska, 1998). It is unlikely that a student with an IQ of 50 would be in an inclusion classroom with no services or accommodations. A student with an IQ of 150, however, is often in an inclusion situation with no services or accommodations. Their IQs are equally different from those students who are considered average (IQ 100); however, the attention paid to their educational needs is vastly unequal (Silverman, 1993). Webb et al. (1994) explain: "Gifted children are not simply decorated normal children—they are, indeed, fundamentally different. A child with IQ 145 is as different from the normal IQ of 100 as the child of IQ 55" (p. 31).

CHARACTERISTICS OF STUDENTS WHO ARE GIFTED

Behavior

Students who are gifted possess some similar behavior traits. For example, they are very active, often questioning, and continue to question all day while demanding answers. This active questioning can exhaust teachers and parents. In addition, gifted students often prefer the company of older children and/or adults to children of the same chronological age.

In the music classroom, the behavior of some gifted students can appear to be rude, attention-seeking (or defiant), and developmentally inappropriate. The asynchronous characteristics of students who are gifted can pose some challenges in the music classroom. Gifted students often ask detailed questions that may not seem pertinent to the lesson or activity. They may blurt out responses even when no question has been asked. Alternatively, their responses may be seemingly unrelated to the question asked.

Music educators need to know their gifted students' relative strengths and challenges. Once these specific needs are known, it becomes easier to be aware of possible behavioral triggers for a specific student and ways to lessen the effect these behaviors may have on other students in music. It is helpful for those who teach gifted students either to be ready with responses to questions and concerns posed by a student or to set an appropriate time to work with these students in an individual or small group setting. Developing meaningful relationships with students who are gifted can significantly enhance the teaching and learning relationship with individual students and preserve class and rehearsal time for the musical goals necessary for the development of all students.

Learning

Students who are gifted often possess an extreme attention span when engaged in activities that interest them. They learn material faster and earlier and remember information without review. They can comprehend and manipulate concepts that are too abstract and complicated for others the same age. They are passionate about one or more areas of interest or study and spend a great deal of time working and studying in their area of interest. They multitask and multi-process at a greater rate than other students (Sousa, 2003; Winebrenner, 2001).

Observing a highly gifted student encounter a new intellectual challenge in the music classroom can be fascinating and slightly disconcerting. The amount of time necessary for mastery of a concept is often a fraction of the time needed for students who are not gifted. Moreover, once a gifted student has learned the concept, the rest of the time needed by others in the music classroom to absorb, apply, and master is often wasted for this student.

For example, the amount of time a gifted student needs to memorize the names of the lines and spaces on the treble clef may be minuscule. If this lesson is being taught with a visual focus on a staff at the front of the classroom, students who are gifted will begin to tune out the lesson shortly after learning the concept. To continue engaging gifted students, new challenges will be posed (e.g., ledger lines, bass clef notes, or alto and tenor clef). Using learning centers, or small group work, can greatly increase the amount of class time that is actually useful for students who are gifted.

Differentiating educational experiences in the music classroom can benefit all learners. When planning lessons, activities, and rehearsals, considering the variant needs of students with differences and disabilities is essential. Many music educators who are successful in differentiating instruction write essential questions that are appropriate for various levels of understanding and comprehension. By preparing these questions and experiences in advance, the process of truly teaching to the variant needs of all students in the classroom can begin.

Creativity

Students who are gifted have an almost limitless capacity for creativity in their area of giftedness. They often enjoy discovery and can create many items or products as a result of their creative interests. They can easily generate and develop ideas, are able to elaborate and add detail to their creations, and often challenge others to practice divergent thinking skills (Winebrenner, 2001).

Music educators who teach gifted students are sometimes challenged by the depth of creativity and divergent thinking presented by students during instruction. Providing regular opportunities for students who are gifted to develop these strengths may lead to benefits for all students in the music classroom. These opportunities can be created in the areas of composition, improvisation, performance, recording and technical creativity, literary arts, and the relationships between music and other art forms.

An example of an extension opportunity for students who are gifted is to ask them to research repertoire chosen for a concert. Gifted students may enjoy creating audio/video files of compositions, performances, or rehearsals. The possibilities are as divergent as the creativity of the students. A caveat to offer is for the music educator to ensure that gifted students are invested and interested in these additional opportunities. Often teachers assume that a greater workload equals a challenge for gifted students. More work does not necessarily mean a student is learning or is engaged. Students who are gifted can begin to feel their giftedness is a punishment if they are consistently asked or required to complete a greater quantity of work. Choosing quality opportunities that match the interest of students will genuinely be of benefit to students who are gifted.

Emotion

Hollingsworth (1975) stated, "To have the intelligence of an adult and the emotions of a child combined in a childish body is to encounter certain difficulties" (p. 21). Students who are gifted are, by nature, asynchronous in their development. For example, a student may have a chronological age of

10 and the mental age of 15. This can cause great difficulty when processing information and overcoming emotional situations. Hallmarks of the emotional lives of students who are gifted include asynchronous development; perfectionism, which can lead to a lack of risk-taking; imposter syndrome; extreme frustration when work is incorrect or not perfect; and extremes in emotions and reactions to events and situations. These students may also have difficulty winding down for the day and/or sleeping at night.

Many gifted students experience intense perfectionism along with the imposter syndrome daily, and the possibility of failure can lead to some unusual and distracting emotional situations. Students who are gifted have often been told from a very young age that they are smart or geniuses. These laudatory comments can become a heavy mantle for gifted students as they may begin to define their self-worth through their successes and the number of intellectual feats they accomplish.

For some gifted students, the music classroom may pose the first real challenge they have experienced. Music performance requires a unique set of skills; these new skills and expectations may challenge an intellectually gifted student. Playing a musical instrument can be difficult, and the mastery of an instrument does not occur in a short amount of time. For students unaccustomed to this process, extreme frustration, inordinate feelings of inadequacy, and a palpable fear of being discovered as not being as gifted as the school community had assumed are genuine concerns.

Being aware of intellectually gifted students in the music classroom, adjusting vocabulary, and using positive reinforcement with students for demonstration of musical skills can lead to increased well-being and acceptance for all students. Students who are gifted may need to be reminded frequently that musical performance skills take years to master and that everyone improves at his or her own rate. In addition, they may not understand that while technical skills may be difficult now, it does not mean they have no potential for music success. Because of the possibilities of real challenges, the music classroom can be a powerful and affirming experience for students who are gifted. Being introduced to a process that is new and that possibly may require a new set of strategies for success can truly change the way a student who is gifted views others around him or her and the challenges they face.

General Intellectual Ability

Students who are globally gifted often display the following characteristics at a young age: excellent attention and recognition memory, preference for novelty, precocious physical development, complex oral language, hypersensitivity and possible overreaction to stimuli and events, an ability to learn with minimal instruction, extreme curiosity, persistence and concentration, an abundance of energy, metacognitive awareness, and obsessive interests (Winner, 1996).

When most teachers think of students who are gifted, students who are globally gifted come to mind. Students who are globally gifted are gifted in almost every area of intellectual pursuit. They will have relative strengths and areas of challenge, but also consistently demonstrate their inherent characteristics in all academic areas. These students are not necessarily gifted in the area of music, yet their skills from other intellectual pursuits often provide an excellent level of basic preparation for the academic skills required for success in the music classroom.

The ability of students who are globally gifted to comprehend complicated and multi-step processes in music is very high. They learn quickly and completely. They are insatiably curious about everything, and using this curiosity and ability to become hyper-focused in an area of interest can allow a music educator the opportunity to create a meaningful and enduring set of experiences for a student who is gifted. Finding the access point for a student who is gifted (an area of interest that intersects with music) is an excellent starting place for these experiential pursuits.

Specific Academic Aptitude

Students who demonstrate precociousness in a single area (verbal, mathematical, etc.) are not always globally gifted. This sometimes leads to frustration on behalf of both teachers and students because the gifts a student displays in one area may not generalize to a holistically gifted student (Winner, 1996). It can be difficult for a student who is extraordinarily gifted in one academic area to understand that he or she is not necessarily as gifted in all areas.

Strategies for students who are gifted in one academic area are similar to those discussed previously regarding students who are globally gifted. It is helpful to introduce an expanded or augmented project or curriculum using the area of giftedness possessed by the student. These experiences, again, can be very meaningful for students who are often not challenged by the general curricula in place in public schools.

INSTRUCTIONAL DELIVERY/PACING/PROCESS/MODIFICATIONS

Students who are gifted may need changes in the way their instruction is presented and paced. It is possible that some students who are gifted may be able to learn without intense modifications in the general education classroom. For students who are highly or profoundly gifted, a change in placement (LRE) may be necessary. These placement options are discussed next. There are also several options in the general classroom for enhancing the teaching and learning environment for students who are gifted.

Grouping Options

There are several options for grouping students who are gifted. They include within-class grouping, gifted pull-out (once or twice a week), enrichment classes, resource room, and mentoring (Winner, 1996). Other options include separate classes (self-contained gifted class, advanced placement classes), separate programs within schools (International Baccalaureate, gifted programs), separate schools (magnet), acceleration (by subject or by grade), "testing out," concurrent high school/college enrollment, independent study, and compacting (by subject or by grade). In the music classroom and ensemble setting, students who are gifted can benefit from occasional homogenous grouping strategies. These strategies can include grouping for chamber music, grouping by centers, whole-class grouping (sometimes already in place in center-based elementary schools for students who are gifted), and grouping by music theory achievement levels.

Some research has shown that students who perform at an average to below-average level in the inclusion classroom benefit more from a heterogeneous classroom. For gifted students, however, the opposite is true. They benefit more from homogeneous grouping with other students who are gifted (Winebrenner, 2001). A few guidelines for working with students who are gifted include less emphasis on drills and repetition in the classroom. Furthermore, students who are gifted respond to increased opportunities to demonstrate mastery and to differentiation strategies that include adaptations to content, process, product, environment, and assessment (Winebrenner, 2001). Using grouping strategies in the music classroom will benefit the academic enrichment of students who are gifted.

TEACHER CHARACTERISTICS THAT ARE SUCCESSFUL WHEN TEACHING STUDENTS WHO ARE GIFTED

Music educators who work with students who are gifted will be more successful if they possess a specific set of behaviors and dispositions. Some of these characteristics are inherent, and some are learned and strengthened through experience and purposeful planning. These characteristics are delineated next, and while they are specified for teachers who work with students who are gifted, many are also beneficial for all teachers.

Walker (1991) recommends the following characteristics:

- Understand and respect the student who is gifted.
- Encourage while challenging students to achieve.
- Provide depth in assignments.
- Include specific comments on student work to note level of achievement.
- Be a responsible, efficient, gifted, loving, and caring teacher.

Webb et al. (1994) make the following suggestions to teachers of students who are gifted:

- Communicate that the student's beliefs, feelings, and behaviors are important.
- Facilitate identification, expression, and acceptance of feelings.
- Convey understanding and acceptance of their feelings.
- Make it clear that you value the whole student rather than just abilities and achievements.
- Express that you value the uniqueness of the student.
- Encourage pursuit of the student's special interests.
- Create time to share with the student.
- Encourage students for attempts rather than merely successes.
- Emphasize the value of productive cooperation and model these traits for students.

Winebrenner (2001) shares these suggestions for teachers:

- Have enthusiasm for teaching and the subject being taught.
- Be a lifelong learner.
- Be flexible in your teaching style.
- Hone your listening and inquiry strengths.
- Increase your knowledge of the characteristics of students who are gifted.
- Possess an interest in adapting and accommodating students who are gifted.
- Have a strong sense of humor.
- Demonstrate excellent organization and time management skills.
- Be an effective advocate for students.

VanTassel-Baska (1998) found the following characteristics to be beneficial for teachers when working with students who are gifted:

- Maturity and experience; self-confidence
- High intelligence
- Non-academic interests that are intellectual in nature

- High achievement needs; desire for intellectual growth
- Favorable attitude toward gifted students
- Systemic, imaginative, flexible, and creative in attitudes and responses
- Sense of humor
- Willingness to be a "facilitator" rather than a "director" of learning
- Capacity for hard work; willingness to devote extra time and effort to teaching
- Wide background of general knowledge; specific areas of expertise (particularly secondary teachers)
- Belief in understanding of individual differences

TWICE EXCEPTIONAL

Students who are designated as "twice exceptional" are intellectually gifted and also possess a special need that requires an Individualized Education Program (IEP) or 504 Plan for appropriate inclusion in public school classrooms. These "unevenly gifted" (Winner, 1996) students are sometimes misdiagnosed or undiagnosed as their strengths and areas of challenge sometimes mask each other. Until recently, the "global giftedness" premise was the accepted norm, and many students who had disabilities and were gifted were only recognized for their giftedness. This sometimes led to uneven learning needs that were labeled underachievement, laziness, or a behavior disorder. Students who are twice exceptional also are often adept at hiding their disabilities by utilizing their giftedness and strengths as often as possible (Winner, 1996).

As seen in Vignette 8.2, it is also possible that students can have an unidentified disability that is masking their giftedness. In these cases, some students are never appropriately identified as "twice exceptional" because their disability becomes the focus of instructional interventions and amelioration efforts (Winebrenner, 2001). If a student is undiagnosed or misdiagnosed (e.g., attention deficit/hyperactivity disorder rather than gifted), he or she can be labeled as having behavior issues and may feel increasingly isolated and different from peers. These feelings can lead to depression and thoughts of suicide (Webb et al., 1994). Moreover, the asynchronous development often seen in students who are gifted is multiplied in students who are twice exceptional (Kay, 2000). What follows is a chapter authored by Alice M. Hammel that was published by Oxford University Press in 2016.

Vignette 8.2 District Band Auditions

David was excited to have auditioned well enough to play in District Band as a ninth-grade student. Being second chair trombone in ninth grade was quite an achievement. He was also happy to be able to miss a day of school to rehearse as part of the weekend band event. He was definitely eager to be away from the teachers at school who were constantly telling him to pay attention and that he was not performing up to his potential. How boring! Well, those teachers would just have to find someone else to pick on today.

On the way to the event, David had a great time talking to the other students. They were polite to him; however, it was clear to everyone but David that he was talking too much and that his impulsiveness was intruding on the personal space and conversations of others. The band director had told the other students to be nice to David and that the bus ride was only 45 minutes long.

Once David arrived at the site of the rehearsals, he ran through the auditorium to see his friends from other schools. He tripped over some backpacks, spilled a set of folders onto the ground, and ended up rolling down the aisle toward the stage. The conductor learned his name very early in the rehearsals and knew his band director and school name within the first hour.

David's excitement was soon lessened as he settled into the long (excruciatingly long to him) two days of rehearsals. He then realized that this event was going to be the same as many others he had experienced. His intellectual abilities and talents often earned him honors and experiences that his brain and body were not able to handle. How embarrassing to have both the band director and District Band conductor talk to his mom about his behavior ("hyperactive" and "impulsive" were the words they used) at the end of the day. Suddenly, David hated band and was ready to quit. He knew he wouldn't be allowed to quit because he had already quit soccer, baseball, violin, and the chess team. Maybe he could fake sick tomorrow morning to get out of his second day of District Band.

Questions for Consideration:

1. How can a director or music teacher prepare a student who is "twice exceptional" for an experience that may be difficult? What strategies can be put in place to increase the possibility that this will be a positive experience?

(continued)

Vignette 8.2 Continued

2. How can the five areas highlighted in this book (cognition, communication, sensory, behavioral/emotional, and physical) be addressed in these situations?
3. When is it appropriate for a music educator to intervene in a situation like this to protect a student from embarrassment, a negative experience, or his own impulsiveness?
4. What are the signs that a student is frustrated or struggling in an honor ensemble situation?

Twice Exceptional

Alice M. Hammel

From Blair, D. V., McCord, K. A. (2016). *Exceptional music pedagogy for children with exceptionalities: International perspectives.* New York: Oxford University Press.

She was 6 weeks old as I held her and she instinctively grasped my finger with her hand.

I looked at her beautiful face and suddenly had a deep feeling that this child was going to need more and better from me than I ever thought I could provide.

Hollie

When our first daughter was born, we thought the "what your baby will do this month" books were extraordinarily cautious with skills they predicted she would display each month. Her older sister, Hannah,[1] easily breezed past each expectation and was months ahead of the expected benchmarks by the time she was 4 months old. Because of this experience, we were unprepared for the struggle we witnessed as our younger daughter worked herself to exhaustion to achieve each milestone. We began reading the books again with new eyes and took note of each small achievement made, almost always after great energy and practice had enervated her in the process. It was at Hollie's 8-month well-baby appointment that I first voiced our concerns and requested a referral to a developmental pediatrician.

After months of providing data and documentation and delivering increasingly distressed pleas for assistance, we were finally referred to a developmental pediatrician and placed on the waiting list for an appointment. Hollie was 13 months old when we began the rounds of developmental and medical testing to discern the cause of the developmental delays my daughter was experiencing. Two months later, we received a diagnosis of pervasive developmental disorder (PDD) and began occupational, speech, and sensory integration therapies. It was then that the work really started.

Our lives began to revolve around regular trips to the children's hospital for therapy. Therapists also visited our home each week to monitor her progress. I knew we were racing against time to make gains because each month of delays let the sand sift further underneath Hollie's developmental feet. It was during this time that we began to notice her uncanny sense of timing and comedy as she drew everyone who knew her into her world with her bright eyes and silly faces. These abilities confused doctors and therapists, who were looking for a simple diagnosis; our daughter was anything but simple.

In preschool, Hollie loved being a part of the classroom and enjoyed silly songs and games, as well as arts and crafts projects. We were concerned, however, when, at age 4, Hollie brought home a painting with her friend Emily's name on it insisting she had drawn it. Hollie finally admitted switching pictures because "Emily was a good drawer"—she wanted me to be proud of the drawings that came home from preschool. This began our introduction into the world of a child who is twice exceptional.

Introduction

This chapter will focus on the needs of students who are intellectually or musically gifted and present unique challenges that must be met within the music classroom. Teacher qualities necessary for successful educational experiences, as well as specific needs and issues that can arise when teaching students who are twice exceptional, will be addressed. Research and best practice will be framed within the narrative of a family experiencing the daily challenges posed by a child who is intellectually and musically gifted and who has other differences and disabilities.

Intellectual Giftedness

Testing to determine speed of cognition and processing began in the late 1800s. Alfred Binet (1894) designed a test to determine whether children were considered educable. Children who did not score well were then considered unsuitable for formal education. Lewis Terman standardized the intelligence test created by Binet that became known as the Stanford-Binet Intelligence Scale (Winner, 1996). Through this process, Terman determined that intelligence is fixed, and he defined intellectual giftedness as the top 1% of scores on the Stanford-Binet scale (Terman Oden, 1947).

In the past, schools utilized an IQ testing process that included group and/or individual testing of students in schools with results often used to determine the children eligible for gifted programs in schools. Most schools established the initial level of giftedness as those students with an IQ of at least 125; however, students from diverse backgrounds traditionally scored lower on these tests. As a result, tests of nonverbal language ability began to be used in addition to IQ testing to identify students who may have otherwise gone unnoticed (Webb, Meckstroth, & Tolan, 1994).

Some schools request individual testing for students. This can be time-consuming and expensive; however, it is often more accurate than group testing (Winner, 1996) at finding a precise level of giftedness. The use of augmented teacher narratives, standard achievement testing scores, and products created by a child are now utilized (Walker, 1991). Intellectual giftedness, when thinking in quantitative terms, occurs according to the universal bell curve (Figure 8.1 above).

Most students in school, as with most of the general population, demonstrate IQs between 85 and 115, whereas those most often identified as having intellectual giftedness possess an IQ between 125 and 200 (Hollingsworth, 1975). Issues sometimes arise when students who are exceptionally or profoundly gifted are found within an inclusive population of students (Box 8.1 above). These can include underperformance, a need for perfection, behavioral issues, and a feeling of disrespect by these students because their intellectual needs are not being met. While school systems use a multiple-method approach to finding students in need of gifted services, the presence of giftedness in the general population does fall along a universal curve.

Some researchers have determined that students with exceptionally high IQs may "waste" most of their time in school because they have already learned the material being taught (Hollingsworth, 1975; Silverman, 1993; Winner, 1996). When students who have IQs of 120 are offered the same educational differentiation as students who have IQs of 160, we should look to the other side of the bell curve and consider the commensurate differentiation for students who have IQs of 40 to 80 (VanTassel-Baska, 1998).

Definitions and common practices regarding the identification of students who are gifted have varied. For example, the Marland Report (Marland, 1971/1972) defines students who are gifted as those who score in the 95th percentile or above on an IQ test or demonstrate achievement or potential for achievement in one or more of these areas:

- General intellectual ability
- Specific academic aptitude
- Creative or productive thinking
- Leadership ability
- Visual and performing arts
- Psychomotor ability.

Their recommendation was that students be evaluated according to objective measures and professional evaluation. A few years later, Renzulli (1977) posited a theory of giftedness. His markers for giftedness include above-average ability, creativity, and task commitment. This theory began to be applied in identification procedures in some school systems and is still highly regarded by some. Others have posited further conceptions regarding giftedness, and scholars in the field are still somewhat in disagreement on the matter.

Some in the field recommend that students be identified through a demonstration of exceptional performance or the potential for exceptional performance. Others contend that truly intellectually gifted students often refuse to display their true ability in an environment that is not intellectually or creatively stimulating (Tolan, 1999). Through use of the Torrence Tests of Creative Thinking and the Structure of Intellect Learning Abilities Tests, students have been identified as creatively talented by school systems. These tests, however, have not been proven to show high correlation with subsequent creative production by students (Silverman, 2013).

The widespread use of various markers to identify students who are intellectually gifted began in the 1990s. This shift led to the inclusion of some or all of the following indicators by some school systems when identifying students who are gifted (Silverman, 2013):

- Top 10% of the school population
- Domain-specific giftedness
- Achievement or the potential for achievement
- Student motivation displayed
- External manifestations of giftedness apparent
- Observable in adolescents and/or adults
- IQ scores used as partial evidence of giftedness.

This current thinking is disputed somewhat by another group of researchers and thinkers in the field of giftedness who counter that children who are intellectually gifted are inherently different and can be identified through that giftedness (Gallagher, 2000):

- Can be identified through developmental differences in abstract reasoning, emotional sensitivity, and intensity
- Can be observed in very young children
- Can be documented on measures of IQ
- Is lifelong
- Encompasses 2% to 3% of the population
- Creates qualitative different life experiences
- Leads to a set of unique life situations
- Requires early intervention and accommodation.

In my experience with my daughter and with other intellectually gifted children, the Gallagher premise has been the most useful.

Twice Exceptional

It can be difficult to identify students who have learning differences and are intellectually gifted because strengths and deficits often mask each other. Silverman (2013) notes, "When IQ testing is abandoned, when children are only deemed gifted on the basis of demonstrated performance, when they are not qualified as disabled unless they are performing significantly below grade level, and when psychologists are left out of the process, most twice exceptional children are imperceptible" (p. 13). In addition, Merrill (2012) finds that "highly gifted is not the same as high achieving. Highly gifted is how a person is wired, not what a person produces" (p. 8). Through a combination of testing, teacher narratives, parental input, and student achievement, it is difficult yet possible to accurately identify students who are twice exceptional.

If a student has been identified as being intellectually gifted and also has a 504 Plan or IEP, the designation of twice exceptional may be utilized. Researchers have found that 2% to 5% of students who are intellectually gifted also have a disability (Dix Schafer, 2005; Whitmore, 1980). A child who is twice exceptional may have a more difficult time being admitted into a program for students who are intellectually gifted. If a student has significant gaps in knowledge and/or moderate to severe differences in attention, standardized testing may not accurately measure the cognitive abilities of that student (Bisland, 2004). The gaps may occur because of a specific learning disability or other difference that does not correctly measure the overall achievement levels of a student who is twice exceptional.

The identification of students who are gifted and have learning differences is problematic and may require new or revised methods for identification (Karnes, Shaunessy, & Bisland, 2004). Observations, portfolios, and anecdotal data provide invaluable information to supplement standardized testing (Silverman, 1989). Moreover, a comprehensive evaluation that includes multiple quantitative and qualitative measures and allows students to demonstrate both their strengths and challenges is the most reliable way to appropriately identify students who are twice exceptional.

Hollie: Elementary School

Before Hollie entered kindergarten, we endured another round of psychological and educational testing that included IQ and achievement measures, video and photographic data, and two visits by the public school special education teacher to the preschool classroom. We learned that Hollie was highly gifted intellectually; however, we were told that she would probably never test to her actual aptitude level because of her differences.

Other deficits including low muscle tone and gross motor problems surfaced. Sensory integration therapy did much to improve these conditions; when funding for this ended, we enrolled Hollie in a gymnastics class. While she had some obvious gross motor development differences from her classmates, she was an affable and energetic little girl who loved nothing more than to spring unannounced into the arms of her teachers to display her unbridled affection. I applauded her early use of social charms to mask difficult tasks.

Music was an early and important part of Hollie's life. Growing up in a house with parents who are professional musicians and music educators facilitated this early interest. I will never forget the day I first heard Hollie babble. She had struggled to say "mama" and "dada" and was working very hard in speech therapy to learn to talk. While teaching a flute lesson, I began to hear a very musical set of babbling from across the room. I asked my student to stop playing, and we listened to Hollie literally sing before she could speak. Her expressive language soon began to increase rapidly and was almost always preceded by vocal explorations and improvisatory singing. As a result, we sang many words and phrases to her, and her sister began to create "Baby Hollie Songs" to sing to Hollie.

Hollie possessed a social awareness far beyond that of many of her friends. With the reality of kindergarten looming large the summer after preschool graduation, I revisited the idea of enrolling Hollie in another year of preschool. Her understanding that most children would advance to kindergarten but those not ready would be held back kept me focused toward kindergarten. She had set kindergarten as an immediate goal.

I was grateful for the opportunity to have Hollie enter kindergarten with an IEP in place and a caring kindergarten teacher who collaborated well with the special education teacher. Social issues became more apparent as Hollie became tired and distracted during the day and was sometimes unable to make and sustain friendships. Hollie met academic goals on time yet struggled with testing and long-term summative assessments. An example is the time-honored "count to 100" that kindergarten students experience each spring. Hollie was able to count to 100 but was not able to do it "in the moment" when the teacher was there with her. She eventually succeeded when allowed to go to a quiet hallway without the distractions of other students in the classroom. This difference widened as timed math tests, multiplication tables, Virginia history state-standardized testing, and multistep science experiments became realities during elementary school.

Musically, Hollie excelled. Her singing voice was always on pitch, and she loved to express herself through song. In second grade, she scored in the 98th percentile for her grade level on the Primary Measures of Music Audiation (PMMA; Gordon, 2012). It was a liberating moment to have her aptitude revealed free of qualifiers. Hollie began piano lessons and continued to sing almost as much as she spoke.

The moments of greatest happiness for Hollie in elementary school often involved music. We were all thrilled when she was chosen to sing at various school events, and we beamed with pride from the front row of the audience when she sang with the All-Virginia Elementary School Choir in the fifth grade. Hollie resisted learning to read music, and memorization was difficult. She played the flute in the school band and easily learned everything she performed by ear. Her flute lessons with me were similar because she had heard the melodies and exercises for years. Hollie auditioned for a summer choral camp and used word rhythms to read a portion of her entrance exam. The examiner asked why she had used unusual words for her rhythms ("puppy puppy cat cat" for "ta-ti ta-ti ta ta"). Hollie's response was that she liked animals better than vegetables. Her sense of humor and aptitude for antics increased as her personality began to bloom.

Elementary school was also the time when Hollie worked her way out of her PDD diagnosis and into three new diagnoses—developmental delay, severe attention deficit hyperactivity disorder combined (hyperactivity/impulsivity and inattention), and generalized anxiety disorder. We spent 2 years trying to find the correct medication and dosage to assist Hollie with attention while maintaining a balance emotionally. The frightening reality came to us suddenly as we were watching our home video of Hollie in the third-grade PTA program. She was the sun in the production and was responsible for striking a large drum on cue. As we watched the video, we could see her holding her breath for lengthy periods followed by a quick exhalation and another held inhalation. After speaking to her doctor, we realized that she was attempting to slow her heart rate because the medication was causing it to race.

In general, we were very fortunate that Hollie attended an outstanding elementary school with a caring staff and an approachable administration. Hollie thrived during those years, and we were satisfied with her academic progress. Socially, Hollie struggled because her peers did not always understand her behavior. We continued to help make connections with peers and provide happy play dates when friends would visit our home.

Characteristics of Students Who Are Twice Exceptional

Students who are twice exceptional often display the characteristics shown in Box 8.2 (Higgins Nielsen, 2000). The following characteristics are also common among students who are twice exceptional (Higgins, Baldwin, & Pereles, 2000; Weinfeld, Barnes-Robinson, Jeweler, & Roffman Shevitz, 2006):

- Have high verbal ability with some language used in an inappropriate way and at inappropriate times
- Display strong observation skills with difficulty in memorization
- Have excellent problem-solving skills when posed with "real world" issues
- Possess outstanding critical thinking and decision-making skills, particularly if compensatory skills have been developed
- Have attention issues (however, hyperfocus is obvious in an area of interest)
- Have strong questioning attitudes that may appear (or be) disrespectful (questions may include facts or other information presented by authority figures)
- Possess an unusual imagination with a high level of originality and a divergent thought process
- Show a lack of risk taking in academic settings but a high level of risk taking in creative or nonacademic situations
- Have an outstanding ability to use humor to deflect, deflate, and defuse situations that may include a lack of academic understanding
- Appear immature and will sometimes use behaviors common in much younger students when stressed or tired
- Constantly ask for support and assurance in area of deficit; may also appear defiant and angry when challenged
- Are highly critical of self and others
- Have difficulty with peer and social groups; may frequently shift friend groups
- May be removed from a friend group by peers if level of intellectual giftedness does not match performance or if social skills are considered inappropriate or immature
- Are often leaders of nontraditional students or of students with lesser cognitive ability who have accepted them in their peer circle and recognize the leadership skills present in the students
- Demonstrate a wide range of interests but often must choose based on area of strength, rather than the interest that is strongest
- May have a strong area of interest that consumes time and energy
- Have difficulty following directions and exhibiting executive function skills in a "step by step" fashion
- Have great difficulty when communicating via written language
- Have difficulty understanding tasks based on written directions due to cognitive functioning and processing delays

- May appear to lack basic language and mathematical skills because of cognitive processing issues
- May excel in music, art, theater, and dance
- Often demonstrate outstanding higher order thinking skills while being unable to process discrete information.

Because of dichotomous behaviors and learning characteristics, students who are twice exceptional are often misdiagnosed or undiagnosed. This complicated learning profile can flummox many teachers, who may resort to labels of behaviors and things that irritate them rather than a thoughtful consideration of the whole child and what he or she brings to the classroom. Moreover, the longer a child traverses a public school system without receiving appropriate services to meet his or her needs, the higher the likelihood of failure, disappointment, decreased self-esteem, and depression.

Behavior

The already complicated behavior profile of students who are intellectually gifted becomes increasingly murky when learning differences are present. Students who are gifted and have learning differences can be exponentially frustrated because they are aware of the standard or level of competence expected but are not able to communicate their level of understanding or the desired response. Attention-seeking behaviors or behaviors that seem rude can occur, resulting in misunderstandings between teachers and students. These developmentally asynchronous events are disruptive to the classroom routine and to the learning process of all students. Moreover, the frustration felt by a student who is twice exceptional can appear to be aggressive, careless, and/or off-task.

An awareness of the asynchronous characteristics of students who are intellectually gifted can lead to an even greater awareness of the compounding asynchronicity inherent within a student who has learning differences. For example, a student who is chronologically 10 years old may have an IQ of 150, thus placing his or her cognitive age at 15 years. On the other hand, if this student has a learning difference in mathematics that places his or her calculating and processing abilities at 7 years old, he or she will demonstrate a compounded asynchronous profile that can be debilitating in an elementary classroom created for students who are neurotypical. Frustration, anxiety, and tension may present in a vicious cycle that leads to behavioral outbursts (Benito, 2003).

The music classroom can be a place of respite and joy for a student who struggles in a traditional classroom. By utilizing multimodal teaching techniques, music educators can increase the potential for every student to obtain competence and demonstrate musical understanding. Many behavioral outbursts and disruptive occurrences can be diminished through choice of modality in expression of understanding, chunking of assignments to decrease anxiety, and an atmosphere of inquiry that encourages freedom to explore through multilevel opportunities. Improvisation and composition are excellent musical activities for differentiation as each student may choose his or her own specific level of comfort in a process-oriented approach (Benito, 2003).

Learning

"Street smart versus school smart" is a phrase used by some students who are twice exceptional to describe themselves. They may be able to expertly travel city streets at an early age, know the exact change necessary to complete almost any transaction, and be able to talk their way out of any number of possibly difficult situations, yet these same students struggle with academic tasks that include memorization, organization of materials, study habits, and use of executive function skills to titrate long-term assignments. The lack of cognition speed to quickly absorb global information becomes debilitating when instruction and expectations become task and sequence oriented (Shore, 1995).

Many students who are twice exceptional must process information several times before making a conclusion or stating a final response (Sousa, 2003). This often causes anxiety and frustration, which leads students to stop processing because of the time it takes to produce an answer or to problem solve a situation. They sometimes find themselves offering an incorrect response after having labored to express it. This, over time, can lead teachers to add another label to this child: lazy.

A student who is twice exceptional can appear unmotivated, disinterested, and disengaged. With a studied and compassionate approach, a teacher can increase the potential for a student to achieve *and* demonstrate understanding at a level closer to his or her aptitude. Creating an atmosphere of collegial inquiry using open-ended questioning and a structure for responses that is clearly organized will benefit students who struggle to acquire and demonstrate knowledge.

Creativity

Students who are intellectually gifted can possess an almost limitless amount of creative potential in their area of giftedness. Likewise, students who have differences in learning may also be extraordinarily creative in one or more areas of scholarly pursuit. With strict guidelines or expectations removed, all students are able to create at a level that is comfortable for them and to fully utilize their creative gifts and strengths.

The music classroom can provide students with many opportunities to create music that demonstrates their level of creativity and their ability to present divergent thought within a musical context. The capacity of a music educator to cultivate creativity can translate to other academic settings. Works created by a student can also be a powerful indicator of creativity that may not be seen in other classrooms. By creating meaningful partnerships with other faculty and staff, evidence of creativity in the music classroom may be shared with everyone who interacts with the student.

Emotion

For students who have been identified as intellectually gifted, the possibility that their giftedness may be "taken" from them can cause significant frustration. Some students will do almost anything to mask their areas of difficulty. The higher the level of intelligence is, the longer a student may succeed in school while not really understanding or mastering certain subject material. Conversely, a student who has a learning difference may never be identified as also possessing a high level of intelligence. This situation can be equally difficult because the student may never know his or her true intellectual potential and, more importantly, may never understand the way his or her brain processes information. This can also lead to depression, despair, and even suicide.

Music is filled with complex emotions and understandings that are multidimensional. By exploring emotion and its relationship to music, students can become familiar with complex and abstract processes inherent in music. Students who struggle yet are also highly capable may benefit from opportunities to search for meaning within masterworks, new creations, compositions, and performances.

General Intellectual Ability and Specific Academic Aptitude

Until recently, many educators assumed that students who are intellectually gifted are equally capable in every academic situation. This premise is only appropriate for some students. Many students are gifted in only one subject area or in a small number of areas. This is also true for students who are twice exceptional. For example, a high level of potential in verbal and written communication does not necessarily transfer to the music classroom. It may be mitigated by a learning difference in syntax, grammar, or other subset of learning. We do not yet know enough about specific connections within the brain to understand exactly how to teach all students, but we do know that each child is different and some children must work harder to learn in certain ways.

Students who are musically gifted may not always demonstrate a global pattern of high performance in the music classroom. This is particularly true for students who are musically gifted and who also have one or more learning differences. Music teachers who use objective data for identifying musical giftedness, as well as music teachers who rely on subjective data, will be most successful if they measure achievement according to the individual profile of a student, rather than an aptitude score or portfolio of process/product accomplishments.

Hollie: Middle School

We were fortunate to live in a diverse, urban school district with many school choice options. Hannah was selected to attend an International Baccalaureate (IB) school program for the 50 top-scoring fifth-grade students from around the city. Hollie soon stated that the IB program was her goal as well. As part of their application process, students took standardized tests to measure aptitude and achievement levels. As a result, not many students with learning differences were admitted. Hollie, however, was admitted, and we spent the next 3 years advocating for her and traveling almost daily to the school to make sure her academic, social, and emotional needs were being met. The teachers in the program were not accustomed to accommodating students with IEPs and 504 Plans. They also were only practiced in accelerating and compacting courses for students who were simply intellectually gifted. The conundrum of a child with multiple areas of gifts and differences was not an opportunity some of the teachers were prepared to accept.

The middle-school-girl carousel of emotions was heightened for Hollie. Her social and emotional development was also uneven, as the "sorting hat" of cliques was confusing and frustrating for her. We had less control over her peer group because middle school is, well, middle school. We continued to support Hollie as much as possible as parents and consoled her when the social sorting made her feel inferior.

During parent/teacher conferences, we would hear of the impulsive, disruptive, and immature behaviors exhibited by our daughter. We would also be told, repeatedly, that her handwriting was unacceptable and her organization skills were lacking. No amount of gentle reminders from us would assuage the blame and judgment in the voices of these teachers. I am convinced our phone number was on speed dial as it rang, almost daily, with new recitations of Hollie's transgressions during school. We had a running agreement with the girls–if they told us what happened at school first, the punishment would be lessened. I lost count of the number of days they flew off the school bus and into the house to explain what happened at school before a teacher had the opportunity to call.

A disappointing accompaniment to the environment of intellectually elite academic situations is that the parents are sometimes more competitive than the children. The totality of this environment included a number of inappropriate assumptions made about Hollie by parents of the peers in her classes. I found myself retreating from volunteer activities and committees at school as I began to see judgment in the eyes of other parents and teachers. Hollie was definitely seen as different in this highly achieving academic environment, and I struggled to not verbally eviscerate anyone who dared counsel me regarding my daughter's behavior and work ethic. In retrospect, choosing an academically elite school for her may have been a mistake; however, I shudder to consider how her intellectual giftedness would have fared in a local neighborhood middle school.

These years were not as musical as her elementary school years. An unfortunate incident with a children's choral director who physically punished Hollie for humming along with a choir singing onstage caused Hollie to stop singing for 3 years. Her middle school band director constantly compared Hollie to Hannah and shook his head while laughing when we walked in the band room for a parent/teacher conference. Hollie quit the flute soon after this. She also stopped taking piano lessons because reading music using a grand staff was still so difficult for her. Lastly, she stopped ballet classes and cited "too many rules" as her rationale. I allowed her to stop her afterschool activities because she was already exhausted from all the requirements of preadolescence, and I could see the daily wear caused by anxiety, frustration, and tension. We did not want to add more to the stresses of her daily life.

Specific Strategies for Engaging Students Who Are Twice Exceptional

Students who are twice exceptional benefit from flexible groups that change according to the situation. Chamber music, music theory, composition and improvisation, and music listening can all be accomplished within flexible groupings that take into account the intellectual, musical, and emotional needs of students who are twice exceptional.

Box 8.2 describes other grouping options (adapted from Tomlinson, 1999).

Box 8.2 Grouping options for instruction

Strategy	Description	Benefits for students who are Twice-Exceptional
Flexible Skills Grouping	Students are placed in groups according to their musical and intellectual needs. Movement among groups is common, based on readiness according to a specific objective.	Students are not expected to perform at the highest musical or intellectual level at all times. They are able to learn in appropriate groups that change according to the task. For students with uneven learning profiles, this allows a label-free and organic system that honors their needs.
Compacting	A three-step process that (1) assesses what a student knows about material to be studied and what the student still needs to master, (2) plans for learning what is not known and excuses a student from what is known, and (3) plans for additional time to spend in enriched or accelerated study.	Students who are twice exceptional often understand the 'whole' of a concept far before the 'part' of a concept. This can create difficulty in the classroom because a student may appear to understand the entire topic or be able to 'talk around' an area without really mastering the concept or skill. Compacting allows the student to pretest for current knowledge and then ameliorate elements that are unclear.
Most Difficult First	Students can demonstrate mastery of a concept by responding to a small number of the most difficult tasks with 85% accuracy (scale, key signature, rhythm, composition). Students who can demonstrate mastery do not need to practice anymore.	Students who struggle with attention, discrete steps, detailed assignments, and memorization will appreciate only being asked to do the most difficult portions of composition, memorization, and series of specific direction activities.

Box 8.2 Continued

Strategy	Description	Benefits for students who are Twice-Exceptional
Orbital Study	Independent projects that are long term. They orbit, or revolve, around some facet of the curriculum. Students select their own topics for orbital, and they work with guidance and coaching from the teacher to develop more expertise on the topic and the process of becoming an independent investigator. Musical examples could include studies of historical performance styles, composers, music concepts, and performance projects.	Individual rather than group projects are often preferred. An opportunity to choose the topic, depth, and breadth for study without the forced community and social issues that arise in a group project can create a true creative and differentiated project. The time to spend studying a musical topic of interest can also lead to a process and product that closely aligns with the intellectual or musical aptitude of the student because she is able to learn and create according to her strengths.
Independent Projects, Group Investigations	Teacher directed individual and group projects allow students the opportunity to demonstrate skills and understandings through verbal, written, aural, and kinesthetic activities.	Student interest and independence can both be encouraged through these active opportunities. The addition of a specific timeline with many checkpoints provides a structure for students who need small chunks of accountability frequently.
Problem Based Learning	Active and 'real world' situations that require inferential learning.	Students who are twice exceptional often tire of exercises they consider meaningless. By providing a 'real world' situation and asking students to use brainstorming and problem solving to resolve an issue, they can see the applicability of the issue to their musical lives.

Agendas	A task analysis or sequence of events necessary to complete and assignment.	Metacognition and executive functioning are often compromised with students who are twice exceptional. Frustration can ensue when specific directions are not provided. An agenda levels the playing field for students who struggle moving from whole to part.
Learning Centers, Interest Centers, Choice Boards	Offer options that include improvisation, composition, singing, playing instruments, listening, and movement.	Student choice is a powerful motivator for students who are often passive in their own learning. Students who are twice exceptional often crave depth of understanding.
Portfolios/ Assessment	Provide a multi-dimensional opportunity to demonstrate knowledge acquisition over time. Assessment procedures are ongoing and do not depend on performance on one day.	Students who vary widely in their readiness to learn appreciate the opportunity to add their best work performed on their best days to their portfolios or assessment charts. This also levels the playing field for students who sometimes have a 'bad day.'

Hollie: High School

Hannah decided in the sixth grade that she wanted to attend the Regional Governor's School for the Arts and Technology; Hollie soon decided that she also wished to attend the same school. Aware of the application process, point distribution for applicants, and competition within each of the seven art areas, I began to search frantically for the area that would best display Hollie's innate talents and gifts. Our local school system had approximately 9 to 14 slots each year for eighth-grade students who wished to attend this school, and the vetting process could be fierce. We chose musical theater and soon after enrolled Hollie in a local class that I knew was taught by the program director of musical theater at the Governor's School.

She did not do well in her first musical theater classes, and I began to see and hear the same familiar weariness from these teachers. Her father and I began engaging in cognitive rehearsal each day after school to help Hollie comprehend her behaviors and the way they were viewed by others. She had a difficult time understanding that her words could be misunderstood and that people around her had their own independent reactions to her language and behavior choices. We began to see improvement within a few months and also began private voice lessons with one of the teachers from the musical theater class. I began to fervently hope we had found the opportunity for excellence Hollie desperately needed.

I continued to remind myself that what Hollie says and what Hollie means are often dissimilar. Through the cognitive rehearsals each day, she began to develop an increased theory of mind and become slightly less impulsive when queried or challenged by someone. The voice lessons went very well and the teacher easily prepared Hollie for an audition at the Governor's School. The audition required singing, dancing, and improvisatory acting. Her father took her to the audition and dawdled afterward hoping to "run into" the director of the program. When he did, he learned that Hollie had received a perfect score on her audition. The combination of her interview, audition, and academic record secured her a space at the prestigious school.

High school began with a flurry of meetings, carpool lists, and orientation activities. Hollie was very excited to be starting a new school and made friends easily with other rising freshmen who were interested in musical theater. In the first round of auditions, Hollie was cast in a touring show opportunity that would end with a statewide competition for awards at the end of the fall. Academically, she did not struggle because much of the coursework had already been introduced during her middle school program. Her stagecraft teacher contacted me in late September with some of the same concerns we had heard during middle school. A notable difference was that this teacher seemed to be contacting me to inform her teaching rather than judge my parenting. The relief in my voice was palpable.

Hollie began to struggle socially and academically in the spring of her freshman year. The unsettled schedule of a musical theater student did not fit her need for consistency and a quiet space each day to complete assignments and study for classes. Hollie's grades began to drop, and she became annoyed with some of the other students who could easily dance, sing, act, and excel in the classroom without seeming to work at any of it. Hollie asked to return to ballet, even with the rules, and then wanted to change her focus area from musical theater to dance. I considered the difference between the daily schedule of an actor and a dancer. The consistency of classes and rehearsals offered at her ballet school would better suit her temperament and anxiety level. Hollie easily convinced the dance department chair to allow her to enter as a sophomore, and we started a new schedule.

Sophomore year was a train wreck. Hollie was doing poorly in her honors trigonometry class and also did not understand the mathematics portions of her chemistry course. Her anxiety worsened and she began experiencing symptoms of panic and distress on days she had assignments due. We asked for a complete re-evaluation including psychological and educational testing to determine the cause of these issues. After months of testing, we learned that Hollie had two learning disabilities in mathematics (processing and computation), as well as chronic depression and acute anxiety. Her functional mathematics achievement levels were at the early fourth-grade level. After receiving the diagnosis of the learning disabilities in math, we met with Hollie at home to talk about it. I expected a dramatic scene that would require reassurance and consolation. Instead, her reaction was "Oh my God! This is awesome! I'm not stupid. I'm LD!" She immediately ran upstairs to post the diagnosis on Facebook. It was such a relief to her to know that her giftedness was not in danger. She was not floundering in math because she was not intelligent enough to understand; she had learning disabilities. We addressed the depression and anxiety through a new psychiatrist, new medication, and new rounds of 24-hour-a-day monitoring for side effects.

We found an excellent math tutor who managed to teach Hollie as she pirouetted and sang around the dining room table. John became a close family friend during the 3 years he guided Hollie through high school math, through the PSAT and SAT (tests for US college admittance), and into college. He was also willing to attend case study meetings and a tension-filled discussion we had with the school administrators and Princeton about accommodations during SAT testing. We were so very fortunate to find John; I now offer his name to anyone who needs a lifeline!

Hollie's junior year was filled with emotional pain. She was acutely aware that the year was very important for college applications and became paralyzed at times with fear and panic during the school day. We received a call one day from school stating that Hollie was underneath a table in the library sobbing. The school nurse called frequently to talk about Hollie or to let me know she was in the clinic again asking to come home for the day. We began allowing Hollie to take days off when she felt overwhelmed with school. She stopped taking dance classes, dropped out of the church band, refused to audition for musicals or other theater activities, and spent a lot of time sleeping and listening to music. Her voice teacher moved to Italy, and her sister was four states away in college.

In an attempt to reach Hollie, I began spending most afternoons watching television with her. We did not do homework or talk about school. We made snacks, snuggled on the couch with blankets, and watched television. I reminded myself of a statement I had made in a case study meeting when she was in the third grade: "I don't care if she ever graduates high school. I just want my child to be happy." I repeated that mantra many times during that difficult year.

Hollie's friends dropped by the wayside during junior year, and a former friend in her dance group orchestrated a "shun" just before the spring dance performances. I kept buying flowers, listening to her music, watching television, and making snacks. Her psychiatrist was helpful, and thankfully, her innate intelligence buoyed her through the coursework. My relationship with my child was the most important thing in the world to me, and as a result, we watched every single episode of the television show *House*.

By the end of the school year, Hollie had qualified to be a lifeguard and spent her summer saving three lives at our local pool. She decided she wanted to major in music in college; however, commercial/popular voice was her route. We began identifying schools and preparing applications. Hollie was heartily accepted at a top university in the area of commercial music. We were elated and terrified at the same time.

Suggested Adaptations and Accommodations for Students Who Are Twice Exceptional

Some common themes permeate the literature regarding best practice for students who are twice exceptional (Baum Owen, 2004; Silverman, 2013). Students who are highly capable and need assistance benefit from:

- Completing only the most difficult questions or examples
- Testing out of an area of study or unit
- Receiving extended time to complete assignments and projects
- Having preferential seating
- Receiving nonverbal cues to signal inappropriate behavior
- Having copies of visuals for study and use during class

- Using repeated self-talk during difficult and stressful tasks (academic and emotional)
- Highlighting areas of music and text
- Using organizational aids to assist with complicated information and large assignments
- Using mnemonics for memorization of notes, keys, circle of fifths, musical terms, and historical performance practice
- Modeling (by teacher) and reviewing organizational skills and techniques
- Making to-do lists—prioritized and possibly color-coded according to musical subject or task
- Having additional copies of materials, instruments, and supplies
- Using a computer or notation software for lengthy written work
- Chunking concepts and skills into small parts.

Students who are twice exceptional often understand an assignment but lack the necessary metacognitive skills to allow them to complete an assignment within the allotted time. Some examples are naming notes on a staff, playing key signature games, marking musical terms and definitions, playing several scales in a short period of time, and memorizing music. Frustration can occur rapidly and behavioral outbursts often follow. By understanding the characteristics of students who are twice exceptional and applying adaptations and accommodations in advance, these episodes can be lessened in duration and frequency.

Teacher Qualities That Foster Learner Success

Some common successful teacher qualities have been noted in research and the literature. They include:

- Teachers who design high-level projects with open-ended product expectations
- Teachers who include a multisensory approach to all objectives
- Teachers who demonstrate and advocate brainstorming opportunities
- Teachers who respect creative thinking
- Teachers who design safe classroom and rehearsal environments that encourage risk taking
- Teachers who recognize effort before achievement
- Teachers who recognize achievement before aptitude
- Teachers who reinforce effort as success
- Teachers who provide opportunities to develop leadership skills
- Teachers who are flexible in the response style expected from students

- Teachers who encourage all students to be aware of the gifts (academic, social, emotional) of every student
- Teachers who are active members of the team of professionals who work with students who are twice exceptional (including the parents/guardians)

Students can be difficult to diagnose and label. Creating differentiated assignments for music classrooms and ensembles can be exhausting. The process is sometimes made more difficult when students have intellectual and musical gifts and comorbid learning challenges. The task is to be the best teacher possible for every child in every class and ensemble.

Knowing your students and their needs can be far more important than the specific labels included in their paperwork, if they are even listed. The music teacher may be the first professional to notice the difference between aptitude and achievement, ability and performance, and motivation and executive function skills. When the profile is apparent to you, make the adaptations and accommodations you consider most appropriate for the student. If the student improves, you have made good choices. If the student does not improve, keep applying different strategies until the student begins to improve in musical and academic skills and understanding.

The reward of this process is to know you have done your very best. By providing your very best each day, you are increasing the possibility that you are creating an environment that will meet the needs of every student. In the end, we teach the students–music is our vehicle.

Hollie: College

Hollie will start college next week. Letting go is never easy, and letting go when a child is twice exceptional can be complicated. Her school is 10 hours from home, and the commercial music students will be talented and focused. Hollie has prepared organizational tools, taken responsibility for finding a job on campus, delivered her college credit courses for transfer consideration, and emailed her voice teacher in advance. We will always be on speed dial, and I imagine there will be some frequent flier miles with my name on them. She is still the beautiful baby who looked meaningfully into my eyes to tell me this wasn't going to be easy, and her journey is partly also my journey. I hope her teachers know that she is loved, valued, and supported. I hope Hollie knows that we love her for who she is rather than the enumeration of her successes. If she can recognize her challenges and utilize her abilities, her life will be happy and whole. I hope those who read this derive a renewed sense of the individual personhood of each young person and the charge we have as educators to meet the needs of every student we teach.

The efficacy of our pedagogy depends on our ability to understand our individual students and to apply teaching and learning experiences that will lead to meaningful musical experiences for them. Our students require individual approaches that are based on research, best practice, and the uniqueness of each person. By continuing to purposefully learn about our students' strengths and challenges, we ensure that their musicianship, divergent thinking abilities, and sense of self will be increased throughout their musical lives.

REFERENCES

Baum, S. M., & Owen, S. V. (2004). *To be gifted learning disabled: Strategies for helping bright students with LD, ADHD, and more.* Mansfield, CT: Creative Learning Press.

Benito, Y. (2003). Intellectual giftedness and associated disorders: Separation anxiety disorders or school phobia. *Gifted and Talented International, 18*(1), 27–35.

Binet, A. (1894). *Psychologie des grandes calculateurs (et de jouers d'echecs) (Psychology of large computers (and chess players).* Paris: Hachette.

Bisland, A. (2004). Using learning-strategies instruction with students who are gifted and learning disabled. *Gifted Child Today, 7*(3), 52–58.

Dix, J., & Schafer, S. (2005). From paradox to performance: Practical strategies for identifying and teaching gifted/LD students. In S. K. Johnson & J. Kendrick (Eds.), *Teaching gifted students with disabilities* (pp. 153–159). Waco, TX: Prufrock Press.

Gallagher, J. J. (2000). Unthinkable thoughts: Education of gifted students. *Gifted Child Quarterly, 44*, 5–12.

Gordon, E. E. (2012). *Learning sequences in music: Skill, content, and patterns.* Chicago: GIA Publications.

Hannah, C. L., & Shore, B. M. (1995). Metacognition and high intellectual ability: Insights from the study of learning-disabled gifted students. *Gifted Child Quarterly, 39*, 95–106.

Higgins, D., Baldwin, L., & Pereles, D. (2000). *Comparison of characteristics of gifted students with or without disabilities.* Unpublished manuscript.

Higgins, L. D., & Nielsen, M. E. (2000). Responding to the needs of twice-exceptional learners: A school district and university's collaborative approach. In K. Kay (Ed.), *Uniquely gifted: Identifying and meeting the needs of the twice-exceptional student* (pp. 287–303). Gilsum, NH: Avocus Publishing.

Hollingsworth, L. S. (1975). *Children above 180 IQ.* New York: Arno Press.

Karnes, F. A., Shaunessy, E., & Bisland, A. (2004). Gifted students with disabilities: Are we finding them? *Gifted Child Today, 27*(4), 16–21.

Marland, S. P. (1971/1972). *Education of the gifted and talented: Report to the Congress of the United States by the US Commissioner of Education, Volume 1.* Pursuant to Public Law 91-230, Section 806. Washington, DC: US Government Printing Office.

Merrill, J. (2012). *If this is a gift, can I send it back? Surviving in the land of the gifted and twice exceptional.* Ashland, OR: GHF Press.

Renzulli, J. S. (1977). *The enrichment triad model: A guide for developing defensible programs for the gifted.* Mansfield, CT: Creative Learning.

Silverman, L. K. (1989). Invisible gifts, invisible handicaps. *Roeper Review, 12*(1), 37–42.

Silverman, L. K. (1993). *Counseling the gifted and talented.* Denver, CO: Love.

Silverman, L. K. (2013). *Giftedness 101.* New York: Springer.

Terman, L. M., & Oden, M. H. (1947). *Genetic studies of genius,* Vol. 4: *The gifted child grows up.* Stanford, CA: Stanford University Press.

Tolan, S. (1999). Self-knowledge, self-esteem, and the gifted adult. *Advanced Development,* 8, 147–150.

Tomlinson, C. A. (1999). *The differentiated classroom. Responding to the needs of all learners.* Alexandria, VA: ASCD.

VanTassel-Baska, J. (1998). *Excellence in educating gifted and talented learners.* Denver, CO: Love.

Walker, S. Y. (1991). *The survival guide for parents of gifted kids.* Minneapolis, MN: Free Spirit.

Webb, J. T., Meckstroth, E. A., & Tolan, S. S. (1994). *Guiding the gifted child.* Scottsdale, AZ: Gifted Psychology Press.

Weinfeld, R., Barnes-Robinson, L., Jeweler, S., & Roffman Shevitz, B. (2006). *Smart kids with learning difficulties: Overcoming obstacles and realizing potential.* Waco, TX: Prufrock Press.

Whitmore, J. F. (1980). *Giftedness, conflict and underachievement.* Boston: Allyn and Bacon.

Winner, E. (1996). *Gifted children: Myths and realities.* New York: Perseus Books Group.

PUTTING IT ALL TOGETHER

Teaching students who are gifted can be a truly enriching experience for music educators. The task assigned to music educators is to channel their cognitive abilities into an artistic endeavor. If music educators are aware of their strengths and areas of challenge, and are mindful of their responsibilities as educators, they have the opportunity to make a real difference in the lives of these learners, as well as those with other cognitive challenges.

Attention to the needs of students who are gifted and who do not possess a high aptitude for music is also important as the awareness that many students are not "globally gifted" may be received by the student with great appreciation. Because of the many areas of potential giftedness, the task for the music educator may be to adapt instruction to the asynchronicity that can occur between intellect and musical ability in a student who is gifted in one area yet more like his or her classmates in others. Modifying teaching practices according to the areas of giftedness and recognizing the possibilities that exist for students who are gifted are important steps in serving as an effective teacher for all students in the music classroom.

CONCLUSION

While we have termed students with superior abilities in the area of cognition as gifted, we also know they are students with differences and disabilities who can be effectively included in music classrooms and ensembles, provided appropriate consideration and strategies are applied to meet their specific needs. The difference in approach involves differentiation, course and concept compacting, acceleration of educational experiences, and a vertical (delving deeply into topics) rather than horizontal (linear) approach to curriculum and instruction. When these general principles are introduced, students with differences and disabilities, and all students, will benefit from the enhanced teaching and learning environment.

DISCUSSION QUESTIONS

1. Please delineate the similarities and differences between qualities of teachers who are effective with students who are intellectually gifted and students who are twice exceptional.
2. What is the difference between intellectual giftedness and musical talent?
3. How can secondary music ensemble conductors differentiate instruction in a small or large ensemble setting to meet the needs of students at various levels of cognitive ability (please remember this is intellectual giftedness and not musical talent)?
4. Please describe the adaptations you would use if Hollie were a student in your classroom (or future classroom)? You may choose the musical setting.

PART IV

RESOURCES FOR MUSIC EDUCATORS

Chapter 9

Resources for Music Teachers and Music Teacher Educators Regarding Teaching Students with Differences and Disabilities

Label-Free Approach

Prepared by Erika J. Knapp, Ph.D.

This chapter consists of two sections. The first section is a comprehensive list (as of the publication date) of internet-based resources for teachers, parents, and students with a variety of students with differences and disabilities. The second section is a resource list of research articles, books, and practitioner articles in the fields of music education and general education related to teaching students with differences and disabilities.

DIGITAL RESOURCES

The following digital resources are grouped into categories in an effort to support a label-free approach to students with differences and disabilities. However, we recognize the occasional necessity of diagnosis and the label attached to it, and many resources are still located through terminology that prioritizes a medical diagnosis over a label-free approach. Furthermore, resources from more than one category may support the same student, as disability is often multifaceted.

Each link was tested and reviewed, and at the time of publication was up to date.

Overarching Organizations on Special Education and Disabilities

Center for Parent Information and Resources
https://www.parentcenterhub.org/

A self-declared hub to support the parents of children with disabilities. It offers family-friendly information and research-based materials, a

Teaching Music to Students with Differences and Disabilities. Third Edition. Alice M. Hammel and Ryan M. Hourigan, Oxford University Press. © Oxford University Press 2025. DOI: 10.1093/9780197689356.003.0009

forum for parents to interact, parent training and webinars, and a bimonthly newsletter.

Council for Exceptional Children (CEC)
https://exceptionalchildren.org/

The largest international professional organization dedicated to improving the success of children and youth with disabilities and/or gifts and talents. They advocate for policy changes, offer professional development and resources for special educators, and provide standards and benchmarks for professionals who want to work with a special population. The CEC has local chapters in all 50 states, as well as in some universities across the United States.

Internet Special Education Resources
http://www.iser.com/

A nationwide directory of other websites and links related to special education and learning disabilities. It also provides links to regional and local services that can support assessment, diagnosis, and instruction.

National Association of Parents with Children in Special Education
http://www.napsce.org/

A membership organization dedicated to providing resources and support to parents whose children receive special education services. It offers networking between parents (as well as between educators and parents), relevant research and publications, and a database to help parents locate professional services in their area. In addition, it provides members a comprehensive overview of special education laws.

Special Education Resources on the Internet
http://www.seriweb.com

This is a collection of internet links and information resources for special education. It catalogs many other websites available on the internet and categorizes the resources according to disability type and the person seeking the information (e.g., parents or teachers).

Special Olympics
http://www.specialolympics.org/

The Special Olympics is an international nonprofit, and the world's largest organization for children and adults with intellectual disabilities. It serves over 5 million participants in 172 partner countries.

United States Government Supported Resources

Center for Disease Control (CDC)
https://www.cdc.gov/

The nation's science-based, data-driven organization focused on public health. It offers specific information about diseases, as well as research on children with disabilities. The CDC offers the latest data and stats on topics related to physical health.

Department of Education
https://www.ed.gov

The Department of Education provides information on all aspects of P–12 education for students with and without disabilities. There are links to educational statistics on students with disabilities, information about laws and public policy, as well as opportunities for grants for research.

Interagency Autism Coordinating Committee
https://iacc.hhs.gov/

A part of the U.S. Department of Health and Human Services, this coordinating committee focuses on coordinating federal efforts on issues related to autism spectrum disorder. The website offers the latest news regarding laws and public policy, access to publications and funding, as well as links to a variety of other autism-related resources.

MedLine Plus
https://medlineplus.gov/

This is an online health information resource for parents and students. It is provided through the National Library of Medicine (NLM), which is a part of the National Institutes of Health (NIH). It offers articles on health and wellness, specific medical conditions, an encyclopedia of terms, as well as information on healthy recipes and current clinical trials.

National Association for the Education of the Young Child (NAEYC)
https://www.naeyc.org/

A professional membership organization that works to promote high-quality learning for all young children, birth through age 8. They offer a Developmentally Appropriate Practice (DAP) framework for educators, research-based publications for parents and teachers, professional development opportunities, and articles on a variety of topics to support children during this critical period of their learning.

National Heart, Lung, and Blood Institute
http://nhlbi.nih.gov

The National Heart, Lung, and Blood Institute focuses on prevention and treatment of heart, lung, blood, and sleep disorders. They offer research, training, and education to enhance health in these areas. Links to research, events, grants, and training are available on their website.

National Institute on Deafness and other Communication Disorders (NIDCD)
https://www.nidcd.nih.gov/

Part of the National Institutes of Health, the NIDCD conducts and supports research on hearing, speech, and language, among other topics. The website provides information on a variety of hearing and communication topics, free publications, information about clinical trials, and links to other sites and resources that support similar goals.

National Institute of Mental Health (NIMH)
https://www.nimh.nih.gov/

A part of the National Institute of Health (NIH), this organization provides funding for research regarding mental health topics. This website provides access to current research and information about clinical trials for a variety of mental health issues. It offers quick links on its homepage to some of the most common mental health needs.

National Library Service for Blind and Physically Handicapped
https://www.loc.gov/nls/

A part of the Library of Congress, this service administers a free national library program that provides Braille and recorder materials to those who are blind or visually impaired. This program includes music materials and, in 2016, began offering refreshable Braille displays. This program is open to any resident in the United States who is unable to read or use regular print materials.

Substance Abuse and Mental Health Services Administration (SAMHSA)
https://www.samhsa.gov/

This website is the information center for the Substance Abuse and Mental Health Services Administration, which is a part of the U.S. Department of Health and Human Services. The website offers information about mental health programs and treatment, training for practitioners, data on mental health, publications, and resources to other branches of the U.S. Department of Health and Human Services

State-Supported Resources

Many states have individual sites to support teachers and parents of children with disabilities. While most link directly to their state government website, some states offer specific sites dedicated to supporting parents and educators. Be sure to check your individual state, as websites often change.

Federation for Children with Special Needs: Massachusetts
https://fcsn.org/

The mission of this organization is to provide information, support, and assistance to parents of children with differences and disabilities. They offer a variety of links to services including early intervention, support navigating medical/insurance needs, a parent training and information center, and links to support programs. While focused primarily on local support based in Massachusetts, many of the resources on the website can support families located anywhere.

New Jersey Autism Center of Excellence
https://njace.us/podcasts/

This website offers free podcasts about autism, neurodiversity, and inclusion. In addition, there are links to current research, and resources for families and researchers. There are funding opportunities and links to other organizations related to autism.

New York Institute for Special Education
http://www.nyise.org/

This website offers educational resources for teachers, support for parents, information about school programs and summer camps in the state of New York, as well as links to advocacy and other state-supported resources for students with disabilities.

Special Education Texas
https://www.spedtex.org/

This site provides information and resources for parents and educators in Texas. There are links to information on different types of disabilities, collaborative webinars, educational tips for teachers, a parent's guide to special education in Texas, and links to locate resources.

International Organizations

Autism One International
https://www.autismone.org/

This website contains media images and links regarding various aspects of autism. There are articles on related topics, including research, treatments, awareness, and social networking for parents and teachers. Links to other notable autism sites are also available.

Center for Autism and Related Disorders (CARD)
http://www.centerforautism.com/

The Center for Autism and Related Disorders (CARD) is an international organization focused on treating children with autism, Asperger syndrome, pervasive developmental disorders, and related disorders. The website offers historical information on the CARD approach and details of their services, including individualized treatment plans. Parents are also offered resources, a glossary, media guide, and information on educational rights.

The Davis Dyslexia Association International
http://www.dyslexia.com/

This website provides resources and research that offer teaching strategies designed to address dyslexia. In addition to resources, the site has links to a library of articles, free software, education, and professional development workshops. There are also links for family support and finding an educational provider.

Deaf-Blind International
http://www.deafblindinternational.org/index.htm

This is a worldwide organization that promotes services for people who are both deaf and blind. It offers membership, links to conferences, publications, and news. Additionally, it provides a list of known conditions and syndromes that can result in deaf-blindness.

Division for Early Childhood of the Council for Exceptional Children

https://www.dec-sped.org/

The Division for Early Childhood is an international organization for those who work with or on behalf of young children (age 0–8) with disabilities and other differences and their families. This membership offers webinars, publications, and scholarly journals dedicated to promoting evidence-based practices and policies that support children at risk for developmental delays. They also offer an eLearning library and a conference.

The National Autism Society of England
http://www.austim.org.uk

This is England's National Autism Society, and the site offers facts about autism, treatment, and current research. The process of diagnosis is presented in clear detail, and this site promotes early intervention and the importance of specialized education as the ideal treatment. The organization also provides a list of resources and support services.

PAMIS
http://www.dundee.ac.uk/pamis/

Formerly the "Profound and Multiple Impairment Society," PAMIS now stands for "Promoting a More Inclusive Society." This group offers family- and self-directed support services, provides current research, and offers links to creative arts opportunities. They also offer a growing library of pamphlets and publications on several topics related to persons with multiple impairments.

Royal National Institute of Blind People
http://www.rnib.org.uk

The Royal National Institute of Blind People is England's leading charity that offers information and support to persons with sight loss. Some of the links focus on general eye information, daily life with vision loss, job opportunities, reading rehabilitation, technology, and citizen's rights.

The International Dyslexia Association
https://dyslexiaida.org/

The International Dyslexia Association is a nonprofit organization dedicated to helping individuals with dyslexia. The website provides a variety of links for information, including interventions, research, a grant program, an online bookstore, a discussion forum, publications, conferences, and membership.

All Together Autism
https://www.altogetherautism.org.nz/

Based in New Zealand, All Together Autism is an information and advisory service funded by the New Zealand government. Their website offers information about autism through different stages of life and development, articles on different topics related to autism, an information hub that includes resources and a newsletter, and links to workshops and events.

The Hanen Centre
http://www.hanen.org/Home.aspx

This nonprofit organization based in Canada is committed to promoting language, social, and literacy skills in young children. They offer programming for parents and educators, as well as guidebooks, professional development, current research, and membership.

Mill Neck International
https://millneckinternational.org/

This international organization seeks to collaborate with partners to mobilize abilities, skills, and resources of Deaf communities worldwide. This online resource center offers stories in both English and sign language, a resource library, webcasts, and toolkits for educators. They also offer information about the Deaf community and Deaf culture.

SENSE
http://www.sense.org.uk/

The National Deaf-Blind and Rubella Association is the world's largest organization of support for persons who are deaf-blind, their families, and professionals. A wide variety of resources are available through this comprehensive website.

Developmental Delays/Early Intervention Resources

American Academy of Pediatrics
http://www.aap.org/

An organization of more than 67,000 pediatricians, the American Academy of Pediatrics is dedicated to the health of all children and includes many resources for parents and professionals on nearly every health issue facing children today. Specific details on education, publications, and advocacy, as well as quick topic search, are included.

First Signs
http://www.firstsigns.org/

The mission of this organization is to provide information about early warning signs for developmental delays. They have a video glossary, recommended readings, and a developmental milestones guide. The website also provides a wealth of vital resources, covering a range of issues from monitoring development, the screening and referral process, and how to share concerns with a medical professional.

Zero to Three
http://www.zerotothree.org/

This site is sponsored by the National Center for Infants, Toddlers, and Families. Their goal is to support all infants and toddlers in reaching their full potential. They offer resources for families and professionals, as well as links on topics such as child welfare, trauma, and early intervention.

Professional Development Resources for Teachers

National Professional Development Center (NPCD) on ASD
https://autismpdc.fpg.unc.edu/national-professional-development-center-autism-spectrum-disorder

Funded by the Office of Special Education Program as a part of the U.S. Department of Education, the NPCD provides free professional resources for teachers, therapists, and other providers who work with children on the autism spectrum. The website includes information on how to plan, implement, and monitor specific evidence-based practices. It also provides links to learning modules for those seeking additional training.

Teaching Tips by Temple Grandin
https://www.lcsc.org/cms/lib/MN01001004/Centricity/Domain/15/Teaching_Tips.pdf

Temple Grandin, Ph.D., is a prominent speaker and author about autism, and offers a set of teaching tips to those who work with students with autism. Many of these tips could also be applied to working with students with other disabilities as well.

Research Resources and Peer-Reviewed Research Journals

In this section, the aims and scope of each research interest group or journal are summarized as stated on their main "aims and scope" page. Please consult each respective journal for more details about individual topics or article fit.

Children with Exceptionalities Special Research Interest Group
https://sites.google.com/view/exceptionalities-srig?pli=1

The National Association for Music Education hosts a special research interest group site featuring links to research related to teaching music to students with disabilities. There are also links about adaptive musical instruments, assistive devices, apps, films, and movies, as well as ways to join this interest group.

Disability Studies Quarterly
https://dsq-sds.org/

This is the peer-reviewed journal of the Society for Disability Studies (SDS). It is a multidisciplinary and international journal of interest to social scientists and those in humanities and arts, disability rights, and others studying people with disabilities.

International Journal of Disability, Development, and Education
https://www.tandfonline.com/journals/cijd20

This is a multidisciplinary peer-reviewed journal with an international focus that centers around the education and development of persons with disabilities. It reflects a variety of topics, disciplines, research methods, and cultural perspectives.

International Journal of Inclusive Education
https://www.tandfonline.com/journals/tied20

This journal offers a forum for international and multidisciplinary dialogue on inclusive education and educational policy. This peer-reviewed journal focuses on research into pedagogies, curricula, organizational structure, and policy to include all students in education, and questions the nature of exclusion in schools.

International Journal of Special Education
http://www.internationalsped.com/ijse

The International Journal of Special Education is a peer-reviewed, open-access journal that offers a wide range of papers on topics regarding education and services for individuals with disabilities. There is a fee to publish in this journal, but reading is free.

Journal of Deaf Studies and Deaf Education
http://jdsde.oxfordjournals.org/

This website is sponsored by Oxford University Press. The *Journal of Deaf Studies and Deaf Education* seeks to integrate and coordinate research related to individuals who are deaf. Links for educators include cultural, developmental, and linguistic topics.

Journal of Special Education
https://journals.sagepub.com/home/SED

The *Journal of Special Education* publishes peer-reviewed research and scholarly reviews on improving education and services for individuals with disabilities. This is the official journal for the Division for Research Council for Exceptional Children.

Teaching Exceptional Children
https://journals.sagepub.com/home/tcx

Teaching Exceptional Children features research-to-practice articles and educator materials for classroom use. This peer-reviewed practitioner journal is published six times a year and focuses on practical content and immediate application of ideas.

Neurodiversity Resources

AAPC Publishing
http://www.aapcpublishing.net/

AAPC Publishing specializes in providing information regarding autism spectrum disorders to parents and educators. The books and multimedia that they publish are more practical than technical and address the issues around autism from many different angles.

Asperger Syndrome Education Network (ASPEN)
http://www.aspennj.org

The Asperger Syndrome Education Network (ASPEN) is a nonprofit organization that provides individuals and families affected by Asperger syndrome with education, support, and advocacy. The website provides media links and recommended readings. There are also links to local chapters and membership information.

Attention Deficit Disorder Association
http://www.add.org/

The Attention Deficit Disorder Association is the world's leading adult ADHD nonprofit organization. Their website offers support, resources, and connection to adults with ADHD and their family members. There are links to a virtual support group, a directory of professionals, workshops, and a resource library.

Autism/Asperger Network (AANE)
https://www.aane.org/

This network provides individuals, families, and professionals with information, education, community support, and advocacy on topics related to autism and Asperger syndrome. Links on the website include a directory of diagnosticians, specific resources for individuals, parents, and educators, and a link to related research studies. They also hold events for individuals and families.

Autism Navigator
https://autismnavigator.com/

This website offers information to families and professionals about autism spectrum disorders. Links include information sheets about autism signs and diagnosis, resources for families including a how-to guide and a glossary of terms, courses and webinars for professionals, and a provider directory.

Autism Now
www.autismnow.org

This national autism resource and information center offers resources to families and professionals regarding supporting individuals with autism spectrum disorder and other developmental disabilities. They have a collection of articles on topics related to autism, a directory to find local resources, a referral call center, and a section of specific resources categorized for families, educators, and adults in the community.

Autism Research Institute
https://www.autism.com/ari/

Although this site identifies current autism research as its main topic, it also includes concise information about autism, treatment options, and frequently asked questions. Triggers for autism and dietary treatment, as well as links to articles on many topics related to autism, are embedded in this site.

Autistic Self-Advocacy Network
https://autisticadvocacy.org/

This nonprofit organization seeks to advance the principles of the disability rights movement and believes that people on the autism spectrum should have equal access, rights, and opportunities. This is run by and for autistic people, and offers links to a resource library, accessibility tools, and ways to get involved with policymakers at the local and national level.

Autism Society of America
https://autismsociety.org

This site offers basic information about autism and signs for early identification. It also includes information on education laws, family issues, and links to the greater autism community. There are current research articles on autism, resources for parents, and a database of autism-related services and support.

Autism Speaks
https://www.autismspeaks.org/

Autism Speaks contains a variety of information about autism, including treatment options and links to related websites. The rights of children with autism and families of children with autism are presented in a direct manner, as are resources for living with autism and other family services. Finally, this site includes links to current research and information about conferences on autism.

Future Horizons
http://www.fhautism.com/

Future Horizons was created to help educators, therapists, and families who face challenges associated with autism spectrum disorders. They provide books, videos, and conferences that emphasize the most current information for dealing with these challenges.

Help with Autism, Asperger Syndrome, and Related Disorders
http://www.autism-help.org/

This site offers over 350 fact sheets about autism and autism-related disorders. It emphasizes practical strategies for families that cannot afford expensive interventions or may be geographically isolated.

The National Autism Association
http://www.nationalautismassociation.org/

The National Autism Association offers abundant information regarding many aspects of autism. Details about terminology, diagnosis, and research are available. Also, this website offers numerous autism resources and family support services.

One ADD Place
http://www.oneaddplace.com/

This is a collection of external links related to all things ADD and ADHD. There is information about testing, alternative remedies, products, and services, learning disability resources, and a virtual library. They also include a calendar of events, and a directory for professional services.

Organization for Autism Research (OAR)
https://researchautism.org/

The Organization for Autism Research (OAR) seeks to use science to address social, education, and treatment concerns of autistic individuals, parents, and professionals. The website offers introductions to autism, family guidebooks, resources and grants for educators, and grants for researchers.

Tourette Association of America
http://www.tourette.org/

This national organization seeks to raise awareness, advance research, and provide ongoing support to individuals and families impacted by Tourette Syndrome. Their website offers an overview of symptoms and treatment, a set of resource tools for parents and educators, and a link to local chapters and support groups. They also offer a provider database of medical professionals.

Sensory Resources

This section includes resources for working with children who have a variety of sensory needs, including visual, hearing, speech and language, and other sensory processing needs.

A-Z of Deaf-Blindness
http://www.deafblind.com/

This site contains an up-to-date listing on the internet of links to websites supporting those who are deaf-blind. Almost every kind of service, from education and devices to international organizations and research groups, has links on this website. The site also offers translations in French, German, Italian, Portuguese, and Spanish.

American Association of Deaf-Blind
http://www.aadb.org/

This site offers information regarding publications, conferences, emergency preparations, FAQs, communication technology, and articles related to people in the deaf-blind community.

American Council of the Blind
http://www.acb.org/

The American Council of the Blind is one of the leading organizations for persons who are blind or visually impaired. They strive to improve the well-being of persons who are blind by promoting education, building morale, coordinating services, and fostering greater understanding of blindness. They support the *Braille Forum*, a monthly magazine, and the website also contains links to state organizations, audio recordings, and other helpful resources.

American Foundation for the Blind

http://www.afb.org/

This group is focused on the expansion of possibilities for persons with vision loss. In addition to helpful links for education, Braille sites, technology, employment, and a section on strategies for living with vision loss, there is a Family Connect page to assist parents who are raising children with visual impairments. There is also a Career Connect page to help people with vision loss locate jobs.

American Printing House for the Blind
http://www.aph.org/

American Printing House for the Blind has been the largest provider of educational and daily living products for more than 160 years. Software, large-type books, and many types of learning products are available online. The database contains information in various media formats for over 200,000 publications related to visual impairment.

American Society for Deaf Children
http://www.deafchildren.org/

This society's mission is to ensure that every deaf child can learn sign language right from the start. They are dedicated to helping families raise children who are deaf by providing valuable links to services, camps, conferences, educational sources, and organizations connected to persons in the deaf community.

American Speech Language Hearing Association
https://www.asha.org/

The American Speech Language Hearing Association is a scientific and professional organization composed of speech language pathologists and scientists who strive to improve effective communication for all people. The website offers current research, events, and continuing education for educators and health professionals.

Association of Adult Musicians with Hearing Loss
http://www.musicianswithhearingloss.org/wp/

This organization seeks to create opportunities for adult musicians with hearing loss to discuss the challenges they face in making and listening to music. They offer opportunities for public performance, research on hearing and assistive technology, and educational opportunities for hard of hearing and deaf adults to appreciate and make music. They also offer publications, recordings, and hearing-impaired concerts.

Blindness Support Services
http://www.blindnesssupport.com/

This organization seeks to teach those who are blind or visually impaired to become more independent and adapt to the challenges they have. The website offers links to a variety of services, including assistive technology and travel training and Braille instruction. There are also links to outside sources of assistance, such as YouTube videos, essential apps, on-demand transportation services, and other agencies working to support the blind and visually impaired.

Bookshare
https://www.bookshare.org/cms/

A website designed to help make reading easier for people with dyslexia, blindness, cerebral palsy, and other reading barriers. They can customize a reading experience with eBooks, audio books, Braille, and large font, and other formats, as well as provide the materials on a variety of devices. Currently they have access to over 1,000,000 titles.

Boston University Deaf Education Library
http://www.deafedlibrary.org/

This bilingual ASL-English Deaf education library is supported by Boston University. Here, teachers, parents, and students can share educational materials for children. The website offers ASL readings of books, educational lessons, teaching materials, and an event calendar. The best part is anyone who knows ASL can contribute to this growing resource.

Braille Authority of North America (BANA)
https://www.brailleauthority.org/

The Braille Authority of North America (BANA) promotes the standardization of Braille and tactile graphics. They offer scholarly research on Braille, policy opinions related to the creation of materials, position statements, and guidelines for those who seek to use Braille.

Central Institute for the Deaf
http://www.cid.edu/

This is a school for the deaf located in St. Louis, Missouri. In addition to the physical school, their website offers many online resources for parents, and strategies for educators and schools to support students who are deaf.

Deaf Culture That
https://deafculturethat.com/

This website offers a partnership between the Deaf and hearing communities and has a range of educational materials. They offer resources including books and online programs that teach the hearing community about Deaf culture, educational materials, a blog, and links to other Deaf culture resources.

Deaf Resource Library
http://www.deaflibrary.org/

This site is an online collection of reference material and links intended to educate and inform people about Deaf cultures in Japan and the United States, as well as deaf- and hard-of-hearing-related topics.

Hands and Voices
https://www.handsandvoices.org/

This organization began as a parent support group in Colorado and now has over 50 chapters across the country. This network of families, professionals, educators, and service providers seeks to share ideas and advice to support those who are deaf or hard of hearing. The website offers a resource library on a variety of topics (in multiple languages), links to training opportunities, scholarships, and local support chapters, and offers opportunities for research.

Hearing Health Foundation.org
https://hearinghealthfoundation.org/

The mission of this nonprofit organization is to prevent and cure hearing loss, and to promote hearing health. The website offers overviews on hearing loss testing, prevention, and treatment. Also, they offer links to relevant research, a blog, webinars, and a magazine.

Helen Keller National Center
https://www.helenkeller.org/hknc/

Helen Keller is the only national rehabilitation program exclusively for children and adults who are deaf-blind. Links to sources for devices, camps, related agencies and services, and Helen Keller National Center publications are provided.

Laurent Clerc National Deaf Education Center
https://www.gallaudet.edu/clerc-center/info-to-go.html

Hosted by Gallaudet University, this site provides information about assistive technology, family resources, cochlear implants, Deaf culture, and legislation. It also includes a state-by-state listing of resources for students who are deaf or hard of hearing.

National Association of the Deaf
http://www.nad.org/

This website represents the National Association of the Deaf, which serves as a civil rights organization to support individuals who are deaf or hard of hearing in the United States. It offers links to resources on education, civil rights, sign language, and health services. It also offers information on state-level resources.

National Braille Press (NBP)
http://www.nbp.org/

The National Braille Press (NBP) is a nonprofit Braille printer and publisher of resources for persons who are blind. They promote literacy for blind children through outreach programs and encourage the teaching of Braille to blind children by providing age-appropriate Braille reading and support materials for caregivers and educators. Links to NBP bookstore, books for children, a special reading program, and a tour of the printing plant are available on their main page.

National Center on Deaf-Blindness
http://www.nationaldb.org

This national technical assistance center works with state and local partners to improve educational results and quality of life for children who are deaf-blind, and their families. Their website offers a list of information services, including support for families and educators, articles on a variety of topics related to deaf-blindness, and professional development opportunities for educators. They also offer an accessibility toolkit and links to outside services that families can access.

National Deaf Center
https://nationaldeafcenter.org/

An organization focused on supporting Deaf students in college and beyond. The website offers interactive games for teens, online learning modules, research and data, and a media library. There is also a resource library that offers evidence-based practices that support post-secondary outcomes for Deaf students.

National Family Association for Deaf-Blind
https://nfadb.org/

This site exists to support people who are deaf-blind and their families through training and support, collaboration with organizations, and advice regarding research. It also offers links to other resources, conferences, and a listserv.

National Federation of the Blind (NFB)
http://www.nfb.org/

The National Federation of the Blind is the oldest nationwide organization of blind Americans. Founded in 1940, the NFB consists of chapters in all 50 states, Washington, DC, and Puerto Rico. Through the network of blind members, the NFB coordinates many programs, services, and resources to defend the rights of blind Americans, provide information and support to blind children and adults, and bridge the knowledge gap for the visually impaired.

National Stuttering Association
https://westutter.org/

The National Stuttering Association is a nonprofit that provides support, friendship, and information to the stuttering community. The website offers information on stuttering, including causes and treatments, connection to local organizations, current research, and conference offerings, as well as links to other stuttering resources.

Paths to Literacy
https://www.pathstoliteracy.org/

This website is designed for teachers, families, and others who are interested in supporting literacy for children and use with visual impairments. Links include practical activities to use at home and in school, fundamentals on a variety of topics related to literacy and visual impairment, lessons and materials, links to apps and technology, and the latest research.

The Seeing Eye
http://www.seeingeye.org/

The Seeing Eye Organization seeks to enhance the independence and self-confidence of persons with vision loss by utilizing seeing-eye dogs. This site guides the reader through the detailed process of applying for a seeing-eye dog and even the possibility of raising a puppy.

The Stuttering Foundation
http://www.stutteringhelp.org/

The Stuttering Foundation provides free resources, services, and support for those who stutter and their families, as well as support for research into the causes of stuttering. The website offers information for parents (categorized by age of the child), resources to support teachers and physicians, as well as links to current research. There are also free materials and virtual learning opportunities for parents and educators.

The Stuttering Homepage
http://www.mnsu.edu/comdis/kuster/stutter.html

Supported by Minnesota State University, the Stuttering Home Page provides information about stuttering and other fluency disorders for both consumers and professionals who work with people who stutter. It includes information about research, therapy, support organizations, resources for professors who teach fluency disorders courses, materials for kids who stutter, and much more.

Emotional Impairment Resources

American Academy of Child and Adolescent Psychiatry
http://www.aacap.org/

The American Academy of Child and Adolescent Psychiatry is a medical health organization that seeks to improve the quality of life for persons affected by mental, behavioral, and developmental disorders. This site includes links to information for professionals and families by supporting education, medication, legislation, and policy.

Internet Mental Health
http://mentalhealth.com/home/index.html/

This site contains extensive descriptions, possible diagnosis, treatment options, related research, and additional resources for the 52 most common mental disorders. They offer facts about mental health in the United States and links to resources for medical or therapeutic interventions.

Mental Health Matters
https://mhmyouth.org/

This website offers information about a variety of mental health disorders, including information on symptoms, treatment, and getting or providing support. There are also links about practicing and managing wellness and self-care, as well as resources such as support groups and call centers.

National Alliance on Mental Health
http://www.nami.org/

This site is supported by the National Alliance of Mental Illness, a nonprofit organization that strives to share information and offer possibilities to the persons and families who suffer from mental illness. Major illnesses are linked to the home page, as well as medication options, support, and programs intended to improve the quality of life for everyone.

Cognitive Impairment Resources

American Association on Intellectual and Developmental Disabilities
http://www.aaidd.org/

The American Association on Intellectual and Developmental Disabilities is an interdisciplinary membership group focused on supporting persons with intellectual and developmental disabilities, and their families. There are links to disability resources, educational conferences and publications, data, and other national resources.

The Arc
http://www.thearc.org/

The Arc is a volunteer nonprofit organization that exists to support persons with intellectual and developmental disabilities. There are links to policy and federal laws, grassroots advocacy, networking through state and local chapters, and other disability resources.

The National Down Syndrome Society
http://www.ndss.org/

This national organization exists to advocate for persons with Down syndrome. Links on the site offer educational resources categorized by life span and category of life, public policy information, peer-reviewed research, and self-advocacy tools.

Physical Impairment Resources

American Academy of Special Education Professionals
http://www.aasep.org/

This website offers educational resources to special education professionals. Resources include links to data on each of the federally recognized disability categories under IDEA, as well as intervention resources for parents and teachers. There are also links to legal issues, transition services, conferences, reading materials, and career opportunities.

Brain Injury Association of America
http://www.biausa.org/

This association supports persons and their families living with a brain injury. The site has links to diagnosing and understanding brain injury, information for medical professionals, public policy, publications, and a library of brain-injury-related resources. They also offer grants for research and opportunities to support their cause with donations.

Center for Neuro Skills
http://www.neuroskills.com/

The Center for Neuro Skills offers information and treatment for people with brain injuries. They have physical locations in seven sites across the United States and offer telerehabilitation. The site also has links to patient videos and experiences, and programs such as community reentry assistance, and family support networks.

The Hydrocephalus Association
https://www.hydroassoc.org/

This site seeks to support persons who have hydrocephalus through research, support, education, and advocacy campaigns. There are extensive links to publications, information about medical procedures, scholarships, events, medical articles, and advocacy materials to help broaden the understanding of hydrocephalus.

Muscular Dystrophy Association
http://www.mda.org/

The Muscular Dystrophy Association offers research and support for persons with neuromuscular disease. The site offers links for family services, access to research and medical support, educational materials, and information about summer camps and regional and local events.

Scoliosis Research Society
http://www.srs.org/

This group is dedicated to the care of persons with spinal deformities. The site offers information for parents and families, medical and educational professionals, links to doctors, and ways to get involved. There is also information about conferences around the world and links to several other related resources.

The Spina Bifida Association
http://www.spinabifidaassociation.org/

This organization is focused on research and support for persons affected by a common birth defect, Spina Bifida. The association promotes prevention and quality of life support, and offers links to research, fact sheets, clinics, publications, news, national resources, and local events.

Traumatic Brain Injury
http://www.traumaticbraininjury.com/

An online resource for people and families of those with traumatic brain injury (TBI). The site offers facts about TBI, including symptoms, diagnosis, treatment options, legal resources, and an extensive video library. They also offer a state-by-state resources guide, as well as an article database.

Traumatic Brain Injury Survival Guide
http://www.tbiguide.com/

This site, run by clinical neuropsychologist Dr. Glen Johnson, offers a guide to head injuries. It offers specific information about how brain injuries occur, understanding how the brain works, recovery, and information for family members. There is also information about returning to school/work, and tips for communicating with medical professionals.

United Cerebral Palsy
http://www.ucp.org/

A leading site for information and advocacy for people with cerebral palsy. There are links to education, employment, health and wellness, assistive devices, support for parents and families, and other services related to travel, leisure, and quality of life. Additionally, the website offers information about grants, links to current research, and a state-by-state resource guide.

Chronic Medical Condition Resources

American Diabetes Association
http://www.diabetes.org/

This national organization is committed to helping persons with diabetes manage their lives. Both type I and type II diabetes are explained. The website offers extensive information about managing diabetes, such as nutrition, fitness, and lifestyle. There is also information about research, local advocacy, parenting tips, and support systems.

American Heart Association
http://www.americanheart.org/

This national group promotes healthy lifestyles and knowledge as keys to a better heart. The site provides a list of warning signs for heart attack and stroke, as well as information on cardiopulmonary resuscitation (CPR), heart disease, children's heart health, research articles, and advocacy. There are specific resources for medical professionals, educators, and parents.

American Lung Association
https://www.lung.org/

This site contains information about lung health and diseases for persons of all ages. They offer information about quitting smoking, and lung conditions such as asthma and lung cancer. There are links to current research and medical reports, public policy and advocacy, clean air initiatives, and clinical research centers across the United States.

Epilepsy Foundation
https://www.epilepsy.com/

The Epilepsy Foundation has shone a light on epilepsy by promoting awareness and understanding, advocating for laws that support people with epilepsy, and funding epilepsy research. The site contains information about seizures, diagnosis, treatments, current research, and ways to get involved in advocacy.

Leukemia and Lymphoma Society
http://www.lls.org/

The Leukemia and Lymphoma Society is dedicated to funding blood cancer research, education, and support. There are links to information about blood diseases and diagnosis, finding a caregiver, research, and advocacy. The site offers information for parents and caregivers, including support networks, podcasts, and other helpful links.

Learning Disabilities Resources

Learning Disabilities Association of America
https://ldaamerica.org/

This organization seeks to provide information regarding learning disabilities to parents, students, educators, and professionals. The website offers information about different types of learning disabilities, links to policy and advocacy materials, resources in the form of publications and partnerships, and event information.

LD Online
http://www.ldonline.org/

The website contains a wide variety of information for parents, teachers, and students about learning disabilities. There is a section on different types of learning disabilities and an overview of each one. There are links to frequently asked questions, and a glossary of terms. Teachers are offered links to instructional strategies, broken down by subject matter, as well as current articles and research. Parents are given tips for supporting learning disabilities at home.

LD Resources
https://www.ldrfa.org/

This nonprofit organization seeks to find solutions for those affected by learning disabilities, dyslexia, and ADHD. There are links to frequently asked questions, information about assistive technology, a blog, and a substantial resource page that offers related links to assessment, research, policy, and events.

The National Aphasia Association
http://www.aphasia.org/

The National Aphasia Association promotes public education, research, rehabilitation, and support services to assist persons with aphasia. This website contains links to diagnosis and treatment of aphasia, as well as the law, support materials, how to connect to a health professional or rehabilitation services.

The National Center for Learning Disabilities
http://www.ncld.org/

The National Center for Learning Disabilities works to improve the lives of children and adults with learning disabilities in the United States. The website offers advocacy materials, scholarships, research, and information for those wanting to get involved in policy actions. It also offers a learning disability checklist for parents and caregivers to aid in deciding how to support a child that is showing signs of a learning disability.

RESEARCH WITHIN MUSIC EDUCATION PERTAINING TO STUDENTS WITH DIFFERENCES AND DISABILITIES

Below is a list of research, dissertations, practitioner articles, and books within music education pertaining to students with differences and disabilities, from 2010 to time of publication. While there are certainly substantial contributions to scholarship on this topic from before 2010, much of what is included below has built upon it and is reflective of both changing terminology and continued efforts toward changes that benefit students with differences and disabilities.

Research Within Music Pertaining to Students with Differences and Disabilities

Allan, A. A. (2022). Vision 2020: A review of 20 years of inclusion studies in music education. *Update: Applications of Research in Music Education, 40*(2), 47–55. https://doi.org/10.1177/87551233211040088.

Allen, R., & Heaton, P. (2010). Autism, music, and the therapeutic potential of music in alexithymia. *Music Perception: An Interdisciplinary Journal, 27*(4), 251–261. https://doi.org/10.1525/mp.2010.27.4.251.

Au, T., & Lau, N. (2021). Private music teachers' knowledge of and attitudes towards students with autism spectrum disorder. *Journal of Autism and Developmental Disorders, 51*(12), 4551–4559. https://doi.org/10.1007/s10803-020-04809-5.

Baker, D., & Green, L. (2016). Perceptions of schooling, pedagogy, and notation in the lives of visually-impaired musicians. *Research Studies in Music Education, 30*(1), 77–91. https://doi.org/10.1177/1321103X08089891.

bell, a. p. (2017). (dis)ability and music education: Paralympian Patrick Anderson and the experience of disability in music. *Action, Criticism, & Theory for Music Education, 16*(3), 108–128. https://doi.org/10.22176/act16.3.108.

bell, a. p., Bonin, D., Pethrick, H., Antwi-Nsiah, A., & Matterson, B. (2020). Hacking, disability, and music education. *International Journal of Music Education, 38*(4), 657–672. https://doi.org/10.1177/0255761420930428.

Bernabé-Villodre, M. d. M., & Martínez-Bello, V. E. (2018). Analysis of gender, age, and disability representation in music education textbooks: A research update. *International Journal of Music Education, 36*(4), 494–508. https://doi.org/10.1177/0255761418763900.

Bremmer, M., Hermans, C., & Lamers, V. (2021). The charmed dyad: Multimodal music lessons for pupils with severe or multiple disabilities. *Research Studies in Music Education, 43*(2), 259–272. https://doi.org/10.1177/1321103X20974802.

Brown, L. S., & Jellison, J. A. (2012). Music research with children and youth with disabilities and typically developing peers: A systematic review. *Journal of Research in Music Therapy, 49*(3), 335–364. https://doi.org/10.1093/jmt/49.3.335.

Cano, M., & Sanchez-Iborra, R. (2015). On the use of a multimedia platform for music education with handicapped children. *Computers & Education, 87*, 254–176. https://doi.org/10.1016/j.compedu.2015.07.010.

Cassidy, J. W., & Colwell, C. M. (2012). University students' perceptions of an inclusive music production. *Journal of Music Teacher Education, 21*(2), 28–40. https://doi.org/10.1177/1057083711411714.

Churchill, W. N. (2015). Deaf and hard-of-hearing musicians: Crafting a narrative strategy. *Research Studies in Music Education, 37*(1), 21–36. https://doi.org/10.1177/1321103X15589777.

Churchill, W. N., & Bernard, C. F. (2020). Disability and the ideology of ability: How might music educators respond? *Philosophy of Music Education Review, 28*(1), 24–46. https://doi.org/10.2979/philmusieducrevi.28.1.03.

Culp, M. E., & Salvador, K. (2021). Music teacher education program practices: Preparing teachers to work with diverse learners. *Journal of Music Teacher Education, 30*(2), 51–64. https://doiorg/10.1177/1057083720984365.

Dingle, G., Brander, C., Ballantyne, J., & Baker, F. (2012). "To be heard": The social and mental health benefits of choir singing for disadvantaged adults. *Psychology of Music, 41*(4), 405–421. https://doi.org/10.1177/03057356.11430081.

Dobbs, T. (2012). A critical analysis of disabilities discourse in the journal of research in music education. *Bulletin of the Council for Research in Music Education, 194*, 7–30. https://www.jstor.org/stable/10.5406/bulcouresmusedu.194.0007.

Draper, A. R. (2021). Educational research for students with autism spectrum disorder: Recommendations for music education. *Bulletin of the Council for Research in Music Education*, 230, 22–46. https://doi.org/10.5406/21627223.230.02.

Draper, A. R., & Bartolome, S. J. (2021). Academy of music and arts for special education (AMASE): An ethnography of an individual music instruction program for students with disabilities. *Journal of Research in Music Education, 69*(3), 258–283. https://doi.org/10.1177/0022429421990337.

Draper, E. (2017). Observations of children with disabilities in four elementary music classrooms. *Update: Applications of Research in Music Education, 36*(1), 12–19. https://doi.org/10.1177/8755123316660594.

Gerrity, K., Hourigan, R., & Horton, P. (2013). Conditions that facilitate music learning among students with special needs: A mixed-methods inquiry. *Journal of Research in Music Education, 61*(2), 144–159. https://www.jstor.org/stable/41999574.

Greher, G. R., Hillier, A., Dougherty, M., & Nataliya, P. (2010). SoundScape: An interdisciplinary music intervention for adolescents and young adults on the autism spectrum. *International Journal of Education & the Arts, 11*(9), 1–27. http://www.ijea.org/v11n9/.

Grimsby, R. (2020). "Anything is better than nothing!": Inservice teacher preparation for teaching students with disabilities. *Journal of Music Teacher Education, 29*(3), 77–90. https://doi.org/10.1177/1057083719893116.

Grimsby, R. (2022). "A meeting of equals": Music educators and special education paraprofessionals in a community of practice. *Research Studies in Music Education, 45*(3), 497–511. https://doi.org/ 10.1177/1321103X221078521.

Grimsby, R., & Knapp, E. J. (2022). A comparison of federal and state special education laws: Implications for music educators. *Arts Education Policy Review*, 1–11. https://doi.org/10.1080/10632913.2022.2077872

Hammel, A. M., & Gerrity, K. W. (2012). The effect of instruction on teacher perceptions of competence when including students with special needs in music classrooms. *Update: Applications of Research in Music Education, 31*(1), 6–13. https://doi.org/10.1177/8755123312457882.

Hammel, A., & Hourigan, R. (2011). The fundamentals of special education policy: Implications for music teachers and music teacher education. *Arts Education Policy Review, 112*(4), 174–179. https://doi.org/10.1080/10632913.2011.592463.

Hillier, A., Greher, G., Poto, N., & Dougherty, M. (2011). Positive outcomes following participation in a music intervention for adolescents and young adults on the autism spectrum. *Psychology of Music, 40*(2), 201–215. https://doi.org/10.1177/03057 35610386837.

Hillier, A., Greher, G., Queenan, A., Marshall, S., & Kopek, J. (2016). Music, technology, and adolescents with autism spectrum disorders: The effectiveness of the touch screen interface. *Music Education Research, 18*(3), 269–282. https://doi.org/

10.1080/14613808.2015.1077802.Jellison, J., & Draper, E. (2015). Music research in inclusive settings: 1975 to 2013. *Journal of Research in Music Education, 62*(4), 325–331. https://www.jstor.org/stable/43900262.

Jones, S. K. (2015). Teaching students with disabilities: A review of music education research as it relates to the Individuals with Disabilities Education Act. *Update: Applications of Research in Music Education, 34*(1), 13–23. https://doi.org/10.1177/8755123314548039.

Laes, T., & Westerlund, H. (2018). Performing disability in music teacher education: Moving beyond inclusion through expanded professionalism. *International Journal of Music Education, 36*(1), 34–46. https://doi.org/10.1177/0255761417703782.

Lanovaz, M. J., Sladcezek, I. E., & Rapp, J. T. (2011). Effects of music on stereotyping children with autism. *Journal of Applied Behavioral Analysis, 44*(3), 647–651. https://doi.org/10.1901/jaba.2011.44-647.

Levy, S., Robb, A. J., & Jindal-Snape, D. (2017). Disability, personalisation, and community arts: Exploring the spatial dynamics of children with disabilities participation in inclusive music class. *Disability & Society, 32*(2), 254–268. https://doi.org/10.1080/09687599.2016.1276433.

Nabb, D., & Balcetis, E. (2010). Access to music education: Nebraska band directors' experiences and attitudes regarding students with physical disabilities. *Journal of Research in Music Education, 57*(4), 308–319. https://doi.org/10.1177/0022429409353142.

Nelson, P. N., & Hourigan, R. (2015). A comparative case study of learning strategies and recommendations of five professional musicians with dyslexia. *Update: Applications of Research in Music Education, 35*(1), 1–12. https://doi.org/10.1177/8755123315581341.

Parker, E. C., & Draves, T. J. (2017). A narrative of two preservice music teachers with visual impairment. *Journal of Research in Music Education, 64*(4), 385–404. https://doi.org/10.1177/0022429416674704.

Pickard, B. (2019). A framework for mediating medical and social models of disability in instrumental teaching for children with Down Syndrome. *Research Studies in Music Education, 43*(2), 1–19. https://doi.org/10.1177/1321103X19855416.

Pierce, A., & Abramo, J. (2012). An ethnographic case study of music learning at a school for the blind. *Bulletin of the Council for Research in Music Education, 195*, 9–24. https://www.jstor.org/stable/10.5406/bulcouresmusedu.195.0009.

Power, A., & McCormack, D. (2012). Piano pedagogy with a student who is blind: An Australian case. *International Journal of Music Education, 30*(4), 341–353. https://doi.org/10.1177/0255761412459163.

Preis, J., Amon, R, Robinette, D. S., & Rozegar, A. (2016). Does music matter? The effects of background music on verbal expression and engagement in children with autism spectrum disorders. *Music Therapy Perspectives, 34*(1), 106–115. https://doi.org/10.1093/mtp/miu044.

Rauscher, F. H., & Hinton, S. C. (2011). Music instruction and its diverse extra-musical benefits. *Music Perception, 29*(2), 215–226. https://doi.org/10.1525/mp.2011.29.2.215.

Robinson, C. R., Belgrave, M. J., & Keown, D. J. (2019). Effects of disability type, task complexity, and biased statements on undergraduate music majors' inclusion decisions for performance ensembles. *Journal of Music Teacher Education, 28*(2), 70–83. https://doi.org/10.1177/1057083718811396.

Salvador, K (2010). Who isn't a special learner? A survey of how music teacher education programs prepare future educators to work with exceptional populations. *Journal of Music Teacher Education, 20*(1), 27–38. https://doi.org/10.1177/1057083710362462.

Salvador, K. (2015). Music instruction for elementary students with moderate to severe cognitive impairments: A case study. *Research Studies in Music Education, 37*(2), 161–174. https://doi.org/10.1177/1321103X15613645.

Salvador, K., & Pasiali, V. (2017). Intersections between music education and music therapy: Education reform, arts education, exceptionality, and policy at the local level. *Arts Education Policy Review, 118*(2), 93–103. https://doi.org/10.1080/10632913.2015.1060553.

Simpson, K., & Keen, D. (2011). Music interventions for children with autism: Narrative review of literature. *Journal of Autism and Developmental Disorders, 41*(11), 1507–1514. Retrieved from https://link.springer.com/article/10.1007/s10803-010-1172-y.

Taylor, D. M. (2016). Learning from parents of children with disabilities. *Journal of Music Teacher Education, 172*, 9–23. https://doi.org/10.1177/1057083716638489.

VanWeelden, K., & Whipple, J. (2013). Music educators' perceptions of preparation and supports available for inclusion. *Journal of Music Teacher Education, 23*(2), 33–51. https://doi.org/10.1177/1057083713484585.

VanWeelden, K., & Whipple, J. (2014). Music educators' perceived effectiveness of inclusion. *Journal of Research in Music Education, 62*(2), 148–160. https://doi.org/10.1177/0022429414530563.

Wan, C. Y., Rüber, T., Hohmann, A., & Schlaug, G. (2010). The therapeutic effects of singing in neurological disorders. *Music Perception, 27*(4), 287–295. https://doi.org/10.1525/mp.2010.27.4.287.

Whipple, C. M., Gfeller, K., Driscoll, V., Oleson, J., & McGregor, K. (2015). Do communication disorders extend to musical messages? An answer from children with hearing loss or autism spectrum disorders. *Journal of Music Therapy, 52*(1), 78–116. https://doi.org/10.1093/jmt/thu039.

Whipple, J., & VanWeelden, K. (2012). Educational supports for students with special needs: Preservice music educators' perceptions. *Update: Applications of Research in Music Education, 30*(2), 32–45. https://doi.org/10.1177/8755123312436987.

Wong, M. W. (2021). Fostering musical creativity of students with intellectual disabilities: Strategies, gamification, and re-framing creativity. *Music Education Research, 23*(1), 1–13. https://doi.org/10.1080/14613808.2020.1862777.

Wong, M. W. (2022). The ecology for fostering the musical creativity of students with intellectual disabilities. *International Journal of Music Education, 40*(2), 190–204. https://doi.org/10.1177/02557614211031255.

Wrazen, L. (2016). Spiraling to redefine (dis)ability: A case study in summer music programming for children. *Yearbook for Traditional Music, 48*, 167–185. Retrieved from https://www-proquest-com/scholarly-journals/spiraling-redefine-dis-ability-case-study-summer/docview/1886300555/se-2?accountid=12598.

Dissertations Within Music Education

Barksdale, A. L. (2021). *Self-efficacy beliefs of university music majors with disabilities* (Publication No. 28770823) [Doctoral dissertation, Boston University]. ProQuest Dissertations and Theses Global.

Barnes, J. P. (2010). *Moments of meeting: Difficulties and developments in shared attention, interaction, and communication with children with autism during two years of music therapy in a public preschool class* (Publication No. 862650757) [Doctoral dissertation, Lesley University]. ProQuest Dissertations and Theses Global.

Cannon, M. L. C. (2018). *The effects of instrumental music instruction on the neurophysiological responses and adaptive behaviors of children with autism spectrum disorder* (Publication No. 10751498) [Doctoral dissertation, The University of North Carolina at Greensboro]. ProQuest Dissertations and Theses Global.

Cardella, C. (2014). *Musical ensemble participation and social behaviors in autistic children: Collective case study* (Publication No. 3648826) [Doctoral dissertation, University of Idaho]. ProQuest Dissertations and Theses Global.

Chang, A. C. (2017). *String teachers' perceptions of inclusion of students with autism in classroom settings* (Publication No. 10266847) [Doctoral dissertation, The Florida State University]. ProQuest Dissertations and Theses Global.

Churchill, W. N. (2016). *Claiming musical spaces: Stories of deaf and hard-of-hearing musicians* (Publication No. 10117030) [Doctoral dissertation, Columbia University]. ProQuest Dissertations and Theses Global.

Cólon-León, V. (2018). *A model of parental involvement in the music education of students with special education needs* (Publication No. 10824052) [Doctoral dissertation, University of Miami]. ProQuest Dissertations and Theses Global.

Davilla, G. A. (2013). *A graduate course on inclusion: Four elementary/general music educators' perceived attitudes and applications in the classroom* (Publication No. 3608227) [Doctoral dissertation, University of Iowa]. ProQuest Dissertations and Theses Global.

Davis, R. E. (2019). *Approaches to teaching music reading to piano students with autism spectrum disorder* (Publication No. 27546247) [Doctoral dissertation, University of South Carolina]. ProQuest Dissertations and Theses Global.

Delaney, C. A. (2016). *Patterns of activity and practice among music educators concerning instrumental music students with disabilities* (Publication No. 10131342) [Doctoral dissertation, George Mason University]. ProQuest Dissertations and Theses Global.

Douglas-Kline, M. A. (2015). *The perceived value of music teacher input during IEP meetings: Special education teacher survey responses* (Publication No. 3736871) [Doctoral dissertation, Indiana University]. ProQuest Dissertations and Theses Global.

Draper, A. R. (2020). *Music education for students with disabilities* (Publication No. 28089178) [Doctoral dissertation, Northwestern University]. ProQuest Dissertations and Theses Global.

Duffy, V. A. (2012). *Musical social stories and the preschool child with autism spectrum disorder* (Publication No. 3504191) [Doctoral dissertation, Alliant International University]. ProQuest Dissertations and Theses Global.

Farrell, R. J. (2013). *Accommodating Asperger's: An autoethnography on the learning experience in an e-learning music education program* (Publication No.

3575263) [Doctoral dissertation, Boston University]. ProQuest Dissertations and Theses Global.

Grimsby, R. (2020). *"Because we are important!": Music educators and special education paraprofessionals in a community of practice* (Publication No. 27962769) [Doctoral dissertation, Michigan State University]. ProQuest Dissertations and Theses Global.

Hahn, K. R. (2010). *Inclusion of students with disabilities: Preparation and practices of music educators* (Publication No. 3420149) [Doctoral dissertation, Pennsylvania State University]. ProQuest Dissertations and Theses Global.

Hamblin, C. L. (2013). *Teachers' attitudes concerning students with special needs in area special classes* (Publication No. 3550960) [Doctoral dissertation, Walden University]. ProQuest Dissertations and Theses Global.

Hoffman, E. C. (2011). *The status of students with special needs in the instrumental musical ensemble and the effect of selected educator and institutional variables on rates of inclusion* (Publication No. 3465567) [Doctoral dissertation, University of Nebraska-Lincoln]. ProQuest Dissertations and Theses Global.

Hughes, A. (2019). *The inclusion of all students in a music curriculum for California public comprehensive high schools* (Publication No. 13885874) [Doctoral dissertation, Concordia University]. ProQuest Dissertations and Theses Global.

Jemison Pollard, D. (2010). *The use of music to improve social skills development in children diagnosed with autism* (Publication No. 3536911) [Doctoral dissertation, Texas Southern University]. ProQuest Dissertations and Theses Global.

Joseph, C. K. (2011). *Integrating music education, music therapy and special education in a music classroom* (Publication No. 3475951) [Doctoral dissertation, Union Institute and University]. ProQuest Dissertations and Theses Global.

Knapp, E. J. (2022). *"I want to be a better person and a better teacher": Exploring the constructs of race and ability in a music educator collaborative teacher study group* (Publication No. 29170065) [Doctoral dissertation, Michigan State University]. ProQuest Dissertations and Theses Global.

Laird, L. A. E. (2016). *A little bit more the same than yesterday: A mixed methods exploration of choir member empathy and attitudes towards individuals with disabilities* (Publication No. 10103359) [Doctoral dissertation, University of Nebraska-Lincoln]. ProQuest Dissertations and Theses Global.

McDonald, S. G. (2021). *Accommodating learning differences in the clarinet studio: Private teacher experiences and pedagogical guidelines* (Publication No. 28494687) [Doctoral dissertation, University of Miami]. ProQuest Dissertations and Theses Global.

Mitofsky Neuss, L. K. (2021). *A proposed approach for teaching music students with dyslexia using Orton-Gillingham techniques* (Publication No. 28319667) [Doctoral dissertation, The Florida State University]. ProQuest Dissertations and Theses Global.

Mullins, W. D. (2017). *A survey of piano teachers whose students have ADHD: Their training, experiences, and best practices* (Publication No. 10801039) [Doctoral dissertation, The Ohio State University]. ProQuest Dissertations and Theses Global.

Nelson, K. (2014). *Successful strategies of individuals with dyslexia in the field of music: A comparative case study* (Publication No. 3581077) [Doctoral dissertation, Boston University]. ProQuest Dissertations and Theses Global.

Norris, S. (2020). *Private studio music teachers' attitudes regarding students with disabilities: A descriptive analysis* (Publication No. 28028090) [Doctoral dissertation, The University of Arizona]. ProQuest Dissertations and Theses Global.

Nospal, T. (2022). *Social capital and inclusive music settings: A case study of two paraprofessionals and a music teacher's collaborative practices* (Publication No. 29162402) [Doctoral dissertation, Boston University]. ProQuest Dissertations and Theses Global.

Perry, S. E. (2015). *Musical engagement of children with sensory processing disorder: A multiple case study* (Publication No. 3704513) [Doctoral dissertation, Columbia University]. ProQuest Dissertations and Theses Global.

Powell, L. (2021). *Inclusion practices for students with autism in the music classroom: A survey of K-6 music educators' perceptions, training, and strategies* (Publication No. 29396214) [Doctoral dissertation, Auburn University]. ProQuest Dissertations and Theses Global.

Rathgeber, J. (2019). *Troubling disability: Experiences of disability in, though, and around music* (Publication No. 13857765) [Doctoral dissertation, Arizona State University]. ProQuest Dissertations and Theses Global.

Rice, N. M. F. (2020). *Beyond the IEP meeting: Parents' perceptions of music education for individuals with exceptionalities* (Publication No. 28026957) [Doctoral dissertation, Boston University]. ProQuest Dissertations and Theses Global.

Rodríguez Aedo, P. (2021). *Music teaching strategies for students with low vision, including blindness* (Publication No. 28317447) [Doctoral dissertation, Teachers College, Columbia University]. ProQuest Dissertations and Theses Global.

Smith, J. C. (2017). *The status of music therapists and music educators working with children with autism spectrum disorders in school settings* (Publication No. 10278128) [Doctoral dissertation, University of Hartford]. ProQuest Dissertations and Theses Global.

Soja, M. C. (2015). *The effect of timbre and pitch-pattern difficulty on the pitch perceptions of elementary-aged users of cochlear implants* (Publication No. 3708183) [Doctoral dissertation, University of North Carolina at Greensboro]. ProQuest Dissertations and Theses Global.

Stafford, K. (2019). *Music teachers' perceptions of their involvement in the implementation processes of Individualized Education Programs* (Publication No. 13885951) [Doctoral dissertation, University of Kansas]. ProQuest Dissertations and Theses Global.

Tindell, K. W. (2010). *Comparison of music-based curriculum versus an eclectic curriculum for speech acquisition in students with autism spectrum disorder* (Publication No. 3413582) [Doctoral dissertation, Boston University]. ProQuest Dissertations and Theses Global.

Vinciguerra, S. (2016). *Lived experiences of secondary instrumental music teachers who teach students with disabilities* (Publication No. 10135023) [Doctoral dissertation, Boston University]. ProQuest Dissertations and Theses Global.

Vladikovic, J. (2013). *Gifted learners, dyslexia, music, and the piano: Rude, inattentive, uncooperative, or something else?* (Publication No. 3567890) [Doctoral dissertation, Arizona State University]. ProQuest Dissertations and Theses Global.

Witmer, N. S. (2015). *Music lessons from a tablet computer: The effect of incorporating a touchscreen device in teaching music staff notation to students with dyslexia* (Publication No. 3686102) [Doctoral dissertation, Boston University]. ProQuest Dissertations and Theses Global.

Selected Research Within General Education

Banks, J. (2017). "These people are never going to stop labeling me": Educational experiences of African American male students labeled with learning disabilities. *Equity & Excellence in Education, 50*, 96–107. https://doi.org/10.1080/10665684.2016.1250235.

Banks, J., Frawley, D. & McCoy, S. (2015). Achieving inclusion? Effective resourcing of students with special education needs. *International Journal of Inclusive Education, 19*(9), 926–943. https://doi.org/10.1080/13603116.2015.1018344.

Beach, K. D., Sanchez, V., Flynn, L. J., & O'Connor, R. E. (2015). Teaching academic vocabulary to adolescents with learning disabilities. *Teaching Exceptional Children, 48*(1), 36–44. https://doi.org/10.1177/0040059915594783.

Berchiatti, M., Ferrer, A., Badenes-Ribera, L., & Longobardi, C. (2022). Student-teacher relationship quality in students with learning disabilities and special educational needs. *International Journal of Inclusive Education, ahead-of-print*, 1–19. https://doi.org/10.1080/13603116.2022.2135779.

Brooks, S. W., Schwartz, R., Ampuero, M., & Kokina, A. (2022). Teacher perspectives on partnerships on families of children with autism. *Journal of Research in Special Educational Needs, 23*(2), 79–89. https://doi.org/10.1111/1471-3802.12581.

Byrnes, L., & Rickards, F. (2011). Listening to the voices of students with disabilities: Can such voices inform practice? *Australasian Journal of Special Education, 35*(1), 25–34. https://doi.org/10.1375/ajse.35.1.25.

Connor, D., & Gabel, S. (2013). "Cripping" the curriculum through academic activism: Working toward increasing global exchanges to reframe (dis)ability and education. *Equity and Excellence in Education, 46*(1), 100–118. https://doi.org/10.1080/10665684.2013.750186.

Cooc, N. (2023). National trends in special education and academic outcomes for English learners with disabilities. *The Journal of Special Education*, 57(2), 106–117. https://doi.org/10.1177/00224669221147272.

Cooper-Duffy, K., Szedia, P., & Hyer, G. (2010). Teaching literacy to students with significant cognitive disabilities. *Teaching Exceptional Children, 42*(3), 30–39. https://doi.org/10.1177/004005991004200304.

Coviello, J., & DeMatthews, D. E. (2021). Failure is not final: Principals' perspectives on creating inclusive schools for students with disabilities. *Journal of Educational Administration, 59*(4), 514–531. https://doi.org/10.1108/JEA-08-2020-0170.

Delmolino, L., Hansford, A. P., Bamond, M. J., Fiske, K. E., & LaRue, R. H. (2013). The use of instructive feedback for teaching language skills to children with autism. *Research in Autism Spectrum Disorders, 7*(6), 648–661. https://doi.org/10.1016/j.rasd.2013.02.015.

DeMatthews, D:, & Serafini, A. (2020). Leading inclusive schools: Principal perceptions, practices, and challenges to meaningful change. *Educational Administration Quarterly*, 57(1), 3–48. https://doi.org/10.1177/0013161X20913897.

Donmez, M. (2022). A systematic literature review for the use of eye-tracking in special education. *Education and Information Technologies, 28*, 6515–6540. https://doi.org/10.1007/s10639-022-11456-z/

Erevelles, N., & Minear, A. (2010). Unspeakable offenses: Untangling race and disability in discourses on intersectionality. *Journal of Literary & Cultural Disability*

Studies, 4(2), 127-145. Retrieved from https://www-proquest-com/scholarly-journals/unspeakable-offenses-untangling-race-disability/docview/737523739/se-2?accountid=12598.

Glasby, J., Graham, L. J., White, S. L. J., & Tancredi, H. (2022). Do teachers know enough about the characteristics and educational impacts of developmental language disorder (DLD) to successfully include students with DLD? *Teaching and Teacher Education, 119*, 103868. https://doi.org/10.1016/j.tate.2022.103868.

Goddard, Y. L., Ammirante, L., & Jin, N. (2022). A thematic review of current literature examining evidence-based practices and inclusion. *Education Sciences, 13*(1), 38. https://doi.org/10.3390/educsci13010038.

Green, J. G., McLaughlin, K. A., Alegria, M., Costello, E. J., Gruber, M. J., Hoagwood, K., . . . Kessler, R. C. (2013). School mental health resources and adolescent mental health service use. *Journal of the American Academy of Child & Adolescent Psychiatry, 52*(5), 501–510. https://doi.org/10.1016/j.jaac.2013.03.002.

Guardino, C., Cannon J. E., & Eberst, K. (2014). Building the evidence-base of effective reading strategies to use with deaf English-language learners. *Communication Disorders Quarterly, 35*(2), 59–73. https://doi.org/10.1177/1525740113506932.

Gulya, N., & Fehérvári, A. (2023). The impact of literary works containing characters with disabilities on students' perception and attitudes towards people with disabilities. *International Journal of Educational Research, 117*, 102132. https://doi.org/10.1016/j.ijer.2022.102132.

Gupta, P. (2022). Cognitive profiles of students with hearing loss as a pathway for differentiated instruction. *International Journal of Special Education, 37*(2), 55–66. https://doi.org/10.52291/ijse.2022.37.40.

Hudson, M. E., Browder, D., & Wakeman, S. (2013). Helping students with moderate and severe intellectual disability access grade-level text. *Teaching Exceptional Children, 45*(3), 14–23. https://doi.org/10.1177/004005991304500302.

Johnsen, S. K., Parker, S. L., & Farah, Y. N. (2015). Providing services for students with gifts and talents within a response-to-intervention framework. *Teaching Exceptional Children 47*(4), 226–233. https://doi.org/10.1177/0040059915569358.

Kasari, C. & Smith, T. (2013). Interventions in schools for children with autism spectrum disorder: Methods and recommendations. *Autism: The International Journal of Research and Practice. 17*(3), 254–267. https://doi.org/10.1177/1362361312470496.

Kauffman, J., & Badar, J. (2013). How we might make special education for students with emotional or behavioral disorders less stigmatizing. *Behavioral Disorders, 39*(1), 16–27. https://doi.org/10.1177/019874291303900103.

Lindsay, S. Proulx, M. Scott, H., & Thomson, N. (2014). Exploring teachers' strategies for including children with autism spectrum disorder in mainstream classrooms. *International Journal of Inclusive Education, 18*(2), 101–122. https://doi.org/10.1080/13603116.2012.758320.

Lubet, A. (2011). Disability rights, music, and the case for inclusive education. International *Journal of Inclusive Education, 15*(1), 57–70. https://doi.org/10.1080/13603110903125178.

Lundqvist-Persson, C., & Holmqvist, G. (2022). Music education contributes to development and personal change in young adults with disabilities. *Frontiers in Rehabilitation Sciences, 3*, 1–11. https://doi.org/10.3389/fresc.2022.1046480.

Mason, E. N., & Connor, K. E. (2022). The persistence of deficit language: An investigation of general education preservice teachers' shifting talk about disability. *Teacher Education Quarterly, 49*(4), 6–27. Retrieved from https://www.proquest.com/docview/2743533549/fulltextPDF/84CDC5D2BDD3499APQ/1?accountid=7113.

McDowell, C. (2010). An adaptation tool kit for teaching music. *Teaching Exceptional Children Plus*, 6(3), 1–20. Retrieved from https://files.eric.ed.gov/fulltext/EJ879595.pdf.

Nevill, T., & Forsey, M. (2022). The social impact of schooling on students with dyslexia: A systematic review of the qualitative research on the primary and secondary education of dyslexic students. *Educational Research Review*, *38*, 100507. https://doi.org/10.1016/j.edurev.2022.100507.

Peine, M. E., & Coleman, L. J. (2010). The phenomenon of waiting in class. *Journal for the Education of the Gifted*, *34*(2), 220–244. https://files.eric.ed.gov/fulltext/EJ910193.pdf.

Rensfeld Flink, A., Thunberg, G., Nyman, A., Broberg, M., & Åsberg Johnels, J. (2022). Augmentative and alternative communication with children with severe/profound intellectual and multiple disabilities: Speech language pathologists' clinical practices and reasoning. *Disability and Rehabilitation: Assistive Technology, (19)*3, 962–974. https://doi.org/10.1080/17483107.2022.2137252.

Roy, A., Guay, F., & Valois, P. (2013). Teaching to address diverse learning needs: Development and validation of a differentiated instruction scale. *International Journal of Inclusive Education*, *17*(11), 1186–1204. https://doi.org/10.1080/13603116.2012.743604.

Scheef, A. R., Hollingshead, A., Malone, K., Sherman, W. M., Seamans, A., Sabala, T., & Carson, J. (2022). Increasing the independence of students with disabilities in the classroom through indirect paraprofessional support. *Teaching Exceptional Children*, *56*(2), 82–88. 4005992211434. https://doi.org/10.1177/00400599221143457.

Singleton, S. M., & Filce, H. G. (2015). Graphic organizers for secondary students with learning disabilities. *Teaching Exceptional Children, 48*(2), 17–32. https://doi.org/10.1177/0040059915605799.

Skinner, S. Y., Katz, J., & Knight, V. F. (2022). Meaningful participation in a general education classroom of a student with significant disabilities: Bridging the fields of occupational therapy and inclusive education. *International Journal of Inclusive Education*, 1–22. https://doi.org/10.1080/13603116.2022.2137589.

Smucker, A. D. (2022). Exploring the growth of inclusive curriculum: A systematic review of scholar and practitioner perspectives. *International Journal of Inclusive Education*, 1–15. https://doi.org/10.1080/13603116.2022.2121988.

Stark, K., Bettini, E., & Chi, O. (2022). Momentary affective experiences of teachers serving students with emotional and behavioral disabilities in self-contained settings. *Remedial and Special Education*, *44*(5), 381–394. 74193252211356. https://doi.org/10.1177/07419325221135613.

Zhang, D., Wang, Q., Stegall, J., Losinki, M., & Katsiyannis, A. (2018). The construction and initial validation of the student teachers' efficacy scale for teaching students with disabilities. *Remedial and Special Education*, *39*(1), 39–52. https://doi.org/10.1177/0741932516686059.

Books Within Music Education and Music Therapy

Adamek, M. S., & Darrow, A. A. (2018). *Music in special education* (3rd ed.). American Music Therapy Association.

Berger, D. (2016). *Kids, music 'n' autism: Bringing out the music in your child.* Jessica Kingsley.

Blair, D. V., & McCord, K. A. (Eds). (2016). *Exceptional music pedagogy for children with exceptionalities: International perspectives.* Oxford University Press.

Carrico, A., & Grennell, K. (2023). *Disability and accessibility in the music classroom: A teacher's guide.* Routledge.

Cheng, W., & Horowitz, W. (Eds.). (2016). *Making music with a hearing loss: Strategies and stories* (2nd ed.). AAMHL.

De Orio, P. (2014). *Teaching students with disabilities: A resource guide for the strings classroom.* TL Publications.

Hammel, A., & Hourigan, R. (2020). *Teaching music to students with autism.* (2nd ed.) Oxford University Press.

Howe, B., Jensen-Moulton, S., & Lerner, N. (Eds.). (2016). *The Oxford handbook of music and disability studies.* Oxford University Press.

Jacquiss, V., & Patterson, D. (2015). *Addressing special educational needs in the curriculum: Music* (2nd ed.). Routledge.

Jellison, J. A. (2015). *Including everyone: Creating music classrooms where all children learn.* Oxford University Press.

Kern, P., & Humpal, M. E. (2013). *Early childhood music therapy and autism spectrum disorders: Developing potential in young children and their families.* Jessica Kingsley.

McCord, K. (2017). *Teaching the postsecondary student with disabilities.* Oxford University Press.

McCord, K., Gruben, A., & Rathgeber, J. (2014). *Accessing music: Enhancing student learning in the general music classroom through UDL.* Alfred.

McGrath Taylor, M., & Gagne, D. (2014). *Music for inclusive classrooms.* Themes and Variation.

McPherson, G., & Welch, G. (2018). *Special needs, community music, and adult learning: An Oxford handbook of music education*, Volume 4. Oxford University Press.

Lim, H. A. (2010). *Developmental speech-language training through music for children with autism spectrum disorders: Theory and clinical application.* Jessica Kingsley.

Ockelford, A. (2013). *Music, language, and autism: A guide for parents and practitioners.* Jessica Kingsley.

Ott, P. (2011). *Music for special kids: Musical activities, songs, instruments, and resources.* Jessica Kingsley.

Schraer-Joiner, L. E. (2014). *Music for children with hearing loss: A resource for parents and teachers.* Oxford University Press.

Scott, S. J. (2016). *Music education for children with autism spectrum disorder: A resource for teachers.* Oxford University Press.

Strauss, J. (2011). *Extraordinary measures: Disability in music.* Oxford University Press.

Surette, K. (2020). *Creative miracles: A practitioner's guide to adaptive music.* Warrior Woman Press.

Tomlinson, J., Derrington, P., & Oldfield, A. (2012). *Music therapy in schools: Working with children of all ages in mainstream and special education.* Jessica Kingsley.

Vargas, A. (2018). *Disability and music performance.* Routledge.
Walworth, D. (2013). *Bright start music: A developmental program for music therapists, parents, and teachers of young children.* American Music Therapy Association.
Williams, J. (2013). *Music and the social model: An occupational therapy approach to music with people labelled as having learning disabilities.* Jessica Kingsley.

Selected Books Within General Education

Baglieri, S., & Shapiro, A, eds. (2017). *Disability studies and the inclusive classroom.* Routledge.
Bateman, D. F., & Cline, J. L. (2016). *A teacher's guide to special education.* ASCD.
Bateman, D., & Yell, M. L. (Eds.). (2019). *Current trends and legal issues in special education.* Corwin.
Beninghof, A. M. (2022). *Specially designed instruction: Increasing success for students with disabilities.* Routledge.
Berkell, Z. D., Wehmeyer, M. L., & Simpson, R. L. (Eds.). (2012). *Educating students with autism spectrum disorders: Research-based principles and practices.* Routledge.
Browder, D. M., Spooner, F., & Courtade, G. (2020). *Teaching students with moderate and severe disabilities* (2nd ed.). Guilford Press.
Brownell, M. T. (2012). *Inclusive instruction: Evidence-based practices for teaching students with disabilities.* Guilford Press.
Chardin, M., & Novak, K. (2021). *Equity by design: Delivering on the power and promise of UDL.* Corwin.
Davidson, J., & Orsini, M. (2013). *Worlds of autism: Across the spectrum of neurological difference.* University of Minnesota Press.
Ellis, P., Kirby, A., & Osborne, A. (2023). *Neurodiversity and education.* Sage.
Frankel, F., & Wood, J. J. (2012). *Social skills success for students with autism/Asperger's: Helping adolescents on the spectrum to fit in.* Jossey-Bass.
Friend, M., & Bursuck, W. (2018). *Including students with special needs: A practical guide for classroom teachers* (8th ed.). Pearson.
Gargiulo, R. M., & Bouck, E. C. (2021). *Special education in contemporary society: An introduction to exceptionality* (7th ed.). Sage.
Greenstein, A. (2016). *Radical inclusive education: Disability, teaching, and struggles for liberation.* Routledge.
Hall, T. E., Meyer, A., & Rose, D. H. (2012). *Universal design for learning in the classroom: Practical applications.* Guilford Press.
Hallahan, D. P., Kauffman, J. M., & Pullen, P. C. (2015). *Exceptional learners; An introduction to special education.* Pearson.
Ilona, R. (2010). *The autism spectrum in the 21st century: Exploring psychology, biology, and practice.* Jessica Kingsley.
Jorgensen, C. M. (2018). *It's more than "just being in": Creating authentic inclusion for students with complex support needs.* Brookes.
Karten, T. (2017). *Building on the strengths of students with special needs: How to move beyond disability labels in the classroom.* ASCD.
Kluth, P. (2023). *You're going to love this kid! Teaching autistic students in the inclusive classroom* (3rd ed.). Brookes.

Leach, D. (2010). *Bringing ABA into your inclusive classroom: A guide to improving outcomes for students with autism spectrum disorders.* Paul H. Brooks.

Orelove, F., Sobsey, D., & Giles, D. (Eds.). (2017). *Educating students with severe and multiple disabilities: A collaborative approach* (5th ed.). Brookes.

Prater, M. A. (2018). *Teaching students with high-incidence disabilities: Strategies for diverse classrooms.* Sage.

Prince-Sayward, B. (Ed.). (2013). *Same journey, different paths: Stories of auditory processing disorder.* First Edition Design.

Reid, R., Lienemann, T. O., & Hagaman, J. L. (2013). *Strategy instruction for students with learning disabilities* (2nd ed.). Guilford Press.

Richards, G., & Armstrong, F. (2011). *Teaching and learning in diverse and inclusive classrooms: Key issues for new teachers.* Routledge.

Rufo, J. M., & Causton, J. (2021). *Special education: Using inclusion as a framework to build equity and support all students.* Brookes.

Swanson, H. L., Harris, K. R., & Graham, S. (2013). *Handbook of learning disabilities* (2nd ed.). Guilford Press.

Twomey, M., & Carroll, C., eds. (2018). *Seen and heard: Exploring participation, engagement and voice for children with disabilities.* Peter Lang.

Voltz, D. L., Sims, M. J., & Nelson, B. P. (2010). *Connecting teachers, students, and standards: Strategies for success in diverse and inclusive classrooms.* Association for Supervision and Curriculum Development.

Wehmeyer, M. L., Brown, I., Percy, M., Fung, W.L.A., & Shogren, K. A. (Eds.) (2017). *A comprehensive guide to intellectual and developmental disabilities* (2nd ed.). Brookes.

Weinfeld, R. (2013). *Smart kids with learning difficulties: Overcoming obstacles and realizing potential* (2nd ed.). Routledge.

Wilkinson, L. A. (2010). *A best practice guide to assessment and intervention for autism and Asperger syndrome in schools.* Jessica Kingsley.

Williams, B. F., & Williams, R. L. (2011). *Effective programs for treating autism spectrum disorder: Applied behavior analysis models.* Routledge.

Wilmshurst, L., & Brue, A. W. (2018). *The complete guide to special education: Expert advice on evaluations, IEPs, and helping kids succeed.* (3rd ed.). Routledge.

Practitioner Articles Within Music Education

Abramo, J. (2012). Disability in the classroom: Current trends and impacts on music education. *Music Educators Journal, 99*(1), 39–45. https://doi.org/10.1177/0027432115571367.

Abramo, J. M. (2015). Gifted students with disabilities: "Twice exceptionality" in the music classroom. *Music Educators Journal, 101*(4), 62–69. https://doi.org/10.1177/0027432115571367.

Armes, J. W., Harry, A. G., & Grimsby, R. (2022). Implementing universal design principles in music teaching. *Music Educators Journal, 109*(1), 44–51. https://doi.org/10.1177/00274321221114869.

Bennington, P. M. (2017). Still making music: How students with traumatic brain injury can continue with musical activities. *Music Educators Journal, 103*(4), 20–24. http://www.jstor.org/stable/44677941.

Bugaj, K. (2016). Good news in inclusive string music education: Adaptive strategies for the classroom. *General Music Today, 29*(3), 30–32. https://doi.org/10.1177/1048371315625725.

Clipper, J., & Lee, K. (2021). Composing music in special education. *Music Educators Journal, 108*(1), 43–49. https://doi.org/10.1177/00274321211038281.

Coates, R. L. (2012). Accommodating band students with visual impairments. *Music Educators Journal, 99*(1), 60–66. https://doi.org/10.1177/0027432112448478.

Crockett, J. (2017). Legal aspects of teaching music students with disabilities. *Music Educators Journal, 104*(2), 45–50. https://doi.org/10.1177/0027432117712802.

Darrow, A. A. (2010a). Including students with disabilities in music performance classes. *General Music Today, 23*(3), 42–44. https://doi.org/10.1177/1048371309361186.

Darrow, A. A. (2010b). Music education for all: Employing the principles of universal design to educational practice. *General Music Today 24*(1), 43–45. https://doi.org/10.1177/1048371310376901.

Darrow, A. A. (2011). Early childhood special music education. *General Music Today, 24*(2), 28–30. https://doi.org/10.1177/1048371310385329.

Darrow, A. A. (2013). Culturally responsive teaching: Understanding disability culture. *General Music Today, 26*(3), 32–34. https://doi.org/10.1177/1048371312472502.

Darrow, A. A. (2014a). Applying common core standards to students with disabilities in music. *General Music Today, 27*(3), 33–35. https://doi.org/10.1177/1048371313519645.

Darrow, A. A. (2014b). Promoting social and emotional growth of students with disabilities. *General Music Today, 28*(1), 29–32. https://doi.org/10.1177/1048371314541955.

Darrow, A. A. (2015). Differentiated instruction for students with disabilities: Using DI in the music classroom. *General Music Today, 28*(2), 29–32. https://doi.org/10.1177/1048371314554279.

Darrow, A. A. (2016). Unspoken words: Understanding nonverbal learning disabilities. *General Music Today, 29*(2), 35–38. https://doi.org/10.1177/1048371315609960.

Darrow, A. A., & Adamek, M. (2017). Recent and continuing initiatives and practices in special education. Music Educators Journal, *104*(2), 32–37. https://doi.org/10.1177/0027432117733029

Darrow, A. A., & Adamek, M. (2018). Instructional strategies for the inclusive music room. *General Music Today, 31*(3), 61–65. https://doi.org/10.1177/1048371318756625.

Darrow, A. A., & Segall, L. (2015). Students with disabilities: Using music to promote health and wellness. *General Music Today, 29*(1), 34–37. https://doi.org/10.1177/1048371315591054.

Dobbs, T. (2017). Equity in music education: Being "schooled" on disability. *Music Educators Journal, 104*(2), 51–53. https://doi.org/10.1177/0027432117732313.

Draper, E. (2018a). Navigating the labels: Appropriate terminology for students with disabilities. *General Music Today, 32*(1), 30–32. https://doi.org/10.1177/1048371318792230.

Draper, E. (2018b). Meaningful connections: Making inclusion work. *General Music Today, 32*(2), 31–33. https://doi.org/10.1177/1048371318809969.

Draper, E. (2019). Creating a meaningful music curriculum for students with disabilities. *General Music Today, 33*(1), 47–49. https://doi.org/10.1177/1048371319863792.

Draper, E. (2020a). Individual education programs: What music teachers need to know when working with students with disabilities. *General Music Today, 33*(3), 42–45. https://doi.org/10.1177/1048371320902754.

Draper, E. (2020b). Looking to the past to look into the future: Disability rights. *General Music Today, 34*(2), 34–38. https://doi.org/10.1177/1048371320961386.

Draper, E. A. (2022a). Connecting to the general curriculum: Supporting nonmusic goals for students with disabilities. *Journal of General Music Education, 35*(3), 32–35. https://doi.org/10.1177/27527646221079641.

Draper, E. A. (2022b). Supporting students with specific learning disabilities: Strategies for the general music classroom. *Journal of General Music Education, 36*(1), 47–49. https://doi.org/10.1177/27527646221115153.

Draper, E. A. (2023). Working together: Peer interactions to support students with disabilities in the music classroom. *Journal of General Music Education, 36*(2), 38–41. https://doi.org/10.1177/27527646221134042.

Fuelberth, R. (2017). "I dream a world": Inclusivity in choral music education. *Music Educators Journal, 104*(2), 38–44. https://doi.org/10.1177/0027432117735875.

Gilbert, D. (2018). "It's just the way I learn!": Inclusion from the perspective of a student with visual impairment. *Music Educators Journal, 105*(1), 21–27. https://doi.org/10.1177/0027432118777790.

Gonyou-Brown, J. (2016). Incorporating music into individualized programs for students with developmental disabilities. *Canadian Music Educator, 57*(3), 38–40. Retrieved from https://www.proquest.com/openview/d04fa714bcbd935c18e44bda9e709bf1/1?pq-origsite=gscholar&cbl=45770.

Grimsby, R. (2022). Alternative avenues for collaborating with special education paraprofessionals. *Journal of General Music Education, 36*(2), 13–19. https://doi.org/10.1177/27527646221130314.

Heikkila, E., & Knight, A. (2012). Inclusive music teaching strategies for elementary age children with developmental dyslexia. *Music Educators Journal, 99*(1), 54–59. https://doi.org/10.1177/0027432112452597.

Hourigan, R., & Hammel, A. (2017). Understanding the mind of a student with autism in music class. *Music Educators Journal, 104*(2), 21–26. https://www.jstor.org/stable/26588614.

Jellison, J., Brown, L., & Draper, E. (2015). Peer-assisted learning and interactions in inclusive music classrooms: Benefits, research, and applications. *General Music Today, 28*(3), 18–22. https://doi.org/10.1177/1048371314565456.

Knapp, E. J. (2022). Considering the hidden and null curricula in music education: Becoming vigilantly aware. *Music Educators Journal, 108*(2), 16–22. https://doi.org/10.1177/00274321211060064.

McCord, K. (2013). Universal design for learning: Special educators integrating the Orff approach into their teaching. *Approaches: Music Therapy and Special Music Education, 5*(2), 188-193. Retrieved from https://approaches.primarymusic.gr.

Melago, K. (2014). Strategies for successfully teaching students with ADD or ADHD in instrumental lessons. *Music Educators Journal, 101*(2), 37–43. https://doi.org/10.1177/0027432114547764.

Murdock, M. C., Morgan, J. A., & Laverghetta, T. S. (2012). The music student with epilepsy. *Music Educators Journal, 99*(1), 47–53. http://www.jstor.org/stable/41692696.

Nelson, D. (2013). Professional notes: Reaching all students via technology. *Music Educators Journal, 100*(1), 26–29. https://doi.org/0.1177/0027432113496057.

Perlmutter, A. (2016). Using Orff Schulwerk to engage students with disabilities. *Teaching Music, 24*(1), 8. Retrieved from https://link.gale.com/apps/doc/A466519085/ITOF?u =ITOF&xid=1ed80742.

Poliniak, S. (2019). The benefits of interaction: Students with and without disabilities benefit from working together. *Teaching Music, 26*(4). Retrieved from https://go-gale-com /ps/i.do?p=ITOF&u=msu_main&id=GALE%7CA583655114&v=2.1&it=r&sid=summon.

Price, B. (2012). Zero margin for error: Effective strategies for teaching music to students with emotional disturbances. *Music Educators Journal, 99*(1), 67–72. https://doi.org/10.1177/0027432112451620.

Rush, T. W. (2015). Incorporating assistive technology for students with visual impairments into the music classroom. *Music Educators Journal, 102*(2). 78–83. https://doi.org/10.1177/0027432115606181.

Salvador, K. (2013). Inclusion of people with special needs in choral settings: A review of applicable research and professional literature. *Update: Applications of Research in Music Education, 31*(2), 37–44. https://doi.org/10.1177/8755123312473760.

Salvador, K., & Culp, M. E. (2022). Intersections in music education: Implications of universal design for learning, culturally responsive education, and trauma-informed education for P-12 praxis. *Music Educators Journal, 108*(3), 19–29. https://doi.org/10.1177/00274321221087737.

Scott, S. (2014). The challenges of imitation for children with autism spectrum disorders with implications for general music education. *Update: Applications of Research in Music Education, 34*(2), 13–20. https://doi.org/10.1177/8755123314548043.

Steele, A., & Fisher, C. (2011). Adaptive piano teaching strategies: For the physically and cognitively handicapped piano student. *American Music Teacher, 60*(4), 22–25. Retrieved from https://www.proquest.com/docview/873184617?pq-origsite=gscholar&fromopenview=true.

Thornton, L., & Culp, M. (2020). Instrumental opportunities: Music for all. *Update: Applications of Research in Music Education, 38*(3), 48–57. https://doi.org/10.1177/87551233320907140.

VanWeelden, K. (2011). Accommodating the special learner in secondary general music classes. *General Music Today, 24*(3), 39–41. https://doi.org/10.1177/1048371310396707.

VanWeelden, K., & Heath, J. (2013). Low-budget apps for students of all abilities. *General Music Today, 27*(1), 45–47. https://doi.org/10.1177/1048371313493433.

VanWeelden, K., & Heath-Reynolds, J. (2017). Steps to designing authentic assessments for students with disabilities in music classes. *Music Educators Journal, 104*(2), 27–31. https://doi.org/10.1177/0027432117733028.

Walkup-Amos, T. (2020). Creating inclusive music classrooms through peer-assisted learning strategies. *Teaching Exceptional Children, 52*(3), 138–146. https://doi.org/10.1177/0040059919891185.

Notes

CHAPTER 7: TEACHING STRATEGIES FOR PERFORMERS WITH DIFFERENCES AND DISABILITIES

1. Wix.com is a simple website development application for novices (http://www.wix.com).
2. SmartMusic can be found at http://www.smartmusic.com.
3. United Sound: http://www.unitedsound.org.
4. All Access Choir YouTube channel: https://www.youtube.com/playlist?list=PLDLI4xoMrYem1dWjzU6XyyHnGY8K8pNBX.

CHAPTER 8: TEACHING MUSIC TO STUDENTS WHO ARE INTELLECTUALLY GIFTED

1. Hollie's and Hannah's names are used with permission.

References

FOREWORD

Turnbull, R., Huerta, N., & Stowe, M. (2004). *The Individuals with Disabilities Education Act as amended in 2004.* Upper Saddle River, NJ: Pearson Merrill Prentice Hall.

CHAPTER 1

Arnold, M. L., Newman, J. H., Gaddy, B. B., & Dean, C. B. (2005). A look at the condition of rural education research: Setting a direction for future research. *Journal of Research in Rural Education, 20*(6), 1-25.

Blair, D. V., & McCord, K. (2016). *Exceptional music pedagogy for children with exceptionalities.* Oxford University Press.

Colwell, C. M., & Thompson, L. K. (2000). "Inclusion" of information on mainstreaming in undergraduate music education curricula. *Journal of Music Therapy, 37*(3), 205-221.

Davis, W. B., Gfeller, K. E., & Thaut, M. H. (1999). *An introduction to music therapy.* McGraw-Hill.

Dewey, J. (1916/1944). *Democracy and education.* Macmillan.

Diem, S. D., & Welton, A. D. (2020). Anti racism educational leadership and policy. Routledge.

Hammel, A. M. (2001). Preparation for teaching special learners: Twenty years of practice. *Journal of Music Teacher Education, 11*(1), 5-11.

Hammel, A. M., & Hourigan, R. M. (2022). Poverty, race, disability, and intersectionality and participation in the arts: Needed policy changes for the future. *Arts Education Policy Review.*

Hourigan, R. M. (2014). Intersections between school reform, the arts, and special education: The children left behind. *Arts Education Policy Review, 115*, 35-38.

Hourigan, R. M. (2018). Family perspectives on access to arts education for students with disabilities. In J. B. Crockett & S. M. Malley (Eds.), *Handbook of arts education and special education: Policy, research, and practices* (pp. 267-277). Routledge.

Lewis, R. B., & Doorlag, D. H. (2011). *Teaching special students in general education classrooms* (8th ed.). Prentice Hall.

Lipscomb, S. D. (1996). The cognitive organization of musical sound. In D. A. Hodges (Ed.), *Handbook of music psychology* (pp. 133-177). IMR Press.

McLesky, J., Tyler, N. C., & Flippin, S. S. (2004). The supply and demand for special education teachers: A review of research regarding the chronic shortage of special education teachers. *Journal of Special Education, 38*(1), 50-21.

National Center for Education Statistics. (2022). *Students with disabilities.* Retrieved November 2022 from https://nces.ed.gov/fastfacts/display.asp?id=64.

National Education Association. (2022). *English language learners.* Retrieved November 2022 from https://www.nea.org/resource-library/english-language-learners.

Plucker, J. A., Spradlin, T. E., Magaro, M. M., Chien, R. W., & Zapf, J. S. (2007). Assessing the policy environment for school corporation collaboration, cooperation, and consolidation in Indiana. *Center for Evaluation and Education Policy, Indiana University,* 5(5), 1-16.

Salvador, K. (2010). Who isn't a special learner? A survey of how music teacher education programs prepare future music educators to work with exceptional populations. *Journal of Music Teacher Education, 20*(1), 27-38.

Turnbull, R., Huerta, N., & Stowe, M. (2004). *The Individuals with Disabilities Education Act as amended in 2004.* Pearson Merrill Prentice Hall.

U.S. Department of Education. (2022). Section 300.39: Special Education. Retrieved November 2022 from https://sites.ed.gov/idea/regs/b/a/300.39.

VanWeelden, K., & Whipple, J. (2013). Music educators' perceptions of preparation and supports available for inclusion. *Journal of Music Teacher Education, 23*(2), 33-51.

VanWeelden, K., & Whipple, J. (2014). Music educators' perceived effectiveness of inclusion. *Journal of Research in Music Education, 62*(2), 148-160.

Winzer, M. A. (2009). *From integration to inclusion: A history of special education in the 20th century.* Gallaudet University Press.

CHAPTER 2

Adamek, M. S., & Darrow, A. A. (2018). *Music in special education* (3rd ed.). American Music Therapy Association.

Atterbury, B. W. (1990). *Mainstreaming exceptional learners in music.* Prentice Hall.

Burkett, E. I., & Hammel, A. M. (2007). *On music for special learners.* Reston, VA: Connect for Education.

Cartwright, G. P. (1995). *Educating special learners.* Albany, NY: Wadsworth.

Colwell, C. M. (1998). Effects of information on elementary band students' attitudes towards individuals with special needs. *Journal of Music Therapy, 35*(1), 19-33.

Congressional Information Service. (1986). *Abstracts of congressional publications and legislative histories.* Washington, DC: US Government Printing Office.

Congressional Information Service. (1989). *Abstracts of congressional publications and legislative histories.* Washington, DC: US Government Printing Office.

Congressional Information Service. (1990). *Abstracts of congressional publications and legislative histories.* Washington, DC: US Government Printing Office.

Congressional Information Service. (1997). *Abstracts of congressional publications and legislative histories.* Washington, DC: US Government Printing Office.

Council for Exceptional Children. (1998). *IDEA 1997: Let's make it work.* Reston, VA: Author.

Council of Administrators of Special Education. (1992). *Student access: A resource guide for educators. Section 504 of the Rehabilitation Act of 1973.* Author.

Darling Hammond, L. (2007). *Race, inequity and educational accountability: The irony of "No Child Left Behind."* Taylor and Francis. https://www.tandfonline.com/doi/abs/10.1080/13613320701503207

Darrow, A. A. (1999). Music educators' perceptions regarding the inclusion of students with severe disabilities in music classrooms. *Journal of Music Therapy, 36*(4), 254–273.

Endrew F. v. Douglas County School District RE. (2017). No. 15-827. Argued January 11, 2017. Decisis March 22, 2017.

Every Student Succeeds Act. (2017). *National Association for Gifted Children.* Retrieved April 6, 2017, from http://www.nagc.org/get-involved/advocate-high-ability-learners/nagc-advocacy/federal-legislative-update/every-student.

Haager, D., & Vaughn, S. (2013). The common core state standards and reading: Interpretations and implications for elementary students with learning disabilities. *Learning Disabilities Research and Practice, 28*(1), 5–16.

Hallahan, D. (1997). *Exceptional learners.* Boston, MA: Allyn & Bacon.

Hammel, A. M. (2001). Preparation for teaching special learners: Twenty years of practice. *Journal of Music Teacher Education, 11*(1), 5–11.

Hammel, A. M. (2004). Inclusion strategies that work. *Music Educators Journal, 90*(5), 33–37.

Hammel, A. M. (2017). Amy and Drew: Two children who helped determine what free and appropriate public education means. *General Music Today.* National Association for Music Education. doi:10.1177/1048371317735921 journals.sagepub.com/home/gmt

Hammel, A. M., & Fischer, K. (2014). "It's not easy being green": Charter schools, the arts, and students with diverse needs. *Arts Education Policy Review, 115*(2), 44–51.

Hammel, A. M., & Gerrity, K. W. (2012). The effect of instruction on teacher perceptions of competence when including students with special needs in music classrooms. *Applications of Research in Music Education, 31*(1), 6–13.Hammel, A. M., & Hourigan, R. M. (2022). Poverty, race, disability, and intersectionality and participation in the arts: Needed policy changes for the future. *Arts Education Policy Review.*

Heller, L. (1994). *Undergraduate music teacher preparation for mainstreaming: A survey of music education teacher training institutions in the Great Lakes region of the United States* [Doctoral dissertation, Michigan State University]. Dissertation Abstracts International, 56-03A, 858.

Hourigan, R. M. (2011). Race to the top: Implications for professional development in arts education. *Arts Education Policy Review, 112*, 60–64.

Jimenez, L., & Flores, A. (2019). 3 ways Devos has put students at risk by deregulating education. Center for Academic Progress. Obtained May 28th 2024 from https://www.americanprogress.org/article/3-ways-devos-put-students-risk-deregulating-education.

Johnson, C. M., & Darrow, A. A. (1997). The effect of positive models of inclusion on band students' attitudinal statements regarding the integration of students with disabilities. *Journal of Research in Music Education, 45*(2), 173–184.

Kettler, T., Russell, J., & Puryear, J. S. (2015). Inequitable access to gifted education: Variance in funding and staffing based on locale and contextual school variables. *Journal for the Education of the Gifted, 38*(2), 99-117. Retrieved from https://eric.ed.gov/?id=EJ1061271.

Lewis, R. B., & Doorlag, D. H. (2006). *Teaching special students in general education classrooms.* Prentice Hall.

Marland, S. P. (1972). *Education of the gifted and talented: Report to the Congress of the United States by the Commissioner of Education.* Washington, DC: US Government Printing Office.

McNulty, R. J., & Gloeckler, L. C. (2011). Fewer, clearer, higher common core state standards: Implications for students receiving special education services. *International Center for Leadership in Education.* Retrieved July 18, 2016, from https://www.semanticscholar.org/paper/Fewer-Clearer-Higher-Common-Core-State-Standards-Mcnulty-Gloeckler/ca9a19784fb29582af3965e18fb0de20d164d969/pdf.

Melcher, J. W. (1976). Law, litigation, and handicapped children. *Exceptional Children, 43*, 26-130.

No Child Left Behind. (2001). Retrieved March 9, 2009, from http://www2.ed.gov/nclb/landing.jhtml.

Paul, J. L., & Warnock, N. J. (1980). Special education: A changing field. *Exceptional Child, 27*, 3-28.

Senate Committee on Labor and Public Welfare. (1965). *Elementary and Secondary Act of 1965 (45-779 0-65-1).* Washington, DC: US Government Printing Office.

Senate Committee on Labor and Public Welfare. (1977). *The Education of All Handicapped Children Act (121a320).* Washington, DC: US Government Printing Office.

Simpson, R. L., LaCava, P. G., Sampson, P., & Graner, P. (2004). The No Child Left Behind Act: Challenges and implications for educators. *Intervention in School and Clinic, 40*(2), 67-75.

Turnbull, R., Huerta, N., & Stowe, M. (2006). *The Individuals with Disabilities Education Act as amended in 2004.* Prentice Hall.

U.S. Department of Education. (2009). Overview information: Race to the Top Fund: Notice inviting applications for new awards for fiscal year 2010. *Federal Register, 74*, 221.

VanTassel-Baska, J. (1998). *Excellence in educating gifted and talented learners.* Love.

Walker, S. Y. (1991). *The survival guide for parents of gifted kids.* Free Spirit.

Webber, J. (1997). Responsible inclusion: Key components for success. In P. Zionts (Ed.), *Inclusion strategies for students with learning and behavioral problems* (pp. 27-56). Pro-ed.

Wexler, A. (2014). Reaching higher? The impact of the common core state standards on the visual arts, poverty, and disabilities. *Arts Education Policy Review, 115*, 52-61.

Whitcomb, J., Borko, H., & Liston, D. (2009). Growing talent: Promising professional development models and practices. *Journal of Teacher Education, 60*(3), 207-214.

Wilson, B., & McCrary, J. (1996). The effect of instruction on music educators' attitudes toward students with disabilities. *Journal of Research in Music Education, 44*(1), 26-33.

Winner, E. (1996). *Gifted children: Myths and realities.* Perseus Books Group.

Zigmond, N. (1997). Educating students with disabilities: The future of special education. In J. W. Lloyd, E. J. Kameenui, & D. Chard (Eds.), *Issues in educating students with disabilities* (pp. 377-390). Lawrence Erlbaum Associates.

Zirkel, P. (2008a). What does the law say? New Section 504 and student eligibility standards. *Teaching Exceptional Children, 41*(4), 68–71.

Zirkel, P. (2008b). What does the law say? *Teaching Exceptional Children, 41*(5), 73–75.

Zirkel, P. (2009). Section 504/ADA student eligibility form. *Teaching Exceptional Children, 41*(4), 70.

CHAPTER 3

Gerrity, K. W., Hourigan, R. M., & Horton, P. W. (2013). Conditions that facilitate music learning among students with special needs: A mixed-methods inquiry. *Journal of Research in Music Education, 61*, 144–159.

Heller, L. (1994). *Undergraduate music teacher preparation for mainstreaming: A survey of music education teacher training institutions in the Great Lakes region of the United States* [Unpublished doctoral dissertation]. Michigan State University, East Lansing, MI.

Hourigan, R. M. (2007). Music majors as paraprofessionals: A study in special needs field experience for preservice music educators. *Contributions to Music Education, 34*, 19–34.National Center for Educational Statistics. (2022). Fast Facts. Retrieved December 2022 from https://nces.ed.gov/fastfacts/display.asp?id=64.

Peebles, J., & Mendaglio, S. (2014). Preparing teachers for inclusive classrooms: Introducing the individual direct experience approach. *Inclusive Education: Socially Just Perspectives and Practicices,* 7(2), 245–257.

United States Department of Education. (n.d.). Sec. 300.115 Continuum of alternative placements. Retrieved May 28th 2024 from https://sites.ed.gov/idea/regs/b/b/300.115.

VanWeelden, K., & Whipple, J. (2005). The effects of field experience on music education majors' perceptions of music instruction for secondary students with special needs. *Journal of Music Teacher Education, 14*(2), 62–68.

York, J. L., & Reynolds, M. C. (1996). Special education and inclusion. In J. Sikula (Ed.), *Handbook of research on teacher education* (2nd ed., pp. 820–836). Simon & Schuster Macmillan.

CHAPTER 4

Adamek, M. S., & Darrow, A. A. (2018). *Music in special education* (3rd ed.). American Music Therapy Association.

Biel, L. (2017). *Students with sensory processing challenges.* Routledge

Hammel, A. M. (1999). *A study of teacher competencies necessary when including special learners in elementary music classrooms: The development of a unit of study for use with undergraduate music education students* [Doctoral dissertation, Shenandoah University]. Dissertation Abstracts International, 40-10A, 5299.

Hammel, A. M. (2004). Inclusion strategies that work. *Music Educators Journal,* 90(5), 33–37.

Hammel, A. M., Hickox, B., & Hourigan, R. M. (2016). *Winding it back: Pedagogical implications of sequencing instruction for* all *students.* Oxford University Press.

Heller, L. (1994). *Undergraduate music teacher preparation for mainstreaming: A survey of music education teacher training institutions in the Great Lakes region of the United States* [Doctoral dissertation, Michigan State University]. Dissertation Abstracts International, 56-03A, 858.

Hourigan, R. M. (2009). Preservice music teachers' perceptions of a fieldwork experience in a special needs classroom. *Journal of Research in Music Education, 57*(2), 152–168.

Hourigan, R. M. (2024). Understanding music and universal design for learning: Strategies for students with learning differences in the 21st century. In C. M. Conway (Ed.), *Musicianship focused curriculum and assessment* (2nd ed.), 317–336. GIA Publications.Lewis, R. B., & Doorlag, D. H. (2006). *Teaching special students in general education classrooms.* Prentice Hall.

Pressley, M., Raphael, L., Gallagher, J. D., & DiBella, J. (2004). Providence-St. Mel School: How a school that works for African American students works. *Journal of Educational Psychology, 96*(2), 216–235.

Rozalski, M., Stewart, A., & Miller, J. (2010). How to determine the least restrictive environment for students with disabilities. *Exceptionality, 18*(10), 151-163.

Sausser, S., & Waller, R. J. (2005). A model for music therapy with students with emotional and behavioral disorders. *The Arts Psychotherapy, 33*(10), 1-10.

Shellard, E., & Protheroe, N. (2000). *Effective teaching: How do we know it when we see it?* The Informed Educator Series. Educational Research Service (monograph).

Stronge, J. H. (2007). *Qualities of effective teachers* (2nd ed.). Association for Supervision and Curriculum Development.

Turnbull, A., Turnbull, R., Shank, M., & Leal, D. (2002). *Exceptional lives: Special education in today's schools* (3rd ed.). Prentice Hall.

U.S. Department of Education. (2023). *Protecting students with disabilities.* Retrieved January 2023 from https://www2.ed.gov/about/offices/list/ocr/504faq.html.

Valdes, G., Bunch, G., Snow, C., Lee, C., & Matos, L. (2005). Teaching diverse learners. In L. Darling Hammond & J. Bransford (Eds.), *Preparing teachers for a changing world* (pp. 126–168). Jossey-Bass.

Van Garderen, D., & Whittaker, C. (2006). Planning differentiated, multicultural instruction for secondary inclusive classrooms. *Teaching Exceptional Children, 38*(3), 12–20.

Wehmeyer, M. L. (2002). *Teaching students with mental retardation.* Baltimore, MD: Brooks.

Weiss, I. R., & Pasley, J. D. (2004). What is high-quality instruction? *Educational Leadership, 61*(5), 24–28.

CHAPTER 5

Adamek, M. S., & Darrow, A. A. (2018). *Music in special education* (3rd ed.). American Music Therapy Association.

Allen, B. (2004). *Difference matters.* Waveland Press.

Bambara, L. M., & Kern, L. (2021). *Individualized supports for students with problem behaviors.* Guilford Press.

Barnhill, G. P. (2005). Functional behavior assessment in schools. *Intervention in School and Clinic, 40*(3), 131-143. https://doi.org/10.1177/10534512050400030101

Boyle-Baise, M. (2005). Preparing community-oriented teachers: Reflections from a multi-cultural service-learning project. *Journal of Teacher Education, 56*(5), 446–458.

Colvin, G., Ainge, D., & Nelson, R. (1997). How to defuse confrontations. *Teaching Exceptional Children, 29*(6), 47–51.

Conroy, M. Sutherland, K., Snyder, A., & Marsh, S. (2008). Classwide interventions: Effective instruction makes a difference. *Teaching Exceptional Children, 40*(6), 24–30.

Cotton, K. (2000). *The schooling practices that matter most.* Northwest Regional Educational Laboratory, and Association for Supervision and Curriculum Development.

Dewey, M. (1991). Living with Asperger's syndrome. In U. Frith (Ed.), *Autism and Asperger's syndrome* (pp. 184–206). Cambridge University Press.

Eckert, P. (1989). *Jocks and burnouts: Social categories and identity in the high school.* Teachers College Press.

Goldson, E. (2001). Maltreatment among children with disabilities. *Infants and Young Children, 13*(4), 44–54.

Gustein, S. E. (2000). *Autism: Asperger's: Solving the relationship puzzle.* Future Horizons.

Hammel, A. M., & Hourigan, R. M. (2022). Poverty, race, disability, and intersectionality and the participation in the arts: Needed policy changes for the future. https://www.tandfonline.com/doi/full/10.1080/10632913.2022.2059731.

Hamre, B. K., & Pianta, R. C. (2005). Can instructional and emotional support in the first grade classroom make a difference for children at risk of school failure? *Child Development, 76*(5), 949–967.

Hobbs, T., & Westing, D. L. (1998). Promoting successful inclusion through collaborative problem solving. *Teaching Exceptional Children, 34*(2), 12–19.

Hogg, M. A., & Terry, D. J. (2001). *Social identity processes in organizational contexts.* Psychology Press.

Horner, R., Strain, P., & Carr, E. (2002). Problem behavior interventions for young children with autism: A research synthesis. *Journal for Autism and Developmental Disorders, 32*, 423–446.

Horner, R. H., Sugai, G., & Anderson, C. M. (2010). Examing the evidence for schoolwide behavior support. *Focus on Exceptional Children, 42*(6), 1–14.

Langer, J. A. (2000). Excellence in English in middle and high school: How teachers' professional lives support student achievement. *American Educational Research Journal, 37*(2), 397–439.

Marriage, K. J., Gordon, V., & Brand, L. (1995). A social skills group for boys with Asperger's syndrome. *Australian and New Zealand Journal for Psychiatry, 29*, 58–62.

Marzano, R. J. (2003). *What works in schools: Translating research into action.* Association for Supervision and Curriculum Development.

Marzano, R. J., with Marzano, J. S., & Pickering, D. J. (2003). *Classroom management that works: Research-based strategies for every teacher.* Association for Supervision and Curriculum Development.

Noddings, N. (1984). *Caring: A feminine approach to ethics and moral education.* University of California Press.

Ozonoff, S., Dawson, G., & McPartland, J. (2002). *A parent's guide to Asperger syndrome and high-functioning autism: How to meet the challenges and help your child thrive.* Guilford.

Ozonoff, S., & Miller, J. (1995). Teaching theory of mind: A new approach to social skills training for individuals with autism. *Journal of Autism and Developmental Disorders, 25*, 415-433.

Perry, D., Marston, G., Hinder, S., Munden, A. C., & Roy, A. (2001). The phenomenology of depressive illness in people with learning disability and autism. *Autism*, 5, 265-275.

Shellard, E., & Protheroe, N. (2000). *Effective teaching: How do we know it when we see it? The Informed Educator Series.* Educational Research Service.

Shores, R. E., Gunther, P. L., & Jack, S. L. (2017). Classroom management strategies: Are they setting events for coercion? *Behavior Disorders, 18*(2), 92-102. https://doi.org/10.1177/019874299301800207.

Sokal, L., Smith, D. G., & Mowat, H. (2003). Alternative certification teachers' attitudes toward classroom management. *High School Journal, 86*(3), 8-16.

Southwest Center for Teaching Quality (SECTQ). (2003). Alternative certification teachers' attitudes toward classroom management. *High School Journal, 86*(3), 8-16.

Stainback, W., & Stainback, S. (1990). Facilitating peer supports and friendships. In W. Stainback & S. Stainback (Eds.), *Support networks for inclusive schooling* (pp. 51-63). Paul Brookes.

Sugai, G., Simonsen, B., & Horner, R. (2008). Schoolwide positive behavior supports: A continuum or positive behavior supports for all students. *Teaching Exceptional Children, 40*(6), 4.

Thompson, M., & Cohen, L. (2005). When the bullied must adjust. *Education Digest: Essential Readings Condensed for Quick Review, 70*(5), 16-19.

Vygotsky, L. S. (1934/1978). *Mind in society.* Cambridge, MA: Harvard University Press.

Walls, R. T., Nardi, A. H., von Minden, A. M., & Hoffman, N. (2002). The characteristics of effective and ineffective teachers. *Teacher Education Quarterly, 29*(1), 39-48.

Weinstein, C. S., Tomlinson-Clarke, S. & Curran, M. (2004). Toward a conception of culturally responsive classroom management. *Journal of Teacher Education*, 55(1), 25-38. https://journals-sagepub-com.proxy.bsu.edu/doi/10.1177/0022487103259812.

Zeichner, K. M. (2003). Pedagogy, knowledge, and teacher preparation. In B. Williams (Ed.), *Closing the achievement gap: A vision for changing beliefs and practices* (2nd ed., pp. 99-114). Alexandria, VA: Association for Supervision and Curriculum Development.

CHAPTER 6

Dewey, J. (1929). My pedagogic creed. *Journal of the National Education Association, 18*(9), 291-295.

Garrison, C., & Ehringhaus, M. (2009). *Formative and summative assessments in the classroom.*: National Middle School Association. Retrieved April 9, 2009, from http://www.nmsa.org/Publications/WebExclusive/Assessment/tabid/1120/Default.aspx.

Labuta, J. A., & Smith, D. A. (1997). *Music education: Historical contexts and perspectives.*: Prentice Hall.

National Association for Music Education. (2014). *The 2014 music standards.* Retrieved February 20, 2017, from http://www.nafme.org/my-classroom/standards/core-music-standards.

Oosterhof, A. (2001). *Classroom applications of educational measurement.*: Prentice Hall.

Scott, S. (2006). A constructivist view of music education: Perspectives for deep learning. *Journal of General Music Education, 19*(2), 17-21.

Shively, J. (2015). Constructivism in music education. *Arts Education Policy Review, 116*(3), 128-136. https://doi.org/10.1080/10632913.2015.1011815.

Walker, J. F., & Soltis, J. F. (2004). *Curriculum and aims* (5th ed.). Teachers College Press.

CHAPTER 8

Binet, A. (1894). *Psychologie des grandes calculateurs (et de jouers d'echecs) (Psychology of large computers (and chess players)).* Hachette.

Hollingsworth, L. S. (1931). *Gifted children: Their nature and nurture.* Macmillan.

Hollingsworth, L. S. (1975). *Children above 180 IQ.* Arno Press.

Kay, K. (2000). *Uniquely gifted: Identifying and meeting the needs of the twice-exceptional student.* Avocus.

Kerr, B. A. (1994). *Smart girls: A new psychology of girls, women and giftedness.* Gifted Psychology Press.

Renzulli, J. S. (1977). *The enrichment triad model.* Creative Learning Press.

Renzulli, J. S. (1986). The three-ring conception of giftedness: A developmental model for creative productivity. In R. J. Sternberg & J. Davidson (Eds.), *Conceptions of giftedness* (pp. 53-92). Cambridge University Press.

Silverman, L. K. (1993). *Counseling the gifted and talented.* Love.

Sousa, D. A. (2003). *How the gifted brain learns.* Sage Publications.

Terman, L. M. (1925). *Genetic studies of genius,* Vol. 1: *Mental and physical traits of a thousand gifted children.* Stanford University Press.

Terman, L. M., & Oden, M. H. (1947). *Genetic studies of genius,* Vol. 4: *The gifted child grows up.* Stanford University Press.

Terman, L. M., & Oden, M. H. (1959). *Genetic studies of genius,* Vol. 5: *The gifted group at mid-life: Thirty-five years' follow-up of the superior child.* Stanford University Press.

VanTassel-Baska, J. (1998). *Excellence in educating gifted and talented learners.* Love.

Walker, S. Y. (1991). *The survival guide for parents of gifted kids.* Free Spirit.

Webb, J. T., Meckstroth, E. A., & Tolan, S. S. (1994). *Guiding the gifted child.* Gifted Psychology Press.

Winebrenner, S. (2001). *Teaching gifted kids in the regular classroom.* Free Spirit.

Winner, E. (1996). *Gifted children: Myths and realities.* Perseus Books Group.

Index

For the benefit of digital users, indexed terms that span two pages (e.g., 52-53) may, on occasion, appear on only one of those pages.

Tables, figures, and boxes are indicated by an italic *t*, *f*, and *b* following the paragraph number.